EVANGELISM IN ECLIPSE

World Mission and the World

Council of Churches

EVANGELISM IN ECLIPSE

World Mission and the
World Council of Churches

HARVEY T. HOEKSTRA

Exeter
The Paternoster Press

ISBN: 0 85364 265 6

*All Rights Reserved. This British edition is published by The Paternoster
Press Ltd., Paternoster House, 3 Mount Radford Crescent, Exeter, Devon,
UK, by arrangement with Tyndale House Publishers, Wheaton, Illinois 60187.
Published in the US under the title "The World Council of Churches and the
Demise of Evangelism".*

First published November 1979.

AUSTRALIA
*Emu Book Agencies Pty., Ltd.,
63 Berry Street, Granville, N.S.W. 2142.*

SOUTH AFRICA
*Oxford University Press,
P.O. Box 1141, Cape Town.*

British Library Cataloguing in Publication Data

*Hoekstra, Harvey T
Evangelism in eclipse.
1. Missions
I. Title
266   BV2061*

ISBN 0-85364-265-6

*Made and Printed in Great Britain for
The Paternoster Press Ltd., Paternoster House,
3 Mount Radford Crescent, Exeter, Devon by
Redwood Burn Limited, Trowbridge & Esher.*

CONTENTS

A New Mood
The "Call to Confess and Proclaim"

ABBREVIATIONS

AACC	All Africa Conference of Churches
CCPD	Commission on Churches' Participation in Development
CICARWS	Commission on Interchurch Aid, Refugee and World Service
CWME	Commission on World Mission and Evangelism
DICARWS	Division of Interchurch Aid and Refugee World Service
DPOF	Dialogue with Peoples of Other Faiths
DWME	Division of World Mission and Evangelism
EACC	East Asia Christian Conference - now Christian Conference of Asia
EPS	Ecumenical Press Service
ESP	Ecumenical Sharing of Personnel
FMCNA	Foreign Missions Conference of North America
IMC	International Missionary Council
IRM	International Review of Mission
JAM	Joint Action for Mission
PBS	Portfolio for Biblical Studies
PCR	Programme to Combat Racism
RAM	Rural Agricultural Mission
TEF	Theological Education Fund
UIM	Urban and Industrial Mission
WCC	World Council of Churches
WSCF	World Student Christian Federation

INTRODUCTION

This study of the World Council of Churches, its member churches, and the unfinished missionary task is made in the context of a rising tide of commitment to evangelism at all levels in the life of the churches. Many of us recognize that God is continuing to call his people to new efforts designed to reach out with the Gospel. Our interests and concerns converge in evangelism.

Recent waves of renewal evidence a joyful witness of God's people to his dynamic love in Christ. These fresh awarenesses of the wonder of God's saving power and of the realities of being alive in Christ provide incentive and concern for sharing with people everywhere a valid opportunity to know the Savior. Many are challenged and even convicted by the disturbing thought that unless they go, some they could reach will have no opportunity to know Christ. The conviction haunts them that people without Christ are lost; and they know the power of God's Gospel to "save" all who hear, repent and believe. Young people by the thousands are volunteering to serve as missionaries—to share this Good News.

Keen minds and spirits within the churches are assessing the unfinished task realistically. New information is available with more accurate data. There is great rejoicing for what God has done on all six continents. But there is also a realization that in many of the world's countries there is no church at all among many of the cultures and sub-cultures within the political boundaries. Cultural, linguistic, geographic barriers exist between ethnic and cultural groupings. Many within the churches fear they are only marginally involved in surmounting these barriers with a Gospel witness. Yet out of their deep commitment they continue to be challenged; feelings of frustration give rise to demands that their church leaders respond with them to what God seems to be saying in this moment of history.

On the one hand they hear that missionaries are no longer wanted or needed. On the other hand, they see other churches sending out more missionaries than at any previous time during the history of the Christian movement. How can this be? They do not want to be left out when others are involved in this unfinished task. If people are not challenged by leadership within their own structures they may well turn to non-denominational agencies and societies who present not only the vision and challenge but the opportunity to be involved. Mainline denominations are actually in danger of losing a vitality and enthusiasm that people with such a vision, challenge and conviction could contribute.

The World Council of Churches, of which these churches are members, is committed by its constitution "to support the churches in their worldwide missionary and evangelistic task." This study grows out of a concern that the present understanding of mission within the WCC, and its programs to carry out that understanding, do *not* provide the churches the support they need for this task. A definition of mission has emerged that many feel is too horizontal—and too closely associated with other ideologies. Those who subscribe to this wider definition seem primarily concerned to work for a better society; they place their emphasis on human dignity and human rights. Such participation in the social struggle is a worthy objective as long as it does not lead to the eclipse or neglect of the churches' responsibility to win others to faith in Christ. But this has often been the result. Rather than giving member churches "support . . . in their worldwide missionary and evangelistic task," WCC programs have too often tended to divert those churches from that task.

In order to deal with these concerns constructively, we need to understand our present historical moment. Where did we come from and where are we now, in the light of the changing world? Has the missionary task changed too? What is the role of the World Council of Churches vis-à-vis this missionary task? Are there areas of neglect? What is needed to do the task more effectively? These were my questions as I moved through this study.

The author of this dissertation is a minister whose church has been a member of the World Council of Churches from its inception. And I intend to remain a part of this church within the Council. As an "insider" then I am primarily addressing my colleagues in the churches that make up the membership of the World Council.

This is not intended to be an exhaustive study of the WCC. Nor is it a study of the missionary movement per se. It is limited to tracing the new concept of mission that has emerged within the structured offices of the WCC. The study will examine the historical context in which this concept evolved; and it will identify theological and ideological assumptions underlying this concept. It will look at key world meetings of the missionary and ecumenical movements, studying the inner dynamics that went into their preparation, the ideas generated and the programs mandated to implement these ideas. Throughout its history, the programs of the WCC reflect its understanding of mission and show the extent of its support for the worldwide missionary and evangelistic concerns of member churches. It is a thesis of this study that these programs need to be refocused, and recommendations to that end are included.

This study has been based on my own participation in 1975 in the Fifth Assembly of the World Council of Churches in Nairobi as a member of the press. Taped interviews, conversations with leading WCC staff at Geneva, archival materials (including typewritten and unpublished papers which may not be quoted directly) and library materials available at Geneva—all have been integral to this study.

I am deeply grateful to Philip Potter, Alan Brash, Emilio Castro, Ans J. Vander Bent and many others in Geneva for cordially receiving me and assisting me by giving of their time and words of wisdom. I am unable to express adequately my appreciation to my dear wife and family who marvelously coped with my absences from home and encouraged me to' pursue the study when, through weakness of the flesh and potential diversions of other unmet challenges, I was tempted to put it aside. I am especially indebted to the School of World Mission at Fuller Theological Seminary and to Donald McGavran in particular for his patience, understanding and assistance. To God be the glory!

Now a word about some of the terms that recur throughout this study.

One of our concerns focuses on the reconceptualization of "mission" within the structured offices of the WCC. The concept of mission that emerged is referred to in this study as *New Mission*. By this term I mean that understanding of mission that lifts up humanization as its goal—and the ultimate objective of which is to bring about a new socio-economic-political world order having a "just, sustainable and participatory society."

By contrast, I will frequently call attention to *classical-biblical mission* (more often shortened to *classical mission*), by which I mean that complex of activities whose chief purpose is to make Jesus Christ known as Lord and Savior and to persuade men to become his disciples and responsible members of his Church.

This classical understanding of mission involves evangelism. Like *mission,* evangelism has been used in various contexts during the last 20 years. But in this study *evangelism* means the communication of the Gospel by word and deed in such a way that this good news from God about Jesus Christ, according to the Scripture, is plainly understood—a communicating that enables those who hear to believe in Christ, become his disciples, be baptized and become members of the community of his people, the Church.

All this leads to a focus on persons of other faiths or no faith whom we will refer to as *unreached peoples*. By this term we mean those who have no way to hear the Gospel effectively—and in most cases have no chance to hear it at all. These are peoples who for various cultural, linguistic, geographical or political reasons are beyond the reach of existing evangelistic programs of churches anywhere in the entire world. They may live in proximity to existing churches but be cut off from them by language, race, educational or economic status. It is recognized that there are unreached peoples among the new pagans in western culture and our churches should respond to this challenge. However, in this study the accent falls on those unreached peoples who *cannot* hear because there are no churches with Christians of like culture among them to share the Gospel—and no one has yet been sent from churches in other places to tell them about Jesus Christ. They are those who will only be reached through the classical-biblical missionary activity of the churches.

Hopefully, this study will suggest positive, practical avenues for both the WCC and the member churches to consider that will enable them to join together in ways appropriate to meet the challenge of reaching those peoples who remain unreached and untouched by the message of Jesus Christ, God's appointed Savior, who alone gives eternal salvation.

ONE
CHURCH AND
MISSION
IN A CHANGING
WORLD

The quest for a new concept of mission did not occur in a vacuum. The ferment of the twentieth century raised troubling questions for concerned Christians. Conscientious church leaders could not just close their eyes and hope the problems would go away. The crises of the century were much too cataclysmic and insistent.

Not that our century began that way. Walter Lord wrote about the first decade in America under the title, *The Good Years*. Across the Atlantic, the Edwardian prosperity and euphoria were in full flower. The superiority of western culture was assumed. Within the churches, an almost-utopian optimism tended to create a "theology" of progress. This was most dramatically illustrated by the expectant naming of a newly-published church journal: *The Christian Century*. Historians will no doubt choose a different title.

Optimism soon turned to pessimism as the slaughter of World War I, the Great Depression, the Hitler madness and the savagery of World War II followed each other in quick succession. And even these dramatic events did not fully reflect the festering social side-effects of the Industrial Revolution. These surfaced in a secular, even atheistic response which contributed to the century not only the revolutions in Russia and China, but also the Cold War, the Korean Conflict and Vietnam. The "Second World" of Communism, in west and east, posed a competitive challenge to the western nations that, in turn, affected the whole world.

It is into this kind of world that the World Council of Churches was born. True, its acknowledged genesis dates back to the optimistic period; for the ecumenical mood and community grew out of that landmark meeting of the missionary movement at its zenith: Edinburgh, 1910. Because the roots of the WCC lie deep within the missionary movement, we shall first examine the effect of the historical context on that movement.

THE WORLD OF MISSIONS

Edinburgh reflected the euphoria of the times—in the form of thanksgiving and praise. But it did not just assume a continued progress. Rather, it was a working conference marked by study and determination—to occupy the unoccupied fields and complete the task of world evangelization. For the agencies represented there, Edinburgh was a beginning. Most of these not only absorbed the early upheavals of the century, but pursued their task with renewed zeal.

Nevertheless, the close of World War II marks the end of an era. The world of nations would never be the same. Heat-of-battle promises of freedom and nationhood could not be evaded in the post war years. Nation after nation threw off its colonial government until by the end of the sixties the colonial system had become just another subject in the history books.

The end of colonialism and the entry of independent nations into international institutions was to have a profound effect upon the missionary movement and the churches. A few large countries closed their doors to missionary activities. Mission schools and hospitals were taken over by post-colonial governments. In some countries, visas were severely limited or at least difficult to obtain.

The fainthearted found ample reasons for pessimism. Some predicted that with the prop of friendly governments removed, national Christians would abandon the Christian faith and churches would no longer grow. But in many instances the exact opposite occurred. In Africa, for example, churches

16

have grown more rapidly under national governments than under colonial powers.

With the mission fields of China, Burma and the Sudan closed, large numbers of missionaries from these fields began to occupy places of leadership and influence in the sending churches to which they returned. Their frustrating and disappointing experience with "closed doors" tended to spread the pessimistic outlook that the opportunities for missionaries to enter foreign countries was fast coming to an end. Some who sacrificially supported mission work in fields now closed began to question the wisdom of long term commitments. These closed fields and the restrictions on the number of missionaries allowed (e.g., India), contributed to a mood of defeatism and despair about missionary sending.

With the rise of the independent nations, there was a mood among some leaders in the younger churches that their churches also needed independence. By similar analogy, the fact that the new nations were gaining membership in the United Nations affected relationships between missionaries, sending church leaders and receiving church leaders. The entire gamut of appropriate structures, patterns of relationships, ownership of property and program, access to funds and independence in their use, freedom to initiate new programs, the search for patterns of partnership, how mission was to be understood—these and many other related problems and challenges grew out of the end of an era.

Many raised serious questions about the relationship of the missionary movement to the colonial movement. On the one hand there were those who believed that the colonial era had been God's chosen historical moment when his people could send messengers of the Gospel everywhere with a freedom and opportunity not likely soon to be repeated. They read the "signs of the times" to mean that the Sovereign God of the nations had prepared a way. In fact, many missionaries went out believing their time was limited—that doors open today would be closed tomorrow.

Others developed serious guilt complexes by assuming that missionaries from Western churches took advantage of the situation by "riding piggy back" on colonial powers. Missionaries and their sending churches were accused of taking an immoral advantage of helpless "natives" who were powerless to deny them entry into their lands. Missionaries were considered guilty accomplices of the exploitative colonial powers and accused of cheating natives out of their latent wealth.

Ultimately, the end of the colonial era turned out to be not only an historical fact with inescapable consequences for the missionary movement, but it also served to raise serious questions about the Church itself and its Mission. The whole concept of New Mission, the development of which we will trace, cannot be understood apart from all these political, economic and social questions—questions rooted in the colonial era and its aftermath.

With the end of World War II and more noticeably after the Korean conflict, yet another event subtly affected the missionary movement. It became fashionable to think in terms of bringing the missionaries back home, just as the government brought home the soldiers who had completed their task—and, earlier, the colonial administrators and officials were returned to Europe. Further, just as national government officials moved into buildings and positions vacated by former colonial people, so mission employees and church leaders should likewise find their appropriate places and roles. Misunderstandings and wrong assumptions colored the thinking of many discussions and confused the issue of whether missionaries were still needed or wanted.

Meanwhile, the theological foundations and convictions that moved men and women to obediently seek the ends of the earth because Jesus Christ had commanded his disciples to "go and preach the Gospel" were, for some sections of the Church, shaken. For others, these convictions remained firm; the biblical mandate had not been abrogated. If we are to think clearly about a missionary and evangelistic task among unreached peoples, it is essential that the political, economic and social factors which affected the missionary movement and the quest for a new understanding of mission be taken into account. But the question arises as to whether these political, economic and social factors should determine and shape our understanding of an unfinished task; or whether our understanding must not, rather, be based on theological affirmations arising out of what God has made known in his Word.

THE WORLD OF THE CHURCHES

As indicated earlier, the modern ecumenical mood is usually traced back to Edinburgh, 1910, where delegates of the missionary community came together to share their joint concerns for the evangelization of the world. The shared experience of that meeting spawned the Faith and Order movement (1920) and gave an assist to the Life and Work movement (1930). These two streams eventually merged to form the World Council of Churches (1948).

But the WCC owes more to the missionary movement than the realized fellowship across a broad spectrum that characterized Edinburgh. Throughout the gestation period, Christian world mission was the common uniting thread.

> At virtually every point, the conviction and impulses of Christian unity originated within the enterprise of Christian mission (Van Dusen 1961:16).

Moreover, this world evangelization produced churches. As more churches were formed, more churches could become part of the ecumenical body of churches. Today representatives come to WCC assemblies from all six continents.

Despite this common ground, it is hardly surprising that by mid-century, church leaders would view their world somewhat differently than the leaders of the missionary movement saw theirs. Concerned and sensitive Christian leaders tried to come to grips with what was happening—and tried to put it all together. They asked basic, essential and inescapable questions that demanded answers. The questions asked by their churches, the cries of the poor and powerless, the violence, the determination to change conditions that had been accepted too long—all these were part of the context for examining the meaning of what was happening.

The questions dealt with what God was doing in the world, and what the churches, the people who claimed to be his, could do to be a part of what God was doing. Those seeking such answers were no longer primarily an elite group from within the life of affluent Western churches. In the ecumenical church, non-western spokesmen told of their experiences from among the poor peoples of the world. They brought different perspectives that contributed just as much in shaping this new understanding as those with keen awarenesses of social demands from the western world.

One fundamental and inescapable fact seemed apparent to those who reflected on the meaning of this new, modern world: it was a world that was rapidly becoming secularized. Age old assumptions no longer held people captive. Van Leeuwen ranks high among those who recognized the full implications of this process of secularization (1964).

The views of Bonhoeffer, Cox, Hoekendijk, Rahner, Moltmann and, more recently, Gutierrez, Miguez and Cone have pushed Calvin, Luther and Barth off the stage. These new voices from within the churches were pounding in one ear while in the other came voices from the world: Marx, Mao, Guevara and others. Always in the background were the cries of the poor, the hungry, the exploited, the powerless; the voices of minorities, youth and women; victims of racism, the imprisoned and the tortured. Earlier optimism had long since given way to misgiving, doubt and stark reality. Hopes too long deferred gave way to hopelessness, apart from major changes in the actual structures of society. The way things were going, the rich were becoming richer and the poor were becoming poorer. These problems were seen to be intricately interrelated, complex, global in nature; furthermore, they involved every structure and institution that shaped people's lives.

Looking out into the world, church leaders from within the WCC saw this new secularized world and asked themselves what the implications were for the churches. They looked at the churches they knew and saw too little correlation between what their churches looked like, did and said, and what they saw happening in the world. They were not relevantly participating in the new world; their structures were geared to another day. In this mood, the call for a reconceptualization of what the churches should be doing was a natural consequence.

In searching for new understandings there was a search for relevance. Brilliant flashes of insight, useful for particular situations, were too frequently made universal. Traditionally, answers had been sought first from the Scriptures. Now it became more fashionable to begin with the world. If one wanted to hear the voice of God, one must listen to him speak through the voices of the poor, the exploited, the powerless. God speaks to us from the world. His concern is for the world. Therefore, to experience Christ, one meets him in other people, especially among the struggling and hurting, the poor.

Those passages in the Bible dealing with God's concern for the poor and liberation took on vast new meanings with their own implications about our understanding of God and his intent for the world. The experience out in the world, followed by the reading of the Bible, focused on a kind of reading that spoke to that situation. Understandably the Bible was read selectively—and seen through different eyes. Many saw new meanings in familiar passages; our presuppositions were said to color the way we have traditionally understood many of the familiar accounts; ways in which our ideology affects our interpretation of the Bible were emphasized. People who didn't like the new selective reading of the Bible were also judged guilty of bypassing large sections of Scripture because of the difficulty in harmonizing them with their other ideological presuppositions. Some even suggested a materialistic Bible study method to show the relevance of many passages in support of positions arrived at on other ideological grounds (Rostagno 1977).

While it is true that the basic approach for some was to look out into the world first and then look into the Bible, it is a fact that the Bible was, and still is, being studied seriously. Many suggested that the approach to take was to be involved at all levels in the struggle with the poor, and then reflect on the meaning of that experience. Their formula was action/reflection. One "does" theology. Theological understandings arise out of experience.

During this quest for a new and more profound understanding of what God was doing in their reading of history and their particular historical moment, some basic assumptions began to emerge. A consensus formed. But it would be a gross over-

21

simplification to think that each of these basic assumptions holds the same implications and ramifications for everyone who holds them. Within the WCC and its member churches there is a tremendous range of backgrounds—a variety of theological orientations, traditions and contemporary experience coming out of many different cultural and ethnic groups. While a consensus seems evident among those who have the power to influence and determine policies, shape programs and tell the listening world what that consensus is, there are within the movement large numbers of people who subscribe only at certain points to that general consensus about God and mission, but have serious reservations at other points. This is important to bear in mind when we are tempted to say that "the WCC believes . . ." Recognizing the complexity doesn't make things simpler. But it does more closely correspond to the realities of the WCC.

CHURCHES ON SIX CONTINENTS

In a recent interview I asked W. A. Visser 't Hooft, honorary president of the WCC, what had happened in the ecumenical movement that he had not anticipated. With no hesitation whatsoever, he stated that it was the speed with which the movement had grown. He referred to the rapid increase in membership among Third World churches and the resulting impact on the WCC's understanding of both itself and of the entire mission of the Church. He also spoke of the tremendous impact of the Orthodox churches upon the WCC and upon the ecumenical movement as a whole.

Yes, the quest for new understandings had broadened. In the past, theologies and statements about God and man had been formulated largely by Christians with a Western perspective. Now Christians from the Third World were equally important in reading the "signs of the times." Basically, these new voices reacted against what appeared to them to be rationalized, propositional statements about God. Speaking from their experiences and from a perception of God that arose out of different cultural and ethnic backgrounds, they suggested that man's understanding of God should be shaped in large measure out of these experiences; that understandings about salvation came out of experiences shared in ecumenical fellowship—experiences arising from their often exploited, racist-enforced structures and out of longings for liberation. In their own way, they were also focused on a "doing" theology. Increasingly, Third World problems and perspectives as voiced by these spokesmen influenced the balance of power in the ecumenical movement in a shift from the west and north to the south and east. Assumptions derived from differing backgrounds both within and without the churches of the ecumenical movement seemed to converge.

Meanwhile, the contribution of western churches seemed blunted by external and internal problems. American churches were deeply involved in civil rights issues—and then came the agony of the Vietnam conflict. Confrontation and polarization between peoples, dissatisfaction of youth with the churches, sit-ins and occupation of church offices and schools were commonplace. Students no longer wanted to attend compulsory chapel; the relevance of prayer, worship and Bible study were questioned. The call was to get involved and find God in the anonymous Christian. Everywhere churches were called on to demonstrate their relevance. A moratorium on new church buildings seemed sensible. Church growth was not on the agenda. Money is better spent in helping people.

As for European churches, many appeared increasingly aloof from the changes taking place in the way people lived and organized their activities. Sermons were dull. Churches were devoid of youth. Traditional forms persisted, but for the majority, the church existed only to perform the ritual duties associated with birth, marriage and death. What took place in religion took place in churches, but among fewer and fewer people. The working classes were hardly represented. Indifference stalked the churches whose bells tolled mournfully of a day that had passed. Churches were said to be relics of the past, completely out of touch with modern man. They were characterized by a kind of "morphological fundamentalism" (Hoekendijk 1952).

Many churches in both America and Europe were experiencing a deadness to spiritual things. In Europe, Christianity was culturally acceptable only for the remaining few, while in America it had become fashionable, particularly among the middle class. Ardent Christians saw nominal Christians leaving the churches as a good thing. Many churches had little real Christian joy to share with anyone else. Preachers were preoccupied and forgot how to proclaim good news; many had nothing gripping to say about Jesus Christ. There was little Gospel to proclaim, for the power had disappeared. Over much of the Church many were ready to write, "Ichabod."

Perhaps this assessment made by large sections of the Church is too grim. It is indisputable, however, that leaders in many churches knew a radical change was mandatory if modern secular man was to again become interested in whatever churches were supposed to be all about.

Stirrings in Third World churches related more closely to the missionary movement itself. While Western church life (both in spiritual quality and in an understanding of how change could be relevant) had direct bearing on their continued participation in missionary involvement, what Third World churches were thinking and saying, in the long run, would be more significant. These churches were concerned about their identity particularly in terms of their freedom.

> The time in which the Christian community was solely under the leadership of European and American Christians is over. Increasingly the "younger churches" have been taking their place in the ecumenical movement. It would not be difficult to mention a number of names of Asians, Latin Americans and Africans who have influenced the life of the Church profoundly in the last years. Theological reflection may still be heavily dominated by Europe and North America, but the matter on which this reflection takes place often originates outside these continents (Vanden Heuval 1973:55).

When their nations gained independence from colonial rule, Third World churches too wanted their freedom from both missions and missionaries. Their governments met in international forums, and heads of government spoke to each other as equals. Could they not have equal partnership relations with Western churches? They wanted opportunities for heads of churches to speak with other heads of churches. So it was that church-to-church relationships replaced the indirect route where the missions and missionaries were the middlemen. This was a normal reaction to paternalistic attitudes where churches in the West made the decisions for their good. They needed what Western churches had to offer, but they wanted no strings attached.

Missionary numbers were progressively reduced, for Western churches felt sure that some of the tensions could be eased by fewer missionaries "interfering" in the life of churches. In many instances they had become too tied to institutions. And missionaries themselves were no longer so keen to be out on the cutting edge. Much of the original idealism and high expectations had faded.

International meetings of government and business leaders, scientists, educators, experts of all kinds grappled with world problems. Ecumenical church counterparts followed suit, dealing with the same or similar problems. Increasingly, thoughts and efforts of church leaders from many parts of the world were devoted to revolution and struggles for freedom from oppressive governments and institutions based on racism. And their awareness of these things happening on a global scale affected everything they discussed. The separation between Church and governments sometimes blurred. Both were tackling the same problems in similar ways. Moreover, Third World church leaders were close to their governments in some instances, particularly in Africa. Most of their government leadership had been trained in mission operated schools. The most prominent Third World church leaders were international in outlook. Naturally, those in the WCC were interested in international issues and saw a relationship between what their churches did and what happened in their countries. Churches became increasingly aware of a comradeship with other churches who shared like expectations, experienced similar frustrations and suffered in the same kind of struggle.

The Third World churches had come of age. An era had ended. In the larger, challenging world there was a danger that both Third World churches and churches of the West would turn aside from the unfinished missionary task. Third World churches were becoming preoccupied with social and political issues, and with relationships and questions about their positions within ecumenical structures. Western churches were so enamored of developing church-to-church relations with these younger churches that they neglected the realities of tiny churches in the midst of vast unevangelized populations. Succeeding ecumenical leaders became so consumed with social issues that this may have diverted Third World churches from evangelizing their own unreached peoples. C. W. Ransom of the IMC spoke for many in reminding all churches that the task of world evangelization was not yet complete. He said:

> If we stand at the end of an era, it is not because the task of world evangelization has been completed. It is true that the Christian Church has taken root in most countries of the world. But in many places it is a very small and tender plant; and there are vast areas of the world in which the task of evangelization has *scarcely begun.* [Italics mine.] Measured in terms of population, the unfinished task is more formidable today than it was when Ziegenbalg and Plutschau set out for Tranquebar. (Ransom 1954).

MISSIONARY INFLUENCE DECLINES

Historically, missions and missionaries had played a central role in developing ecumenical relationships between Western and Third World churches. In the quest for a new understanding of mission, however, this role for missionaries of mainline American churches became increasingly smaller. Many Western church leaders were not intimately involved in the missionary movement that had given rise to Third World churches. They were outside the tradition that brought these churches into being. Third World church roots and early ecumenical relationships grew within the limited structures of the missionary movement. As churches multiplied and formed their own councils, the relationships of these younger churches, to each other and to the churches of the Western world, involved dual relationships with a certain amount of confusion and overlapping.

When Third World churches were "set free" from this am-
bivalent, dual set of relationships by the integration of the IMC
into the WCC, they realized more fully what they had missed
and now knew they wanted to be full members of the ecumenical movement structured in the World Council of Churches.
Pressures from within the Western churches and longings from
within the Third World churches hastened the process.

Mission agencies and missionaries had long enjoyed a
monopoly in their own churches about Third World matters.
When questions arose about missions and challenges in other
places, mission executives and missionaries were the experts.
This began to change as Third World churches became full
members of the WCC. When the IMC was integrated into the
WCC, this had a significant bearing on the quest for a new
understanding of mission. In the transition, the decisions
(about what churches should do and what their mission was)
were increasingly made by people from Western churches who
had not been involved in the missionary movement, and by
people from Third World churches who had been unable to
communicate clearly before, due to the intermediate screen of
the mission organization and the missionaries.

Inevitably, in the integration process, the unfinished worldwide missionary and evangelistic task lost out. It lost its
structure, its visibility and its flexibility—all so vital to missions.

The winds of change were blowing. So strong were they that
the "s" was blown right off the word "missions." The term
missions became *mission*. Only later would many realize that
much more than a change in spelling was involved. But Bishop
Lesslie Newbigin had already in 1960 alerted us that subtle,
crucial differences were implied.

> When we speak of "the mission of the Church" we mean
> everything that the Church is sent into the world to do—
> preaching the Gospel, healing the sick, caring for the
> poor, teaching the children, improving international and
> interracial relations, attacking injustice—all of this and
> more can rightly be included in the phrase "the Mission
> of the Church."

But within this totality there is a narrower concern which we usually speak of as "missions." Let us, without being too refined, describe the narrower concern by saying: it is the concern that in the places where there are no Christians there should be Christians (1960:23).

Peter Wagner also calls attention to the importance of what was meant by this change:

The phrase *the church is mission* is more dangerous than it might first appear. It reflects a subtle but widespread shift in emphasis from making disciples as the top-priority missionary goal to simply doing good works in the world (1971:54).

New understandings about mission were evolving, with new goals and new priorities. Would the new concept which says the whole "church is mission" challenge us to evangelize the three billion who remain without messengers to share the transforming Gospel of Christ? Which priorities would be implemented by programs, people and funds?

It remains to be seen whether the World Council of Churches, or its member churches, can keep alive the vision of an unfinished missionary and evangelistic task aimed to reach these people for Christ. It remains to be seen whether the dictum of New Mission (that the whole Church is mission, or exists for mission) can make it more likely—or less likely—for those yet unreached to have a valid opportunity to come to know Jesus Christ as Savior.

There are missiologists of note who contend that churches, per se, cannot carry out this unfinished missionary and evangelistic task. Church history, they say, shows that apart from the initiatives of the "committed few" (orders, mission boards and societies) there would be no new churches in the Third World to comprise a truly worldwide ecumenical movement—and no World Council of Churches to opine what it thinks churches should be doing. Churches would still be largely confined to the Western world and ancient churches would remain isolated in their ghettos.

Still, the question remains: can churches who believe that

the whole church exists for mission focus on an unfinished missionary and evangelistic task? Is it possible for them to fashion, within the life of the churches and within the World Council of Churches, those instruments for mission that will enable their members to participate with impact in this task? Do we dare to hope that at long last the whole Church will, in everything it does, make evangelism central to its life and work? Will members be challenged, encouraged and assisted to reach out to the "ends of the earth" to communicate the Gospel among otherwise unreached peoples?

Such a task is possible only when hundreds, even thousands of new missionaries go out from within the life of all the churches to peoples yet unreached—when they proclaim in ways relevant to our time the transforming power of the one saving Gospel from God in Jesus Christ. Three billion people are waiting! Each one of these should have a valid option to become a follower of the Lord Jesus Christ. There is no more basic human right!

TWO
MISSION IN
TENSION
The International Missionary Council

In that momentous worldwide missionary conference at Edinburgh in 1910, men and women of great vision and faith dreamed together of evangelizing the world in that generation. Their burning zeal characterized the missionary movement at its best.

The Edinburgh delegates created a Continuation Committee. In 1921 this became the International Missionary Council (IMC). It had one controlling purpose: to encourage and assist churches and mission societies in their missionary task. The core of that task was consistently understood to be sharing with all peoples everywhere the transforming power of the Gospel of Jesus Christ. In other words, IMC was focused on the missionary task.

From Jerusalem (1928) to Ghana (1957), the theological foundations of mission demanded that the churches obey their Lord who had with authority and clarity commanded, "Disciple the nations." Each international meeting focused on major issues of how to best carry out this command within the framework of the classical-biblical understanding of mission. Their biblical foundations were secure. Their directions were clear. Their manner and method however had to adapt to the particular historical moment.

EARLY INTERNATIONAL CONFERENCES

The Jerusalem, 1928, conference dealt with the threat of secularism. In a world where mission and church leaders were perhaps tempted to join with other religions in a common effort to stem the tide of secularism, the IMC clearly affirmed:

> Our message is Jesus Christ. He is the revelation of what God is, and of what man through Him may become . . . He made known to us God as our Father, in Him we find God incarnate, the final, yet ever unfolding, revelation of the God in whom we live and move and have our being (IMC 1928:402).

The Tambaram, Madras, meeting (1938) wrestled with the relationship of the Christian message to the messages of the non-Christian World. Hendrik Kraemer's monumental study on the Christian message and the non-Christian world dominated the conference. The question of the uniqueness of Christ was handled decisively. He was God's appointed Savior intended for the whole world. There was no other Savior.

Events of the day reinforced the reality of man's sin and guilt and his inability to save himself. The world was in the depths of depression. War was imminent. In that atmosphere, leaders of the missionary movement found it easy to affirm that God alone can save. And this affirmation affected the whole conference. Man's lostness apart from God and apart from the hope described in the Bible was confirmed by the then current events. The IMC did not doubt that the solution for man in society, and for the world's problems in general, was found in the saving power of Jesus Christ. This was good news from God—then as now—for a world in desperate need of solutions that man by himself was incapable of providing. The convictions at Madras were based on God's self revelation in the Bible. The realism of the Bible matched the realities of the world.

> Man is the child of God, made in His image. God has designed him for life in fellowship with Himself, and with his brothers in the family of God on earth. Yet in the mystery of the freedom which God has given him, man

chooses to walk other paths, to seek other ends. He defies his Father's will. He seeks to be a law unto himself. This is the deepest cause of the evil and misery of his life. Alienated from God, he seeks his salvation where it cannot be found. Impotent to save himself, he stands ever in need of conversion, of forgiveness, of regeneration.

Who then shall save? God saves, through Jesus Christ our Lord. 'God so loved the world that He gave his only begotten Son that whosoever believeth on Him should not perish but have everlasting life.' This is the heart of the Christian Gospel, the Gospel which we proclaim (IMC 1938:186).

The IMC spoke decisively out of theological convictions shaped by Scripture. At the same time, (and as was true at all IMC conferences) Madras conferences wrestled with questions that defied unanimous views. The ferment of discussion and debate was enlivened and intensified by the growing number of representatives from the younger churches. The result of successful missionary work meant that more and more churches were formed. And the additional voices from these Third World churches rightly and inevitably needed to be heard. It was only a matter of time before the question arose as to whether these spokesmen from Third World churches truly spoke for the churches they represented.

WHITBY 1947

The Whitby meeting in 1947 (Latourette 1948) is especially remembered for its note of "expectant evangelism." The call to renewed efforts in worldwide evangelism was sounded clearly. Churches were reminded of their central task; the world remained largely unevangelized. Encouraged by God's faithfulness in preserving and keeping his people during the terrible war years, with their long periods of separation and isolation, the leaders were eager to move confidently ahead in the power of the Gospel. For was not the task directed by God himself through Jesus Christ? Though war had interrupted and threatened, they were mercifully preserved and marvelously protected by God. Therefore, they should now move ahead with programs of "expectant evangelism."

Those at Whitby also dared to dream of evangelizing the world in such a way that all would soon hear the Gospel. The Whitby meeting was regarded as in the finest tradition of Edinburgh. God's eye was assuredly on the world. Joy and hope filled hearts. The churches, now that the war was over, could expand out into a world once again open to missionaries. Though setbacks in China, Burma and the Sudan lay ahead, they anticipated with joy the task God had for the churches and their mission societies.

Events at Whitby show clearly that IMC's consistent priority was mission, with evangelism the core. The Gospel was to be proclaimed or communicated in such a way as to be good news from God calling all who heard to repent and accept God's offer of eternal salvation through Jesus Christ. These would then become Christ's disciples and members of his Church.

WILLINGEN 1952

It was at the Willingen meeting in 1952 that new theological winds began to blow more strongly. Issues first raised there continued to develop until they eventually dominated later discussions about mission in the Commission on World Mission and Evangelism (CWME) and the WCC.

The Willingen conference addressed itself to the question of the "Missionary Obligation of the Church" (IMC 1952). What was the exact nature of that missionary obligation? The meeting was held in the wake of the closing or threatened closing of many traditional mission fields to Western missionaries. Churches of the West lost their incentive for missions. They increasingly began to place higher priorities on mission to their own neighborhoods and communities. Earlier visions of evangelizing the world dimmed at Willingen.

One question surfacing at Willingen (which became central to the discussions about mission in the post New Delhi, 1961, period) was: Did the missionary obligation of the Church derive from the redemptive purpose and acts of God, or did it arise from the very nature of God himself? In trying to express

the precise relation of the Church to its mission, they found
they could not agree. The entire question of how the Church
relates to the Kingdom of God and the extent to which its
message focuses on future eschatological hope could not be
resolved. Just how much of that message is motivated by
looking to God to establish his kingdom beyond history when
his Christ returns for the final consummation? Statements
carefully designed to reach a consensus were received by the
conference but left unadopted. Raised in incipient form at Willingen were also theological issues related to the tremendous
changes in the whole concept of mission. The Willingen conference was the crack in the door that opened the way for the
classical-biblical interpretation of mission to be supplanted by
"New Mission."

Willingen produced official statements, however, that essentially reflected biblical perspectives. No one reading the
Willingen documents would have predicted what would be said
about mission at Uppsala, only sixteen short years later. The
Willingen statement by no means concluded that "humanization is the goal of mission" (IMC 1952).

In comparing language, style and content of the Willingen
documents with statements made by spokesmen of WCC
member churches in the seventies, one finds the entire concept
of mission changed. However, words have been redefined and
used in new combinations. Language at Willingen reflected
commonly understood classical-biblical perspectives. Theological presuppositions about God, man, the Church and the
world—as shaped by the Bible—were largely unchanged.

GHANA 1957: THE FATEFUL DECISION

At Ghana the assurance was given that the IMC would be able
to do more for "missions and evangelism" from within the
WCC than by remaining outside. The missionary movement
had created its own structures to promote and facilitate the
missionary task. And these structures had served well. Historically and consistently, that task had been undertaken in
response to the vision of a "committed few," or "a spiritual
vanguard," as Max Warren had called them (see below).
Eventually these few created structures appropriate for in-

35

volving increasing numbers of persons. The various mission societies and agencies, denominational boards, national organizations (e.g., the Foreign Missions Conference of North America) and the International Missionary Council related to one another as they sought to carry forward their classical-biblical understanding of mission. From its inception, the International Missionary Council had been concerned preeminently with the unfinished task of carrying the Gospel to the ends of the earth (IMC 1961a:3). Was it possible that the whole church was now ready to wholeheartedly embrace the cause of world evangelization?

The die was cast at Ghana in 1957 (Orchard 1958). There the IMC voted to recommend to its constituent members that it be integrated into the World Council of Churches, though it was not until 1961 (at New Delhi) that the decision became final and the IMC officially became the Division of World Mission and Evangelism within the World Council of Churches.

The question of integration was ultimately a practical one, though both theological and practical arguments suggested that the time had come. Members from the two bodies (the IMC and the WCC) working in a Joint Committee had done the spadework. Some thought this Committee should have been content with seeking only affirmative approval of its recommendations rather than calling for decision.

The WCC promised that the missionary and evangelistic commitment would now become central to its life and work. The outcome, however, proved otherwise. Integration served at the outset to facilitate the new formulations about mission and later led to actual dismantling of the missionary-sending capacity in most member churches. The quest for a new conceptualization of mission took a fateful turn in the wake of the decision at Ghana. What a large door would swing on that small hinge! How prophetic were the voices of those who expressed their concern at that time!

There is no dispute about the depth of thought, prayer and study that went into the matter of integration. A careful reading of the full transcript of prepared statements by member missions, councils and churches, as well as by delegate speeches will show this. Passions ran high among both the proponents and the opponents of integration. Interestingly, both sides agreed that the decision taken would have momentous consequences for the whole missionary movement.

Stephen Neill, for example, believed that integration was a thinly disguised way for the WCC to liquidate the troublesome IMC. He rejected integration because:

> The present attitude of the World Council, however marked by polite phrases, is that the IMC is simply an anachronistic nuisance and the sooner it is liquidated by becoming a part of the World Council, the better . . . (Nissen 1974:546).

And he said the WCC did not show:

> . . . signs of any strong missionary passion . . . responsibility for the international aspect of missionary work cannot yet safely be left in its hands (*ibid.*).

He claimed that integration meant that "the IMC would simply become one department of the WCC among ten or twelve, and by no means the most important" (*ibid.*). Bishop Neill's statement was prophetic! For in 1977 the IMC has disappeared and its successor, the CWME, is merely a sub-unit of a larger unit within the WCC.

H. P. Van Dusen, Chairman of the Joint Committee that prepared the recommendation for integration, spoke as follows:

> Throughout its work the Joint Committee has had before it the conditions which were laid down by the Officers of the I.M.C. in their first discussion of integration. It is: "Before proceeding to submit to its member councils any proposal for a possible integration . . . the I.M.C. must satisfy itself that the result will be to bring the missionary obligation of the Church more sharply into focus as a central responsibility of the entire ecumenical movement. We must be assured that the actual plan of reorganization would promote this outlook, with such changes in the present structure and proceedings of the present Council as would be entailed. There would be required provision

37

for the necessary measure of autonomy for the missionary arm, and adequate representation of missionary
interests in the central bodies of the Council and vice
versa" (Mimeographed papers and notes on Ghana proceedings, WCC Archives, Geneva, p. 4).

In this same major address, Dr. Van Dusen pointed out
another guideline the Joint Committee had set up to insure that
all the IMC had stood for would be preserved in the integration. In this way he attempted to reassure the skeptic and win
over those who had strong reservations. He said:

> . . . the present reality of the I.M.C., not merely its pres-
> ent programme in its full scope and strength, but also its
> present membership and constituency, its traditions,
> loyalties and dedications should be embraced entirely
> within the proposed new organization (*ibid:*4).

Arguments for Integration. Proponents of integration spoke
confidently of the entire WCC being reshaped by this step. The
IMC was not to be viewed as simply an "add on." Basic
changes involving the decision-making process, and a redistribution of power and influence, were envisaged for the enlarged WCC. Honest and good people sincerely believed that
the presence of the IMC in the WCC would enable the entire
work of the Council to take on a more missionary character.
Unless the IMC became an integral part of the Council, the
WCC could not possibly enable the churches to do together all
those things God's people were supposed to be doing.

The social dimension of the Gospel, togetherness among the
churches, and the missionary obligation of those churches all
belonged together as a unit. The logic was irresistible! However, insufficient importance was attached to the committed
few who sparked and kept alive the missionary impetus in
churches everywhere. It had been those few who had been
"fanatic" about missions and then had fashioned instruments
and structures to move ahead with the task who had originally
banded together in the IMC.

A significant number of the keen thinkers and leaders of the
pre-Ghana missionary movement feared that, while it sounded

plausible enough for the whole church to be committed to mission, in practice it wouldn't work. Unless the concept of missions as world evangelization was kept alive and preserved in the churches as the supremely important goal, all that the IMC had been doing in that regard would be lost. As it turned out, advocates of biblical missions within the churches as a whole, and particularly within the integrated council, were outnumbered and outvoted, to the neglect of the unfinished missionary task.

Many convincing reassurances were part of the Ghana debate. Not only did the chairman of the Joint Committee attempt to show that the legitimate concerns and fears of IMC member constituents had been taken into account and provision made to allay such fears, but the WCC Central Committee representative also assured the Assembly that the WCC knew of those fears and was as eager as the IMC to give first place to the missionary obligation of the Church. Franklin Fry, Chairman of the Central Committee of the WCC, spoke as follows:

> We are overwhelmingly convinced that the proposed integration, quite apart from its mechanics, is theologically correct. When we are asked, Is the WCC actually interested in mission?, we feel ourselves restrained because we do not wish to transgress on the rightful territory of the IMC. There are many instances in which we would like to be at the very heart of discussion and action. We believe, with the Joint Committee, that mission as well as unity, belongs to the *esse* of the Church; and find it frequently confusing and embarrassing to separate those things that belong together and handle them in separate, though frequently cooperative organizations. A Church like the one I represent in the WCC is perplexed, with many others, in this situation. Mission is integral to the life of our church and in its operations. . . . There is a large body of opinion in many of the member bodies of the WCC, that the union of the two groups is not only natural but is called for by theological consistency (Unpublished Ghana papers, WCC Archives).

Dr. Fry went on to speak of the appropriateness of the time

for the decision to integrate. He saw this as the Holy Spirit's timing. He spoke of the practical difficulties of delay, of embarrassments and of unnecessary frustrations and irritations experienced by staff of both the WCC and the IMC as their responsibilities or common concerns converged, and yet involved separate organizations. He rightly pointed out the special problems the younger churches faced; they found it particularly offensive and incomprehensible to hold membership in more or less competing organizations. To them this symbolized a disunity within the Church.

The WCC was obviously eager to integrate the IMC into a single structure. The IMC was assured that necessary schedule adjustments for the next Assembly could be made if this would enable a favorable decision. It would then be possible for the IMC and the WCC to meet at the same time and place to consummate the integration of the two bodies. With good humor and charm Dr. Fry persuasively presented the WCC invitation:

> I have been impressed by the repeated emphasis that the IMC has nothing to lose; that it will be carried over intact into the new organization; that it will have more of its present powers enhanced, and that the WCC will be improved in the process! May I suggest with great humility that there may be developments also in the other direction? (Mimeographed papers, WCC Archives, Geneva).

Misgivings about Integration. It was the late M. A. C. Warren, the greatly respected thinker and leader in the missionary movement, who spoke most passionately and eloquently for those who had the gravest misgivings about integration. He recognized the tremendous implications for the future of the missionary movement if integration took place. He feared greatly that the unfinished missionary task would suffer as a result of integration.

Because of his depth of perception in 1957—which was so thoroughly validated by 1977—and because he held these same views until he died, I quote him at length. Hear Dr. Warren's emotion charged voice as he addresses the tension-gripped Assembly in Ghana:

I am standing here with trembling, because we face such tremendous issues; standing under the Holy Spirit of God, and standing thus, it is not easy to know how best to speak the convictions of one's heart, which may all too easily find unhappy verbal expression. But briefly my own position is this:

Of course, I do not know how this debate will develop, but as I see things at the moment, I am disposed to think that I shall cast my vote in favour of integration. But I would like to make it extremely clear that I do it with the most profound regret, believing that we are possibly about to make a very great mistake. It is only because of that regret and that hesitation that I am presuming to address you at all.

I will try and give you my reasons for voting. My first one is a pragmatic reason. I think that things have gone too far for us to avoid the decision in favor of integration. The officers of the IMC who have given enormous thought and care to this issue are, I judge, firmly convinced that integration must proceed. That being the case, supposing this Assembly voted against integration, they would be forced to resign because there would be no mandate in which they had confidence. That would impose an incredibly, absurdly embarrassing position on the IMC. I want to avoid that, and hope and believe there are ways in which embarrassment of that kind can be avoided.

I think it was an error in tactics for the officers of the IMC to present in written form, first of all, a case wholly on one side of the debate.* The case for non-integration has not been presented to the Assembly, and to imagine that a case can be made within the pressure of affairs here, which can do justice to all the arguments is, I think, illusory. It would be very easy indeed for a considered statement to be set before us. You could then have weighed the matter and made your decision; but there has

---

*He is referring to the Payne-Moses pamphlet, FMC.

been no opportunity for you to so judge. I think that was a mistake. I also regret the fact that the presentation of the whole issue yesterday was so heavily loaded on one side, so that almost there was no awareness that there were any new issues which divided us deeply. That, I think, is a pity. That has to be said in all fairness because it lies behind some of the real concern that some of us feel about this whole conclusion. I am concerned that this vital matter should be pushed through in a hurry; and as far as the Assembly is concerned, it is in a hurry. For while those who have been preoccupied with this for some years have come to their conclusions on the matter, to suggest that this has been deeply debated and discussed fully anywhere else I would question.

It is an extraordinarily difficult thing to get a measured judgment by widely disparate groups of people. There is the vast problem of communication of ideas, which have to be translated into other languages than English. That in itself is the task which might be expected to take a good many years. I regret this error in tactics which might be a source of bitterness unless the Holy Spirit is allowed into our hearts and minds (Unpublished Ghana papers, WCC Archives).

Dr. Warren then moves to the theological issues associated with the subject of unity and mission, more specifically the viewpoint presented that mission can only be fulfilled in unity.

Mission and Unity belong together, of course, but there is no obvious necessity for that belongingness to be stressed administratively. There would seem to be two main theological positions, and here, with great presumption, I do not recognize the one which you presented as representing my point of view at all.

To my mind there are two main theological positions on this subject. The one, that only with unity can mission be fulfilled. I deeply and profoundly respect those who hold that judgment, theologically speaking, that only with

42

unity can mission be fulfilled. That that represents eschatological truth I don't question for one moment. I
think we sometimes overlook the fact that what may be
necessary* is not a necessary condition for pursuit. It is a
non sequitur represented by the whole of church history,
that in fact mission can be promoted without unity. May I
remind you of the Apostle Paul in his letter to the Philippians [quoted from Philippians 1:15-18].

. . . I go a very long way, a very long way with those who
feel that only in unity can mission be fulfilled. I respect
that position and am much in sympathy with it, but it
does not correspond with the facts . . . mission can be
pursued without an equal preoccupation with unity. So it
has always been . . . In the providence of God, mission
has been pursued in disunity. The two main groups, on the
one hand the Pentecostals and on the other the Roman
Catholics—neither of whom is particularly concerned
with what we understand by unity—are the ones who are
making the real, growing mission of the Church today.
Those are the two groups who never ask about mission
but get on with it. But we spend conference after conference asking what it is, and set up committees to tell us,
while they are speeding forth. That is one of the tragedies
of the present situation to which we ought to address
ourselves. I state that we are paralyzed while they go
from strength to strength. Is God saying something to His
Church which is disturbing its very foundations? We
have got to ask ourselves that question, and suffer in the
asking of it.

. . . only in the pursuit of mission are we going to be led
into the meaning of unity (*ibid*. WCC Archives).

At this point Dr. Warren spoke to a concern that if the IMC
were to be integrated into the WCC some constituent members
would drop out to the loss of the total missionary effort of the
churches:

*text distorted

I don't think we should fool ourselves for a moment into thinking that if integration was ordered it is possible that this and that council would not disaffiliate itself. That is as certain as that the sun will rise. Let us face that. The facts of the situation are that there is profound suspicion of the WCC, not primarily on theological grounds; the real reason is the profound distrust of mammoth organizations. We have got to take that seriously, notwithstanding the completely honest statements by officers of the WCC and its Committees, that they do not envisage a super-church, and we know they don't. There is, however, a fear on the part of many that we are driving to a super-organization. Many of such Christians are feeling their way into unity, at least into cooperation with those who are deeply committed to the WCC. Why should we, at this moment, choose to stifle a movement towards, a very tentative movement of personal understanding, which I believe will be killed with integration? (*ibid.* WCC Archives).

Dr. Warren did cast his vote for integration, but with the saddest of misgivings. He concluded:

Are you surprised therefore if I view with some misgivings a move towards integration, which I believe will lead to the creation of a new organization?

And yet I think I shall give my vote for integration, with sadness of heart and the deepest misgivings, because I cannot see clearly that this is the leading of the Holy Spirit. I can only act blindly, trying to trust the opinion, as it may well be, of the majority of others as dedicated to the Holy Spirit who, in the end, will give them a vision that I am not receiving. I would certainly want to support the decision of the majority, but if that comes to be taken, I hope it will not be accompanied with the singing of the doxology, because it will be given in many cases by those whose hearts are filled with misgivings that we are giving away a priceless asset of the mission of the Church and are imperiled by fresh organizational developments which will waste manpower at a time when every Christian should be organized in the saving of the world (*ibid.* WCC Archives).

Dr. Warren feared that by attaining integration the missionary vision would dim because it would lose its vitality in the giving up of its freedom, flexibility and visibility. Those deeply committed to the missionary task needed to continue as a "spiritual vanguard" in the churches. They needed their own structures to promote the work and to challenge the whole Church to become a part of it. Perhaps then the whole Church would one day participate in that central task of evangelization to the ends of the earth.

In a personal letter to me dated February 22, 1977, his conviction underlying his concern at Ghana is expressed perhaps even more strongly:

> Mission, understood as Evangelization (the IMC understanding) calls for almost infinite *flexibility*, because no two situations are alike. And flexibility demands, in practice, specialist organs for action *and,* a vital factor, a readiness to take initiatives which may be mistaken! Official bodies have an inbuilt hesitation about ever taking risks!

> This is where, as I see it, the *Voluntary Principle* becomes important. The Church, *qua* Institution, has manifold tasks to discharge, not least the conservation of all that has been achieved in history, the guarding of the Faith; and the continuing ministry to the Christian community whose members are at every stage of spiritual development from spiritual infancy to spiritual maturity.

> This is the essential role of the Church. Only when this role is being adequately discharged can we talk of the Church in a very broad sense as a 'Mission' in its own right. In so far as it is faithful to the Gospel the Church qua Church is a witness.

> The role of the voluntary society within the Church is to serve as a spiritual vanguard, as regards mission.

45

Now it was this role of "spiritual vanguard" as regards world-evangelization, which the IMC was discharging. And I would say that it was discharging it with ever-increasing success. What is more, because it was wholly preoccupied with evangelistic outreach, it held together in a real bond of fellowship those whose doctrinal positions varied from High Lutherans and High Anglicans to Quakers *and* everything in between.

There was a unity of common purpose without any attempt at uniformity of action or doctrine. But in following a common purpose there was, as a sequel, a growing sense of spiritual unity. And, be it noted, it was from such co-operation that such initiatives as the Church of South India became possible. The movement towards Church Union sprang out of mission. Mission has never had to wait for Church Unity. That is an historical fact which is almost totally ignored by those who argue that mission depends on Unity in the sense of organic union. It does not!

As Dr. Warren indicates in his letter, he is not in any way suggesting that attempts be made to restore the IMC. That time has passed. He is suggesting, however, that WCC member churches get on with the task of worldwide evangelization. If the CWME does not provide a dynamic, catalytic leadership which actively assists its member churches in their unfinished missionary and evangelistic tasks, then alternative means must be employed. Somehow, perhaps in new and creative patterns/relationships, these churches may be enabled to make their needed contribution to evangelizing unreached peoples.

Integration Recommended. Ghana will be remembered for that fateful decision to recommend integration. An earlier slogan, "mission in six continents," continued to remain an illusive ideal. For even at Ghana the demands for "international missionary action" were largely unmet. For the commonly accepted understanding of missions (by both "older" and "younger" churches) was still outreach by Western churches. Because these "younger" churches were still strongly influenced by mission societies, many still felt comfortable within their IMC relationships. And because they were apprehensive as to what membership in the CWME within the WCC might mean, a significant number were opposed to integration.* Some, however, particularly from India and Asia, strongly favored integration.

But at Ghana world mission began to be interpreted differently. On the one hand the concept of mission was being broadened until it included, at least in theory, the whole life of all Christians everywhere—i.e., "everything is Mission." On the other hand, the concept was limited to a more specific task defined in terms of evangelism, or proclaiming the Gospel of salvation to non-Christians, particularly to those of non-Christian religious traditions. At Ghana there was already a degree of polarization between these two positions.

Missionaries were inevitably—and increasingly—drawn into the inner life of the churches. Internal church-to-church relationships demanded a certain degree of sophistication for their leaders, and missionaries found their energies going more and more into training the kind of leadership needed for these churches to function within the ecumenical society. Inevitably too, frustrations developed out of these new patterns and were contributing factors in the reevaluation of the entire missionary movement—people, resources and structures as well.

Graaf van Randwijck's paper called attention to churches, particularly in Asia and India, who were no longer satisfied with the label "younger churches" (Orchard 1958:79). Attention was focused again and again on the urgent need for new relationships and for new ways that churches from East and West could join together in the unfinished missionary and evangelistic task.

U Kyaw Than, on behalf of the East Asian churches, highlighted the significance of the joint efforts of both the IMC and the WCC which brought the churches in the East together and resulted in the formation of the East Asia Secretariate. It was especially ironic that those churches which today are at the

---

*The churches of course, as churches were only slightly aware of the momentous issues involved. Their annual meetings devoted very little time to discussion of integrating the IMC into the WCC. It was a very small band of leaders from each denomination who spoke for and acted in favor of it.

forefront of the WCC member churches in calling for a full implementation of the social dimensions of the Gospel, were the same ones in Ghana who were telling of their strong sense of missionary responsibility and of their compulsion to share with all Christians in the evangelization of the world (Orchard 1958:125–137).

Ghana did for relationships and structures what Church and Society would do a decade later for the reconceptualization of mission itself. A new day in missions was fast approaching.

THREE
MISSION IN
TRANSITION
New Delhi and
Mexico City

The Third Assembly of the World Council of Churches met in New Delhi in 1961. This denotes the historic moment when the IMC was integrated into the WCC and became known as the Division of World Mission and Evangelism. Proponents hailed it as an act that would place the missionary and evangelistic task at the center of everything the WCC would now undertake.

> The purpose of Integration is the putting of the missionary obligation of the Church right in the centre of the Ecumenical Movement, so that in all their common thinking and action together in the World Council of Churches the member churches may be constantly aware of the missionary dimension of such thought and action (IMC and CWME Minutes 1961a).

Those opposed to integration feared that the passion for evangelism would be dimmed, and that the missionary obligation would be submerged and obscured by the many other things churches must also do together. John V. Taylor had articulated some of these concerns when he expressed doubts earlier at Ghana.

> The centralized body can only be wholesome if the convictions which underlie and shape its structure are al-

ready so passionately held by the member bodies that they have already given them structural expression at the regional level. . . . If the local and regional churches do not feel the need to have their own agencies and boards devoted exclusively to the missionary task towards the world, I am afraid that the time may come when, as member bodies, they will, after a time, cease to be convinced of the need for a separate Commission on World Mission at the top (Transcribed notes covering the Ghana debate on integration, Archives, WCC Library, Geneva 1957).

Subsequent events serve to confirm the accuracy of Taylor's premonitions. Not only have most mission agencies and boards been structured out of existence in WCC member churches, but even the need for a Commission on World Mission and Evangelism (within the WCC) has been discussed, on more than one occasion, by the WCC staff. More recently, under the dynamic leadership of Emilio Castro, that need for the CWME has been reaffirmed with the result that its specific contribution to WCC life and work may in time be recognized with greater appreciation than was true during the period between Uppsala and Bangkok.*

THE CWME'S CENTRAL AIM

Interestingly, the new CWME was given a stated aim which, surprisingly, the IMC never had:

To further proclamation to the whole world of the Gospel of Jesus Christ, to the end that all men may believe and be saved (IMC and CWME Minutes 1961a).

The statement was in the finest tradition of understandings and assumptions that ever undergirded the missionary movement. In the light of it, no one in New Delhi could possibly have predicted the virtual demise of the missionary movement (so far as WCC member churches from the West are con-

*See CWME files, WCC Archives, Geneva.

cerned)—much less within the next fifteen years. No one at that time could have foreseen the totally redefined goals of mission. But what happened between New Delhi and Nairobi (1961–1975)? A major purpose of this study is to try to ascertain not only what happened, but how it happened and why it happened.

Bishop Newbigin was the Secretary of the IMC and was deeply committed to the historic goals and objectives of the missionary movement. He recognized the validity of the arguments in favor of integration. But with characteristic and perceptive insight he pointed out that integration meant change for both parties:

> For those who have been traditionally related to the IMC, this means a willingness to acknowledge that the particular forms and relationships characteristic of the missionary activity of the past two centuries must be held constantly open to the new insights that God may have to give us in the wider fellowship. . . . For the churches which constitute the World Council this means the acknowledgment that the missionary task is no less central to the life of the Church than the pursuit of renewal and unity (Visser 't Hooft 1962:4).

One who saw the integration positively was Norman Goodall. He had served on both the IMC and the Joint Committee (of the IMC and the WCC) and was involved at the heart of the missionary and ecumenical movement from the beginning of his career. He was convinced that the expertise of the WCC personnel together with available high-level studies (of pressing international, socio-economic and human issues) would be a tremendous contribution to those directly involved in the missionary movement. The whole missionary movement could profit immensely from these closer, more intimate relationships! The result would be broadened understandings for all who were commissioned to communicate the Gospel effectively in this increasingly complex and rapidly changing world. The missionary movement needed the stimulation and larger perspectives that the closer integration in the life of the WCC would make possible.

NEW MEMBERS AND NEW METHODS

Two other significant factors at New Delhi were: (1) the admission of twenty-three new member churches by the WCC, and (2) the CWME's policy statement that mission should now be undertaken by a "Joint Action for Mission."

The addition of these new member churches meant that the balance of power and influence in decision making was shifting rapidly from the traditional and charter member churches of the West to Third World churches. For example, the entry of the Orthodox churches, particularly from Russia, meant that their views would be heard and felt especially as concerned human rights and missionary outreach. The challenge of missionary outreach became much more complicated than it had been for the IMC. Because of Orthodox fears that Western churches would evangelize millions of their nominal members, the CWME found it necessary to soft-pedal the previously aggressive, strategic, evangelistic planning on a worldwide basis. Zones of silence became evident in discussion of human rights violations, of evangelism and even of church renewal.

In attempting to pursue this "Joint Action for Mission," WCC member churches desiring to send out missionaries frequently found it difficult to begin new work in new places. Younger churches, often representing tiny minorities of total populations, actually stood in the way of evangelistic efforts by outside churches and mission agencies. Even though people within their territories remain unevangelized, they clung to the idea of unity and wouldn't agree to let others do it. This was not anticipated when "Joint Action for Mission" was proposed. JAM was intended to facilitate efforts to carry the Gospel effectively to those still without knowledge of Christ. The fact that there is such a vast unfinished task is not disputed. D. T. Niles, as recently as 1968, pointed out that the work of mission in Asia is not finished even in geographical terms.* He spoke of how the missions had concentrated for twenty years on building up the indigenous church. The missionaries became fraternal workers—even virtual employees—of overseas

---

*Notes on a conversation between Niles and others in the CWME, April 10, 1968 (WCC Archives).

churches, to serve the needs of those churches. Unreached peoples were neglected.

Churches became ingrown and all too frequently selfish. Tensions between missionaries and church leaders increased, and energies were sapped by struggles for power and influence. Frustrated missionaries left in increasing numbers for various reasons. This left the national church leaders saddled with institutions they were ill-prepared to handle. Jockeying for advantage and prestige made evangelism among new peoples a chore to be avoided rather than a joy to be embraced.

The missionaries that remained were usually settled in institutions, and found that life comfortable. The evangelistic frontiers were unmanned, effectively cutting the nerve of missionary activity. Joint Action for Mission was scarcely more than an empty slogan. What churches did together was not really mission, but only served the needs of the churches themselves. Their so-called evangelism concentrated on people who were already related to churches in one way or another. Planting new churches and crossing geographical frontiers was left to the "committed few"—mostly of other-than-Council-involved denominations.

Why is it that churches seem so persistently and consistently unaware of the "ripe harvest fields?" Why is it that when churches do things together, their united action appears to involve either the inner life and needs of existing churches or programs limited to social action? Why is it that funds are apparently available for everything except the joint action in mission that sends out and supports evangelists? Should not Joint Action for Mission take new missionaries from the churches on the six continents and send them to proclaim the Gospel among those peoples yet unreached? How realistic are we in our assessments of programs like JAM and ESP?* How many in such programs are actually involved in the cutting edge of evangelism? How much is perhaps only a more sophisticated form of inter-church aid? These programs may have strengths and fill real needs in the life of the churches, but if they do not challenge some from among them to cross frontiers

*Ecumenical Sharing of Personnel

to reach those yet unreached, what programs are there that do this? Are there any that really bring the churches together in that kind of joint action for mission? The official viewpoint sounds impeccable:

> Since New Delhi the term JAM (Joint Action for Mission) has found a wide spread response. It represents a new way of looking at mission and for churches to engage in mission together in new patterns. In essence it means that the churches in any given area look together at the state of God's mission in this area and determine together where the crucial frontiers are. Then in a spirit of self-sacrifice and self-denial, they agree to the redeployment of available resources in personnel and funds to meet the new needs. This may involve winning the cooperation of related bodies at home or overseas (Goodall 1968:233).

Later, at Uppsala, it was specifically urged "that any new undertaking in the field of mission be started in this pattern of JAM" (*ibid.* 1968:234). But this was scarcely ever taken to mean a more effective evangelization of the three billion who have yet to believe.

The ideal goal of a joint action for mission rightly recognized that missions could best be carried out by churches working together—planning and pooling their resources for the common objective. The problem that some churches did not share a vision, or did not permit use of personnel and resources for other tasks within the life of the church or community, frequently brought to mind the New Delhi slogan. In some cases, the use of this slogan (of joint action) actually prevented others from evangelizing peoples that certain churches could not, or did not choose to, reach for Christ.

MEXICO CITY 1963

With a certain degree of innocence "Mexico City" prepared the way for the birth of New Mission. For it was here, at the first full meeting of the Commission on World Mission and Evangelism, that another significant shift took place. The CWME meeting of course involved many delegates who were selected without apparent regard for mission involvement. This contrasted with previous IMC meetings where delegates had direct involvement in the missionary movement. Although Third World churches had always been a part of the IMC by virtue of having a national council involvement with missionary sending churches, they were separated into a somewhat different category from mission agencies and boards. Those directly involved in missions from Western churches had made the decisions on mission matters in IMC meetings.

Different Delegates. Now it was the churches who determined participants, and the CWME delegates represented their own church's involvement. So it was natural that the decisions about mission would be made increasingly by persons not directly involved in the actual missionary endeavor. Many times these had little interest or no enthusiasm for reaching out with the Gospel to the three billion who hadn't heard.

If the whole Church is involved in mission, then it easily follows that everyone in the Church is part of the mission, and one person has as legitimate a right as anyone else in determining what that mission should be. Instead of people sharing together in a common vision and understanding about the missionary obligation of the Church, it is an easy step to entrusting some persons with the responsibility and decision-making power in churches who are actually working against the traditional aims of the missionary movement. The implications of this are enormous. The frustration of those with historic understandings of mission trying to work with persons who were delegated a responsibility for missions but lacked real concern for—or involvement in—missions, has resulted in a defection of people and funds that would normally have been available to WCC member churches.

Mexico City is remembered particularly for the slogan "Mission in Six Continents." Mission clearly belongs to churches everywhere. No country can be said to be completely evangelized or wholly Christian. Partnership in Obedience (Whitby), the Missionary Obligation of the Church (Willingen), Joint Action for Mission (New Delhi) were all subsumed in the new slogan, "Mission in Six Continents." The whole world is a mission field.

The Unresolved Debate. Those at Mexico City were fully committed to the classical goals of the missionary movement. At the same time, they showed a greater awareness of the complexities of a secular world. The mission of the churches somehow needed to be relevant. Debate was intense and disagreements were common. There was an evident restlessness. Pat answers did not satisfy, and delegates searched for new understandings. Discussions included God at work outside of the Church. The feelings at Mexico City were articulated more lopsidedly later in reports by study groups between the Mexico City meeting and the Uppsala Assembly. But at Mexico City they were not quite ready, at this point, to rearrange the order of words from God-Church-World to God-World-Church. Rather, out of their frustration and inability to agree, they said,

> The discussion raised a theological issue which remained unresolved. Debate returned again and again to the relationship between God's action in and through the Church and everything God is doing in the world apparently independently of the Christian community. Can a distinction be drawn between God's providential action and God's redeeming action? If the restoration and reconciliation of human life is being achieved by the action of God through secular agencies, what is the place and significance of faith? If the Church is to be wholly involved in the world and its history, what is the true nature of its separateness? We were able to state thesis and antithesis in this debate, but we could not see our way through to the truth we feel lies beyond this dialectic. Yet we believe that all attempts to adapt the structures or the thinking of the Church to match the great changes that are taking place in the world will be doomed to paralysis until we can find the way through to a truer understanding of the relation between the world and the Church in the purpose of God (Orchard 1964:157).

This was the groundwork. New Mission was emerging. And the pace would accelerate beyond anything anyone at Mexico City could possibly have anticipated. This statement, contained in the final report of Section III and adopted at Mexico

City, provided the opportunity and basis for further study. And this discussion paved the way for a new understanding of mission.

Nine years later, these small beginnings in Mexico City found their way into a paper which formed the basis of discussion and affected the development of the subject "Salvation Today" at Bangkok.

> At the Mexico meeting of the CWME an attempt was made to see mission as directed to all peoples and within an increasingly secular world. One section dealing with "Witnessing to Man in the Secular World" posed the question: "What is the form and content of the Salvation which Christ offers men in the secular world?" The section went on to state: "We at Mexico City were not able to do more than touch the border of this subject." Our task at the next CWME meeting should be to grapple with this question (WCC Archives, Planning for Bangkok 1971/72).

In Mexico City a new wind began to blow. Some CWME leaders believed that the world should have a voice in the Church's agenda. Actually, a new team should decide the agenda. Former members dropped out for various reasons, and were replaced by new faces. These planned a very different agenda.

In Mexico City delegates again raised issues that were central to mission from the beginning. Sometimes these issues were latent, and sometimes explicit. But the shift at Mexico City resulted basically from changes which came in two ways: the world had changed and different people were deciding about mission. Missionaries and those directly committed to world evangelization were no longer in control. It was a new era in world mission. The new understanding about mission presumed that man had come of age: that secularization was setting him free. He no longer needed God. There was great confidence in man's ability to reap the benefits of science.

Not until I attended the Nairobi Assembly did I appreciate the importance attached to statements from documents approved at previous meetings. My observations at Nairobi were further confirmed by my study of archival materials in Geneva. Here I saw how official documents are later studied with extreme care, and the various relevant statements or recommendations are designated as belonging to the purview of a particular person or group. This is not to suggest that there is anything evil or disreputable about this procedure. It was educational for me and helped me to understand more clearly some of the dynamics of an Assembly along with the implications for follow-up.

Of utmost importance is the inclusion in the final documents of certain points which will insure that these matters will receive attention so that they may be dealt with by those concerned. At the same time, I came to realize that opposing positions may safely be included in final reports because later, when the reports are handled, the opposing positions can simply be ignored; they have been stated in the report as a matter of record and that is what is important.

The Department of Studies in Evangelism of the WCC began to consider the Mexico City report. In fact, experts of the European Working Group of the Department met five times between 1962 and 1965. Their final report, "The Church for Others," published in 1967, spoke decisively to an issue left unresolved at Mexico City. We note that the quest for reconceptualization of mission had taken giant strides between 1963 and 1967. Here are the conclusions of that report:

> In the past it has been customary to maintain that God is related to the world through the Church. When we sharpen this view into a formula the sequence would be: God—Church—World. This has been understood to mean that God is primarily related to the Church and only secondarily to the world by means of the Church. Further, it has been held that God relates Himself to the world through the Church in order to gather everyone possible from the world into the Church. God, in other words, moves through the Church to the world. We believe that the time has come to question this sequence and to emphasize an alternative. According to this alternative the last two items in God—Church—World should be reversed, so that it reads instead, God—World—

Church. That is, God's primary relationship is to the world and it is the world and not the Church that is the focus of God's plan.

The old sequence of God—Church—World further tends to falsify the Biblical account of the way God works in the world; it leads one to think that God always initiates change from inside out, from inside the Church to the 'outsiders' in the world. . . . Further, there is a danger of confining God's activity to the Church—this activity in the world being no more than that of the Church itself—so God is refashioned in the image of a residential Deity and the world is left apparently bereft of the divine presence, which is enshrined within and reserved exclusively for the Church (WCC 1967a:16,17).

Traditional and Transitional. Basically, the consensus at Mexico City was in the tradition of the IMC and the classical view of missions. Nevertheless, there was also a restlessness and perhaps even an unwillingness to accept any longer the traditional formulations about missions. Those in Mexico City met in a keen awareness that their rapidly changing, secular society needed to become aware of the significance of Christ in a different kind of way in order to accomplish God's intent for the world. The churches should therefore take stock and shape up for God's mission for them in this new day for missions. Leaders at Mexico City spoke of new frontiers other than geographical ones which churches needed to cross to communicate the Gospel to all peoples. For example, the economic frontier (creating more just pay scales in both field and factory) and the racial frontier (extending equal treatment to minorities).

In many respects, the first meeting of the CWME in Mexico City was exciting. And at least the top leadership in the CWME was still fully committed to the classical understandings about man's need for Christ, the author of eternal salvation. The churches represented there committed themselves afresh to lift up Jesus Christ as Savior and Lord. There was still a confidence in the power of the Gospel and a commitment to make that Gospel known with relevance. The challenge at

Mexico City lay in finding a way for the churches of six continents to participate together in mission.

> We therefore affirm that this missionary movement now involves Christians in all six continents and in all lands. It must be the common witness of the whole Church, bringing the whole Gospel to the whole world. We do not yet see all the changes this demands; but we go forward in faith. God's purpose still stands; to sum up all things in Christ. In this hope we dedicate ourselves anew to His mission in the spirit of unity and in humble dependence upon our living Lord (Orchard 1964:175).

The pity is that as recently as 1977 the associate director of the CWME would have to report:

> "Mission in Six Continents" has become a catch-all slogan for a new look in mission, somewhat analogous to a 'New Economic Order' in the politico-economic field. . . . As far as I can make out there has never been any real definition or a study of what is meant by "Mission in Six Continents!" It does not seem to have been a theme at Mexico City and the report is called "Witness in Six Continents." "Mission in Six Continents" seems to rather have been a slogan to call attention to the fact that with the integration in 1961 the concern of the CWME was now the whole world and not just part of it, and to change the concept of mission as something the affluent West does to the rest of the world, with all its overtones of superiority and condescension, to one of equal partnership (CWME Core Group Meeting 1977).

By its "unresolved dilemma" Mexico City set the stage for a wide range of studies and meetings, sponsored by the WCC, to grapple with questions relating to God and his mission in the world: the Church and its mission, and how the two are related. Meanwhile, urgent issues were brought forward that had been dealt with and either dropped or given incomplete answers at previous IMC meetings. The subject of the witness of Christians to men of other faiths, for example, had not been discussed in real depth since 1938 in Madras. The same sharp differences of opinion were evident now as then. However, bringing the subject forward at Mexico City provided the backdrop for future studies and programs of the CWME. The controversial dialogue program was one such study. Again, the subject, "Witness of Christians to Men in the Secular World," had not been seriously discussed since 1928 in Jerusalem (Gill 1968:344–352). Out of a preliminary discussion of this crucial topic in Mexico City came the question, "What is the form and content of the salvation which Christ offers men in the secular world?" (The Bangkok 1973 meeting with its topic, "Salvation Today," will show what a large place this consideration had in WCC thinking.)

Many subjects touched on at Mexico City became central issues in succeeding years in the WCC's quest for reconceptualization of Mission. These included: 1) Dialogue: the encounter with people of other living faiths and ideologies; the relation of dialogue to proclamation and conversion; the ethics of dialogue. 2) The structure of the missionary congregation: the renewal of the church to give a credible witness to the Gospel. 3) Urban and Industrial Mission: how to bear witness to the Gospel in a world of cities. 4) The proclamation of the Gospel and the social dimension of the Gospel: "holistic evangelism" of Bangkok 1973. 5) Service and Justice: the churches' response to human tragedy, hunger, poverty, earthquake and fire. 6) Secular man and the kind of salvation God intends.

Mexico City delegates recognized the issues in incipient form. They approached the problems and challenges on the assumptions of classical-biblical mission. Their views were shaped by the language and perspectives of Scripture. New Mission was on the way; but no one could have imagined then how near it was.

FOUR
MISSION
RECONCEPTUALIZED:
NEW MISSION
Uppsala, 1968

Why Uppsala? Wasn't Bangkok (1973) the next meeting "like" Mexico City? True, Bangkok was the next meeting of the CWME. But the CWME is not just a successor to the IMC. Integration is a fact. CWME is an integral part of WCC. And if "the Church is mission," the broader forums of the WCC will inevitably influence, even determine, any new understandings of that mission and the programs mandated to implement such understandings.

Since our task is to trace the development of these new understandings, we must look carefully at each of the post-integration Assemblies of the WCC. More specifically, we want to know how the classical missionary task fared in this wider forum—how the advocacy of CWME affected the WCC or vice versa. Who influenced whom?

It was hoped—even expected—that the CWME would influence the WCC to a greater commitment to mission as understood by the IMC. But in actual fact, in the dynamic interaction between the CWME and other divisions of the WCC, the CWME in many respects embraced and implemented the WCC views of mission that focused on humanization and the struggle for a just society. This had not been the intent at New Delhi in 1961. At that time the aim of the CWME was clearly stated:

> . . . to further the proclamation to the whole world the Gospel of Jesus Christ, to the end that all men may believe in Him and be saved (IMC 1961a:143).

The CWME had this mandate:

> To foster the sense of responsibility for the outreach of evangelism by the local church, to assist the churches in any part of the world to bring the Gospel to bear upon situations where there is no effective witness to Christ, and to make the best use of urgent opportunities for evangelism which call for combined action by several churches or other missionary agencies (IMC 1961a:143).

This clear mandate was superseded at Uppsala only a few short years later when the WCC called its member churches to an all-out effort to struggle against injustice and create a more humane social order. WCC leaders felt a different set of missionary priorities was needed for today's revolutionary, often violent, and increasingly secularized society. A massive shift was in the offing for missions and the churches' role in mission.

> Because the world is always changing, it is always necessary to evaluate missionary principles. . . . We suggest the following criteria for such evaluation:
>
> do they place the church alongside the poor, the defenseless, the abused, the forgotten, the bored?
>
> do they allow Christians to enter the concerns of others to accept their issues and their structures as vehicles of involvement?
>
> are they the best situations for discerning with other men the signs of the times, and for moving with history towards the coming of the new humanity? (Goodall 1968:32).

A CRITICAL PERIOD

We must recognize that during the crucial and formative years, when new relationships were being established within the WCC, the CWME somehow lost its dynamic leadership. Those committed to the worldwide missionary and evangelistic task brought over from the IMC dropped out of the CWME for a variety of reasons during those early formative years. During those years, advocates of numerous WCC programs and projects interacted with one another, each determined to show that his or her interest should have top priority. Not only did the CWME lose the experienced and dedicated leaders from the IMC, but these key positions remained vacant for long periods of time. For example, the CWME New York staff dwindled to one secretary. The London office finally closed in March, 1967. A Secretary for Evangelism was not appointed until March, 1968. The search for a Secretary for Information and Interpretation was fruitless. For two years the important portfolio of Joint Action for Mission remained without a secretary. Obviously, the CWME was in no position to boldly advocate its own IMC type program. And it goes without saying that its impact on the rest of the WCC was negligible, when it came to promoting a commitment to evangelism and the unfinished missionary task.

The weaknesses of the CWME during that period are underscored in the report of its Acting Director, Robbins Strong, at the CWME meeting in Geneva in 1966. He referred to staffing:

> . . . we are at rock bottom and weak. This is not said in any sense of criticism of present staff, but simply as a statement of fact. Since Enugu, Lesslie Newbigin, George Carpenter, Ronald Orchard and John Elliott have left the staff. The first three were men of deep and long experience, each with his own gifts, but forming a basic central core of continuity. Tributes will be paid to them on another occasion. As of January 1st, 1966, Gwynth Hubble has moved to Toronto and is now giving only one third of her time to CWME.

Where does this leave us? If one excludes the special committees such as the Theological Education Fund, the Christian Literature Fund and the Committee on the Church and the Jewish People, and thinks only of what I call the basic CWME staff, the picture is not a very encouraging one. There are Victor Hayward (although he is greatly overcharged because of his responsibilities as Acting Director of the Division of Studies), Paul Loffler in London, Joyce Herklots and Alexander John in Geneva, and half of Floyd Honey (a very large half) in New York. Of these, only Victor Hayward and Paul Loffler have been with us for more than eighteen months (CWME 1966:2, Mimeographed paper WCC Archives Geneva).

To make matters even worse, personnel losses continued. During that same year the CWME's magazine lost its editor. Through this magazine the CWME's work and the cause of missions was kept before the WCC and its member churches. And the editorials of its editor, Lesslie Newbigin, were widely read and quoted. In addition, Joan Anderson, his Editorial Assistant who had handled her very complex and demanding job so competently, also left. One cannot doubt the serious implications of the weakened CWME during those critical years of establishing its place within the WCC.

NEW PERSPECTIVES

With the loss of so many experienced and committed staff holdovers from the IMC, the continuity and even the goals of the IMC were largely lost. It is not surprising that changes came about within a few short years. The new CWME staff conceived of mission in different ways. The new staff did not define mission in terms of the biblical-classical understandings.

Philip Potter, the new director of the CWME, was comfortable with the new emphasis of the WCC, that of accenting the need for churches to see their task as participation in the struggles for justice and liberation. He considered himself committed to "evangelism," but he began to see evangelism and mission through new glasses. He easily identified with the hurt and suffering of the peoples of the Third World. Because he himself was of Third World origin, he was inevitably chosen to be the spokesman and symbol of Third World aspirations. Instead of holding to its previous understandings about mission, the CWME views of mission under Dr. Potter's leadership came to closely resemble the views of the rest of the Council.

The new director sympathized with the heightened emphasis which virtually indentified the mission of the Church with the struggle for liberation from all forms of oppression and the goal of a more just society. In fact, Dr. Potter became a most articulate spokesman, and a capable advocate of carrying out the social dimension of the Gospel. But evangelism was neglected in the process.

The implications of all this for the goals and objectives of the missionary movement were depressing. It is not surprising that during this period some WCC member churches once heavily involved in sending and supporting missionaries in evangelistic ministry, withdrew from those activities. We do not necessarily lament the massive withdrawal of missionaries, or the dismantling of the missionary-sending apparatus or of the overseas mission organizations. History demands change in methods, structures and/or institutions required to carry out a task.

We are however deeply concerned that the sharp focus on missions as evangelism be kept before the churches and mission agencies. The CWME has not done this. The promises made at New Delhi have not been kept. True, the record shows a lack of leadership. But even when leadership was provided, its influence diverted member churches away from evangelism and mission as understood by the IMC. The promises and hopes that the CWME would affect the entire life and work of the WCC, and bring to it a new consciousness of the centrality of the missionary and evangelistic task, led to painful disappointment. Instead of influencing the WCC, the CWME—entrusted with carrying on the intent of the IMC—has itself been emasculated. We recall the words at New Delhi when integration took place. The charge given to the CWME was specific and clear:

> To further the proclamation to the whole world of the Gospel of Jesus Christ, to the end that all men may believe and be saved (WCC 1961a).

The WCC churches needed someone among them to be "fanatic"* about the unfinished missionary task given by Jesus the Lord of the Church to his people. The Commission on World Mission and Evangelism could yet be that "fanatic" someone, if it is faithful to the trust given it in New Delhi. By honoring that commitment made in New Delhi, it would honor its Lord in obedience to his command to take the Gospel to all nations.

IMPACT OF STUDIES

Significant studies and meetings formed the background for the documents put on the table at Uppsala. The years between New Delhi and Uppsala were notable for intense activity. Throughout the WCC a great deal of agonizing reappraisal was going on. Where should the Church stand in relation to God and his intent for the world? The CWME, weakened by changeover and lack of staff, produced little, but the rest of the WCC pushed ahead with vision and purpose. Formerly it was the IMC and its constituent members who were the experts on the mission of the Church. Now the other divisions within the WCC were giving more time and thought to what mission entailed. The logic was clear enough. If the whole Church was mission, or was to be engaged in mission (which is what reinterpretation of the term meant), then every division of the WCC was competent to help discover what that mission was. So instead of the CWME infusing the WCC with vision and passion for the unfinished missionary and evangelistic task, other divisions were slowly but steadily shaping the CWME to their concept of mission.

This influence is illustrated by the suggestion of a wide-ranging, WCC-sponsored conference dealing with matters of

---

*Allan Brash, Deputy General of WCC, encouraged the CWME to focus on the unique contribution CWME should give to the rest of the WCC with respect to "Mission and Evangelism." He said, "Someone in the WCC needs to be 'fanatic' about it" (Mimeographed Papers, WCC Archives, Geneva).

development. By the end of that conference Christian mission was defined as "aid for development," and a statement concluded that "the missionary societies should be encouraged to place the work for justice and development in the center of their activity" (WCC 1968:21–27).

These new understandings about mission which were impacting the CWME are perhaps most vividly illustrated in the study report on the missionary structure of the congregation, The Church for Others:

> We have lifted up humanization as the goal of mission because we believe that more than other positions it communicates in our period of history the meaning of the messianic goal. In another time the goal of God's redemptive work might best have been described in terms of man turning towards God. . . . the fundamental question was that of the true God, and the Church responded to that question by pointing to Him. It was assuming that the purpose of mission was Christianization, bringing man to God through Christ and His Church. Today the fundamental question is much more that of true man, and the dominant concern of the missionary congregation must therefore be to point to the humanity in Christ as the goal of mission (WCC 1967a:78).

The acceptance of this point of view by the WCC is evident in the Uppsala preparatory draft, "Renewal in Mission" which used almost identical language:

> We have lifted up humanization as the goal of mission because we believe that more than others it communicates in our period of history the meaning of the messianic goal. In another time the goal of God's redemptive work might have been described in terms of man turning towards God rather than in terms of God turning towards men. . . . Today the fundamental question is much more that of true man and the dominant concern of the missionary congregation must therefore be to point to the humanity of Christ as the goal of mission (WCC 1968b:34).

69

Both are strikingly different from the charge given to the Department of World Mission and Evangelism at New Delhi.

> to help the churches . . . to confront men and women with the claims of Jesus Christ wherever they may live . . . to further the proclamation to the whole world of the Gospel of Jesus Christ to the end that all may believe in Him and be saved (WCC 1961a).

The Church for Others was strongly influenced by Hoekendijk. Actually, Hoekendijk's theology made great inroads into the WCC following the integration. He stated, for example, "mobilizing the people of God for mission today means releasing them from structures that inhibit them in the church" (1950). In certain respects the views of Hoekendijk did the cause of missions great harm. His views resulted in downgrading missionary and evangelistic efforts that were intended to result in a discipleship that leads to church growth. But Hoekendijk saw the church bound by tradition and the accepted ways of doing things; church structures were too rigid to allow God's people "to move out into the world for ministry." By this phrase he meant any ethical action. The Church was characterized by a kind of "morphological fundamentalism." Many of the pre-Uppsala reports reflect his views.

Many of the positions and understandings in these reports found their way into the draft proposals and later became part of the finalized documents as recommendations by the Assembly to member churches. From there they soon reappeared in actions taken by member churches.

Questions giving rise to all these studies were: How shall we interpret what is happening in the world? What are the implications of these interpretations for the Church? It was assumed that the churches would adopt and act on the understanding of God's purposes for the world as formulated by the WCC, even if their own interpretations differed.

In these studies, the starting place was the world. No previous assumptions were accepted no matter how well based on Scripture. In many respects the studies set forth a whole new way of arriving at truth and understanding. No one can read the literature of that period and fail to recognize the radical change in perspective about missions—including the earlier perspective of the CWME meeting in Mexico City.

These studies prepared for Uppsala presented a new way for understanding God, his Church, the world, man (his nature and destiny) and the meaning and goals of history. Previous assumptions upon which the Christian based his understanding about reality were either questioned or cast in doubt. For many, the way one was expected to look at Scripture now differed from the traditional way of arriving at theological conceptions. Theological assumptions and ideological positions coalesced in new understandings about mission.

What avant-garde theologians discussed in a few seminaries, the conciliar leaders implemented into a way of acting. Many of the assumptions and presuppositions were so radically changed that evangelicals wondered about the entire future of the Christian movement. Might it be changed in ways as far reaching as those brought about by the Reformation? Even Dr. Visser 't Hooft acknowledged that without correctives (which appear to have occurred in Nairobi in 1976) and their implementation by the WCC Central Committee, it just might happen. At the same time, he is by no means ready to believe that the aberration at Uppsala is unalterably shaping the future of the Church (Visser 't Hooft 1977).

IMPACT OF "CHURCH AND SOCIETY, 1966"

The World Conference on Church and Society, Geneva, 1966, more than any other single event set the stage for Uppsala. The importance attached to this meeting is apparent in its sheer cost, size and orientation. While the CWME meeting in Mexico City cost $61,000, "Church and Society" cost $241,000.

Altogether there were 420 participants, including 38 observers and 18 guests from 80 nations and 164 member churches. Of the 338 officially nominated church participants attending the Conference, 180 were laymen, 158 theologians. There were 50 political leaders and civil servants, 19 businessmen and industrialists, 28 economists,

71

36 professional men, 9 workers or trade union leaders, 20 social scientists, and 8 natural scientists. Of the theologians and clergy, 20 were pastors, 50 professors of social ethics and 57 church officials and leaders. There were 30 youth participants selected by the World Student Christian Federation and the Youth Department of the WCC; 38 observers, of whom eight were Roman Catholics and five from other non-member churches; six observers from the specialized agencies of the United Nations, and 19 from other fraternal religious organizations.

The official Conference participants divided as follows according to regions and continents: North America 65; Latin America 42; Western Europe (including the UK) 76; Eastern Europe (including the USSR) 45; Africa 42; Asia 46; Middle East 17; Australia and New Zealand 5 (WCC 1968a).

This Conference agenda was divided into four sections:
  I. Economic and Social Development in a World Perspective
  II. The Nature and Function of the State in a Revolutionary Age
  III. Structures of International Co-operation—Living Together in a Pluralistic World Society
  IV. Man and Community in Changing Societies
The Conference activities (including the preparations and the subsequent follow-up work dominated both thought and attention of the WCC Geneva staff in the Department on Church and Society between the New Delhi and Uppsala Assemblies.

The Conference on Church and Society along with the studies, *The Church for Others, Planning for Mission,* and *Becoming Operational in a World of Cities* provided the perspectives and assumptions for the thought, energy and interest of the WCC Geneva Staff in their preparations for Uppsala. Meanwhile, the CWME was limping along, handicapped by discontinuity with its past, and lacking staff to give it direction. During this period Paul Loffler of the CWME staff was also strongly advocating the social dimension of mission.

The impact that the Conference on Church and Society had upon the Fourth Assembly cannot be overestimated. This fact was recognized with appreciation, as follows:

> The Conference on Church and Society (1966) has given to the World Council a great stimulus. While it is still impossible to evaluate the full range of this work, the main reaction of the Assembly can be only to express gratitude for this comprehensive panorama of socio-ethical thinking which has already evoked response all over the world and which will continue to have considerable influence. The findings of Section III and several other Sections of the Assembly were based in a large degree on the conclusions of the Geneva Conference (WCC 1968d:240).

Originally, the Conference was planned in the normal manner. Findings of the conference would be presented as a report of the WCC itself. When those planning the conference recognized that this procedure would restrict their freedom to suggest new ways for the Church to look at the Church and society, they decided it would be better if the report appeared to come as a recommendation from outside of the WCC to the WCC. In other words, they wanted their conference to suggest the ideas for creative new ways—even if controversial and debatable—for the Church to look at itself and what it should be doing. At the same time, they also wanted the freedom to involve, as crucial participants, qualified and key people who would not normally be expected to participate in Church conferences. These participants would include people closely associated with Marxist views of religion, society and economics.

THE THEOLOGICAL/IDEOLOGICAL COMPONENT

The new perspectives which shaped the quest for a reconceptualization of mission owe as much to ideology as theology. The secular became sacred and the sacred became secular. In speaking of man one somehow spoke of God. Man became all important. "Doing theology" became fashionable; one acted first and thought about its significance later. Action/reflection was how one came to understand what God was doing and the manner in which one joined him. Propositional statements about God, the Church, and the world were eschewed. Third World Christians were warned about theologies that suited the Western-oriented view of reality. Instead, experience should be their criteria; one compared experiences to know what God was doing and what was real. Wide varieties of religious or liberating experiences were shared to illustrate the variety of ways in which God's salvation was provided. Proof texts from the Scriptures were cited to confirm assumptions actually based elsewhere.

All these new ways of looking at reality strongly influenced the WCC. In my view, the fundamental change which affected all other understandings about God and man arose from the new assumption concerning the relationship of God to the Church and the world. In fact New Mission flowed from this assumption. There may be other analyses, but in the context of the unfinished missionary task of world evangelization, I believe the changed order of God-Church-world to God-world-Church has wider ranging implications and ramifications for mission or "missions" than does either universalism or secularization, for example.

Some believe universalism served to cut the nerve of missionary passion. This concept is older. But God-world-Church graphically symbolizes in the boldest fashion what is latent in universalism.

Others see the new understanding about mission arising from a theology of secularization. The belief that God is desacralizing the world and liberating man to shape his own future suggests that if this is so, we must run to join God in his mission.

I believe this new assumption about God's relationship to the Church and to the world is the critical point of discontinuity with historic Christianity. The God-world-Church assumption sees God's concern as being primarily for the world and only secondarily for the Church. The Church is not to be regarded as having intrinsic value as such, but only instrumental value as it accomplishes God's purposes for the world.

It then logically follows that God's mission is liberation and desacralization—setting man free from dehumanizing structures, etc.

The view was first given prominence in the study report already referred to, *The Church for Others*. The concept is discussed under the heading, "Re-Thinking the Relationship of Church and World." I quote the section in full that the reader may study it in detail.

> In the past it has been customary to maintain that God is related to the world through the Church. When we sharpen this view into a formula the sequence would be: God-Church-world. This has been understood to mean that God is primarily related to the Church and only secondarily to the world by means of the Church. Further, it has been held that God relates himself to the world through the Church in order to gather everyone possible from the world into the Church. God, in other words, moves through the Church to the world. We believe that the time has come to question this sequence and to emphasize an alternative. According to this alternative the last two items in God-Church-world should be reversed, so that it reads instead God—world—Church. That is, God's primary relationship is to the world, and it is the world and not the Church that is the focus of God's plan. According to the bible, God is the creator and so all creation is his concern. He may use people; he may use individuals, but always it is the whole cosmos that occupies his attention. According to the fourth Gospel, "God loved the *world* so much that he gave his only Son . . . It was not to judge the world that God sent his Son into the world, but that through him the world might be saved" (3:16f). According to Paul, "God was in Christ reconciling the world to himself" (II Cor. 5:19). The Church lives through God's dealing with the world.

> The old sequence of God-Church-world further tends to falsify the biblical account of the way God works in the world; it leads one to think that God always initiates change from inside out, from inside the Church to the

"outsiders" in the world. But God often spoke to Israel through his actions in outside events, e.g. through the actions of a Cyrus or of the Babylonians taking the Hebrews into exile. Further, there is a danger of confining God's activity to the Church—his activity in the world being no more than that of the Church itself—so God is refashioned in the image of a residential deity and the world is left apparently bereft of the divine presence, which is enshrined within and reserved exclusively for the Church.

How then are we to define the relationship between the Church and the world? Again we must distinguish between models that have been adopted in the past and the emphasis that is required today. In former times the Church was viewed as the ark, perilously afloat amidst the turbulent seas of this world; outside the safety of this vessel mankind is going down to destruction and the only safety is to be dragged from the deep into the ecclesiastical ship. Or again, the Church has been seen as an armed camp and individual Christian soldiers are members of the army of the Lord of hosts set in the midst of active enemies. From time to time Christians sally forth from their palisades to rescue from the hostile environment as many as they can. It has to be admitted that some support for these pictures, describing the relationship of Church and world in terms of implacable enmity, may appear to be given by certain New Testament passages. "Do not unite yourselves with unbelievers; they are no fit mates for you. What has righteousness to do with wickedness? . . . Come away and leave them, separate yourselves" (II Cor. 6:14,17, quoting Isaiah 52:11). "Religion which is without stain or fault", according to James, "is to keep oneself untarnished by the world" (1:27) (WCC 1967a:16–17).

The rearranging of the words God-Church-world to read God-world-Church represents a radical discontinuity with the way the Christian Church has traditionally understood these relationships. This rearrangement actually does violence to the

Scriptural message of God and his covenant people. It radically alters the ultimate meaning of history and God's purposes for man. If this view is correct, then many of the basic propositions about God who revealed himself by calling a people to be his own people, distinct from the "nations" are false and must be discarded.

Rearrangement of these words blurs the distinction between the community of God's people and the world. It carries within it implications about the kind of world in which we live, the nature and destiny of man, the goals of human history and God's intent. Who God is, what he is like, what his purposes are and how he accomplishes them—and of who man is, how man can know God, what God may be doing among people outside the Church—all of these are questions of basic, fundamental significance and ultimately involve truth and reality: e.g., the question of how God reveals himself and the place of Scripture in our understanding of God.

MISSION RECONCEIVED

No one reading the story of the ecumenical conferences can fail to realize the change that occurred in language, and even in basic underlying assumptions, after the New Delhi Conference in 1961. These changes were based on a different way of handling and interpreting Scripture, and resulted in new ways of perceiving reality. Words are used differently. They have different connotations and different meanings. The text refers to God, yet the reader strangely feels it is really referring to man. The sacred becomes secularized and, paradoxically, the secular seems sacralized. Verbalization and the tyranny of words is denounced, but somehow words and more words are used to indicate the changes in thinking about a New Mission. Readers are lectured on the limitations of propositional statements. And yet, propositions saying what mission *is* are offered profusely. It is unacceptable to speak of New Mission as a strategy of evangelism aimed at taking the Gospel to the unreached. But it is somehow not wrong to speak freely and dogmatically of strategies to change society.

Nevertheless, in many respects the period between the New Delhi and Uppsala Assemblies was challenging and exciting.

There was a freedom to experiment, to break with the past. To take a fresh look and begin anew. Hallowed beliefs, programs and practices were put to the test in a period of continuous questioning, study and reevaluation. Nothing was sacred! The foundations were being shaken. Perhaps better discretion might sometimes have prevailed, but the Church was attempting to find a new and more relevant way to do God's will in a dangerous, exciting, revolutionary, fearful, painful, promising new world.

Unhappily, the Church was less willing to look back than to look ahead to find its answers in what God was doing or saying to those with spiritual perception. Though much was gained in the process, much also was lost. The pendulum frequently swings too far; but many leaders in the Church and not a few in the world, felt that the Church was getting "with it." The lines between Church and world blurred. It was difficult to discern the spirits! How does one know what results from God's being at work, and what from Satan's activity? For many God seemed either dead or at least unconcerned. It was as if man was left with the world on his own hands.

Nine-tenths and more of the pastors in local member churches had no idea of what was happening at Uppsala. They would have been aghast had they realized the extent to which the classical-biblical concepts were discarded. They would not have believed what was happening. But let us examine more carefully what did happen at Uppsala and what it meant.

Eugene Carson Blake, the General Secretary of the WCC, attempted to allay suspicions and fears about the departure from traditional concepts.

> I am particularly concerned that those who have been especially interested in evangelism and mission will not for a moment suppose that the struggle for new terminology and new programmes better to be understood by the modern world, is, as some fear or charge, a betrayal of the evangelistic task in favour of a materialistic utopia. . . .
>
> In reply then to any who fear or believe that the World Council of Churches is somehow distorting Christianity

by going along with new fads of theology or sociology, I want in this report to make two very simple points:

1. The new emphasis on the social, economic, and political that Uppsala Assembly presses upon the churches is not new in the sense of being novel (and therefore rightly suspect) but new rather in the sense of renewal in the life of the churches of the most ancient truths of the Christian faith.

2. The new in the sense of novel or modern or up-to-date arises from the radically changed world of the late twentieth century in which the churches of Jesus Christ must do their proper work and make their proper witness (*ibid.* 1968d:228).

Dr. Blake's understanding of church "renewal" continued to have an impact long after the Uppsala Assembly was history. To many in the pews, renewal conveyed the idea of a closer walk with God. It had a spiritual connotation; it could lead to a renewed commitment to evangelism and missions. For many in the WCC however—especially those who had been discussing new ways and forms for mission—"renewal of the church" meant their catching a vision of a responsibility to work for a new society, and then joining in that struggle for liberation. No one can quarrel with Dr. Blake's reminder that radically changing times in the world call for an appropriate witness in the light of today's needs. But when both method and objectives change together, serious questions are justified.

Appraisals. Early in the Assembly, retired General Secretary, W. A. Visser 't Hooft laid his finger on the crux of the matter with a timely warning:

There is a great tension between the vertical interpretation of the Gospel as essentially concerned with God's saving action in the life of individuals and the horizontal interpretation of it as mainly concerned with human relationships in the world. A Christianity that has lost its vertical dimension has lost its salt, and is not only insipid

79

but useless for the world; but a Christianity that would use the vertical dimension as a means of escape from its responsibility in the common life of man is a denial of the incarnation of God's love for the world manifested in Christ (*ibid*. 1968d:318).

The findings and views about mission were presented in the reports from Church and Society Conference 1966, *The Church for Others,* and *Planning for Mission.* They appeared prominently in the draft documents and then in the final statements of the Assembly. All were accepted. The concern at Uppsala was not with ecclesiastical or theological questions, but with secular and horizontal issues. The agenda came from the world, and centered on social, economic and political issues. Through it the Church was called to stand at the side of the poor and powerless, the exploited and helpless victims of oppression and racism. The basis was laid at Uppsala for later programs in which the WCC member churches were even more intensely involved in the struggle for liberation and a just society. Unfortunately, this good work was undertaken at the expense of deliberately neglecting the primary task given to the Church by her Lord—that of making known the Gospel to the ends of the earth. Thought, energies and resources of the churches now took aim at improving the quality of life for the millions caught in poverty and trapped by dehumanizing structures in societies beyond their control. But there was no challenge to churches to share the good news of God's offer of eternal life. No challenge to the churches to a new commitment toward making sure that lost men and women without knowledge of Christ have a valid opportunity to experience God's eternal salvation.

We may be thankful for what the churches were urged to do at Uppsala—to side with the poor and deprived in struggles for human values and a better way of life. Churches do need to be shaken out of a comfortable, middle class complacency and mentality. They need to shape both their structures and lifestyles in order to be truly relevant to modern man. The Church needs cultural relevance both in its form and in its message in this generally secularized age. But to have something to say about God in today's world, church people need first of all to be new people of God themselves before they can reflect the heartbeat of Christ to others. God's people need to speak as participants in a world where people despair, suffer and die. They need to relate to people who pursue false visions and seek utopias beyond what can ever happen. The churches need to learn how to conceptualize and communicate as good news today what Jesus Christ did two thousand years ago. The churches need to speak meaningfully to a world where many blasphemously conclude that God is either dead or unconcerned. It was good that Christians were challenged at Uppsala to pour their energies into making the world a better place. Christians should always be at the forefront of all efforts to recognize the enormous complex issues—issues that not only circumscribe our possibilities today, but that determine the kind of world those yet unborn will inherit.

We need to know what repentance from social transgression means. We need shaking out of our small, comfortable, complacent worlds. We must be conscious of the sobs and cries of people who in poverty, hunger and desperation believe nobody cares. Christians must realize that non-participation in the struggle is to be a partner in others' social crimes.

What attitudes should Christian people take toward violence and revolution? The problems in a world of violence and sudden death challenge the Christian to become vulnerable. He must be prepared to suffer as he identifies with Christ who himself suffered death on the cross, rejected by the world but accepted by God. We can be thankful that the WCC at Uppsala called attention to these necessary and urgent challenges.

At the same time, the Uppsala Assembly cannot be thanked for what it failed to say. In its intense emphasis on the horizontal relationships, the vertical dimension and the power of the Gospel to change those who hear and believe into new people in Christ was scarcely mentioned. The challenge to repentance and new birth into the Kingdom of God through belief in Jesus Christ for people everywhere was notably absent. Pity and compassion for the millions upon millions who have never validly heard of Jesus Christ, God's only appointed Savior, was a missing element. Nowhere mentioned was the intent of God that through the proclamation of the Gospel his salvation could reach to the ends of the earth. The great un-

81

finished missionary and evangelistic task of the churches appeared to be deliberately omitted. What happened to the promise at New Delhi that with the integration of the IMC into the WCC evangelism would become central to all the work of the WCC? Christians aware of what was happening felt they had been grievously betrayed.

Uppsala produced statements which may also be faulted for their biblical assumptions and presuppositions. To explain and justify proposals made, there was misuse of the Bible by selective use of Scripture to interpret the perceived signs of what God was doing in the world. The result was a new and highly debatable understanding of mission. Its major assumption was that God is engaged in mission just as much through acts of Mao and Gandhi as he is through acts of ministers and missionaries. And the Church is to join him in that "larger mission." Such assumptions are very often half truths, mixtures of truth and error, or grievous overstatements of truths.

Eugene Carson Blake himself, may have had second thoughts about Uppsala. His references are the more significant when one realizes the prominent role he played in the Fourth Assembly's acceptance of New Mission. He candidly admitted that

> . . . the "first issue" to arise from Uppsala was "Does the Gospel, rightly understood eschatologically and historically really support the present ecumenical preoccupation with social, economic and political questions such as the 'development' commitment of the Uppsala Assembly?" (Blake 1969:333–334).

Blake mentioned a "second issue" when he asked whether the WCC's preoccupation with the study of man is "really more than a passing fashion . . . or worse, an indication that we along with the secularists have become agnostic about God" (Blake 1969:333–334).

Few have analyzed what happened at Uppsala with deeper insights than Canon Douglas Webster. Webster by his own testimony is deeply committed to the ecumenical movement. In a sermon, "The Bible and Mission," which he delivered on the occasion of the 166th anniversary of the founding of the

British and Foreign Bible Societies, he delivered a scathing appraisal of the way the new understandings of mission were based on misuse of Scripture.

A more serious matter arises in connection with the place of the Bible in the theology of mission, in discovering what mission is. It has been pointed out that the words, "mission" and "missionary," "Gospel" and "evangelist" are to be found increasingly in secular use. No one can quarrel with this; Christians have no monopoly of language. But it is high time to draw attention to the increasing secularization of the Christian concept of mission, which is in danger of being *divorced from its roots in the Bible*. [italics mine] Should this continue unchallenged and unchecked, the Church cannot expect to have much of a future, and the Gospel, instead of being preached, would become a subject of research. We are now witnessing a spate of literature on mission which even if quoting from the Bible, has either reversed or ignored at least some of the Biblical perspectives and priorities. The world's agenda is being allowed to take precedence over the Bible's message, and what the world says of itself is not being supplemented by what the Bible says of the world. There was a time when Christians listened chiefly to the Bible and frequently failed to understand what was happening in the world and to relate the two. Today the opposite is true. We are so obsessed with the demands and developments of the secular world as determinative for mission that we have forgotten how often the Bible contradicts the world and diagnoses the world's needs in terms such as repentance and faith which the world continues to reject.

The focal point for this false emphasis and dangerous distortion was reached at Uppsala where the World Council of Churches held its Fourth Assembly in 1968. I take no pleasure in saying this, for I am heart and soul in the ecumenical movement and I rejoice in the existence of the World Council of Churches. But to be committed does not imply being uncritical. After all there are plenty

83

of devout Roman Catholics who are profoundly critical of the Vatican and the papal curia. Unfortunately most of the WCC's critics are opponents from the outside. Real ecumenical commitment should issue in responsible, honest, and searching criticism of what goes on in Geneva and comes out of it. The question has to be asked: "Can those who regard the Bible as in some sense authoritative for the Christian mission be satisfied with what is said about that mission in the Uppsala report?" I would hazard a guess that the time will come—perhaps soon—when those with the most knowledge and experience of real mission will consider the Uppsala report on mission little short of a sell-out to the diseased and confused spirit of our age. Its weakness is less in what it said than in what it refused to say.

Uppsala had compassion and rightly voiced it powerfully. This compassion was for the hungry millions and for those deprived of justice and equality because of race or colour. It had no compassion at all [in its written report] for those deprived of the knowledge of God's love made known in Christ and condemned to live in fear and superstition or by a false faith. Uppsala rightly had a sense of urgency about the evils of world poverty and the iniquities of racist policies. It had no sense of urgency for *preaching the Gospel where it had never been heard* [italics mine]. There may still be a place for the proclamation of the Gospel but today's main approach must be one of dialogue, according to Uppsala.

The Church is sent out into the world to serve people. Uppsala has no doubt about this; but to evangelize people in the hope that they will be converted to Christ? Uppsala had many doubts about this because it could seem to be spiritual imperialism. Uppsala rightly condemned much that was wrong in the Western world (though it seldom explicitly criticized Marxist countries). But the evil it attacked was always social and political; the fact that man, every man, is a sinner and that all sin is first and foremost against God (Psa. 51:4), that man is under judgment and stands in need of divine mercy and pardon every day, is largely ignored. The current inclination would be to dismiss all this as individualism, a pietist hangover, bearing little relation to world need (Webster 1973).

On an earlier occasion, Webster had stated:*

There is a strong tendency today especially by some of the directors of the World Council to dissociate them [evangelism and conversion] altogether from mission and to regard them as defective concepts of mission. They [the directors] assume that mission has nothing at all to do with winning converts or planting churches.

Regrettably, those in positions of power still share the Uppsala point of view. Correspondingly, it is this power that replaced the traditional classical mission with New Mission as the unfinished task of the churches.

Visser 't Hooft, recognized architect of the ecumenical movement, appears to share some of Webster's concern about the place of the Bible in the ecumenical movement. In his book, *Has the Ecumenical Movement a Future?* he appears to raise a word of caution—calling the WCC and the churches back to their roots: "The one distinctive mission given to the Church, and to no other, is to declare the prophetic word of God." (He is obviously speaking of the Word of God known from Scripture.) "This is the prophecy that bears witness to that which God has done, to what God is doing and to what He will do" (Visser 't Hooft 1974:92–93).

It is a timely word of warning. The WCC is in danger of going too far in understanding its zeal for mission to be the struggle for justice. There is danger in neglecting the great central truths of the Bible concerning God, and concerning man and his ultimate destiny. In seeking to speak its own prophetic messages forcefully, the WCC is failing to consider the authoritative "Thus saith the Lord" of Scripture. The accent is too much on what man must do to effect his own deliverance and salvation. This tends to downgrade or leave out

*From an address to a mission society in Germany, 1972.

altogether the glorious good news of what God did to save us in the death and resurrection of his Son. The Church has the one message of salvation the world does not know. It is therefore up to the Church to make it known. There is an agenda the world cannot write. There are questions the world does not even know enough to ask. Moreover, only the Church can give the answers. Through the Church God is pleased to make known his "manifold wisdom" (Eph. 3:10). Since in the wisdom of God the world did not know [him] through wisdom, it pleased God through the folly of what we preach to save those who believe (1 Cor. 1:21).

I hear Visser 't Hooft saying to the Church, "You have been entrusted with the Gospel; proclaim it." It is true that no one else can share this message. This is the Church's unique mission. There is salvation in no one else, for there is no other name under heaven by which we must be saved (Acts 4:12). What if the Church fails to speak God's prophetic voice made clear through Jesus Christ?

The ecumenical movement and the WCC have a future, but it is a future dependent upon bowing before the revelation of God known from Scripture. One cannot but wonder at this point what lies ahead for both the WCC and its member churches.

Repercussions. Up until now it would perhaps appear that the actions of the World Council of Churches and its Commission on World Mission and Evangelism truly represented the convictions of its member churches. I have said, "The younger churches felt strongly" and "the growing conviction of Western churches was . . ."

It is time to be more specific—to examine this matter more closely. In actual fact, only a very few of the ministers, pastors and missionaries—from both Western and Eastern churches—understood clearly the idea of New Mission. They had no idea of the drastic changes that were being conceptualized and made operational in Geneva and in the headquarters of the great boards. They sent their money for missions in complete trust that the good men in charge would spend it wisely and do what the contemporary situation called for.

Familiar terms were used assiduously by the advocates of

the New Mission concepts. "Mission" had never been used so frequently. "Evangelism," if one counted the number of times the word was used, had never been so emphasized. This new mission concept was also concerned, apparently, with "the missionary structure of the congregation." "Salvation," which lay at the heart of the entire traditional concept of classical mission, was being greatly emphasized. In fact, a huge conference was scheduled at Bangkok just to stress its importance for contemporary mission. "Conversion" was used profusely with many references to the Old Testament—as a turning toward what God wanted done. It all seemed so desirable and so necessary for the contemporary situation.

The United Presbyterian Confession of 1967 perhaps best illustrates the process going on in the churches. Those who drafted the new statement felt strongly that the changed world in which Christians lived demanded a new confession. Though designedly supplementary to traditional confessions, "C-67" speaks of "The Mission of the Church" (II-A) primarily as "The Ministry of Reconciliation" (Part II—and the emphasis throughout). This mission of reconciliation, in turn, is seen in terms of the activities of the Church which war against injustice, racism, oppression, poverty and, in fact, against everything that demeans men and women. The framers of Confession 67 did not take "mission" to mean "world evangelization." It did not mean proclaiming Jesus Christ as Lord and Savior and persuading men to become his disciples and responsible members of his Church.

Significantly, the resistance and opposition to Confession 67 was based almost entirely on its view of the Bible. I have not run across any attack on its radical reinterpretation of mission. In short, the thinking in the main boards was disguised by the use of familiar vocabulary. It was so unthinkable that familiar terms would be given radically new meanings that most church leaders, lay and clerical alike, simply did not realize what was going on.

Here I must call attention to a rather disturbing fact: We have seen that the New Mission concept originated with, and was articulated by, ecumenical leaders both at Geneva and at the headquarters of member churches during the sixties and early seventies. Today, in the late seventies, it is being assiduously taught (as we shall see later on) in seminaries, through church papers, in many books and articles and through the media. This means that any corrective changes at the leadership level will be forced to filter slowly to the layman in the pew.

Even conservative evangelicals outside of the conciliar fellowship, many of whom were critical of the World Council of Churches because of low views of the Bible, failed for some years to see or believe what was happening. However, in 1966, the Wheaton Congress on World Mission issued its statement of mission theory and theology. Its sharp variance with New Mission views began to come into focus. Challenges to New Mission followed in various forms.

In 1968, the Church Growth Bulletin printed a now well-known article, "Will Uppsala Betray the Two Billion?" which called on the World Council of Churches to include continuous evangelization in its program. In 1970 came the famed Frankfort Declaration issued in Germany. It not only stated the conservative position but "opposed and denounced" those positions of New Mission which it believed were unbiblical. Greater realization of the theological implications of New Mission and evidences of its effect on world evangelization are appearing increasingly in the seventies.

To a large extent this kind of reaction was anticipated by those architects of New Mission. Already in 1967 they had resolved that when it came it would be parried. The New Mission concept would not be changed, would not be modified to include world evangelization: the sending of missionaries, the increasing of efforts to proclaim the Gospel to the nearly three billion who have yet to believe in Christ. We will see that precisely this program has been carried out as we proceed with the story of the seventies.

FIVE
NEW MISSION
IMPLEMENTED
Bangkok 1973

The Bangkok Conference was ten years in preparation. It was originally planned for 1969 or 1970. But the CWME leaders were not ready; nor was the time ripe for their desired objectives. For the goal of Bangkok was to complete the process that would involve the whole WCC in a common effort: to implement the horizontal understandings of New Mission as laid out in Uppsala; to re-orient and redirect the missionary movement.* A study of WCC staff preparations for Bangkok shows clearly the tremendous importance they attached to this meeting.

> The Bangkok Conference on "Salvation Today," coming as it did midway in the period from Uppsala to Nairobi, has been central to the life of the Commission on World Mission and Evangelism during the period under review, and perhaps, when viewed from the perspective of a greater span of years, pivotal in the history of world mission (Johnson 1975:82).

The announced theme, "Salvation Today," drew a mixed response. Some Asian churches saw the theme as too religious and too traditional; they felt its overtones implied a spiritual,

---

*This bold statement is fully documented in the *Planning for Bangkok* '71/'72 file, Geneva WCC Archives.

non-secular kind of experience. Conservative evangelicals, on the other hand, wanted to believe that the theme offered a grand opportunity for the CWME to reaffirm its commitment to the historic goals of mission and evangelism. They could not know, in advance, the degree to which this meeting had been "orchestrated."

COMPREHENSIVE PLANNING

Archival materials reveal comprehensive preparations. These were not limited to objectives but dealt in detail with how to achieve them, including such matters as timing and mood as well as content. After all, the understandings and goals of mission had been spelled out at Uppsala, and were basically accepted by the CWME staff. Bangkok needed only to formally produce the documents to legitimize and consummate all of this.

When at the close of the Bangkok meeting Emilio Castro, (who was to become the new director of the CWME) speaking in the euphoria of the moment exclaimed, "The missionary era has ended and the era of world mission has just begun," it was evident that Bangkok was judged to have been a success (Castro 1973:140).

The Archives Communicate. WCC staff planning the conference liked the theme, "Salvation Today." It had biblical connotations and offered possibilities to set forth their understanding of what God had in mind for mankind: he was obviously active in liberating people from bondages of various kinds here and now. The Geneva staff clearly felt it necessary that the CWME be given new directions.*

It was Thomas Wieser who edited the study, *Planning for Mission,* as preparation for Uppsala. His paper written in 1968 as part of the Geneva discussions had in mind also the CWME meeting (proposed at that time for sometime in 1969 or 1970). He suggested that the conference should identify salvation as a

---

*Unfortunately, most of the information on which these and the following observations are based are from sources that may not be quoted directly. However, should anyone wish to check the accuracy of these comments, he will find them substantiated by materials in the *Planning for Bangkok* files in the WCC Archives, Geneva.

historical process. This would relate to Marxism's sense of the historical process, and to views about salvation found in other religions as well as to modern (secular) man's apparent freedom from the need of "salvation." Salvation then was directly tied to the concept of *Missio Dei*. Wieser saw "salvation" to be determined by what we believe God is doing in today's world. Such a theme would enable the conference to answer questions of what the Church was supposed to do (its mission) in terms of what God was understood to be doing (his mission). He asked if one could agree that *Missio Dei* was to be identified with the general process of history. Was God working out the purpose of his *shalom* in the secular—in the historical events that shaped people's lives? If so, then to what extent could one say that God is at work in the struggle for humanization, peace and social justice?

These issues and questions needed to be asked. But at the same time we must ask, may *Missio Dei* not also be understood as a process apart from the general involvement of history? God's ways are not that clear and he has his own way of working out his purposes. His actions are to be seen through the eyes of faith, albeit within the context of "salvation history." This is reflected in the fact of a community claiming to be God's people, the Church.

Wieser saw salvation related to mission in terms of the Church engaging in struggles for justice and peace. The world sets the agenda and provides the arena in which the Church goes out to lose itself for the salvation of others. In the discussion, *Missio Dei* is presumed to be the struggle which liberates. The theme "Salvation Today" was not conceived in order to communicate the word about Jesus Christ in such a way that people hear it as God's good news of salvation which is free, eternal and transcends any efforts man can make to achieve it.

The mission in which the Church must engage to be part of *Missio Dei* involves secularizing the ministry. Only in this way can people in the churches become qualified and trained to participate in the secular struggle for liberation. These were the pre-Uppsala views as expressed in 1968 that had to do with what the CWME should communicate in its next meeting.

The theme, "Salvation Today," could be developed in endless ways. It was decided that it should be expressed through a

91

variety of experiences. These "salvation experiences" from various cultures were to be shared in the conference. Through this sharing it would become apparent that there were a great variety of ways in which people of various cultures experienced "salvation." There would however be no attempted consensus of what constituted a genuine, authentic, recognizable Christian experience of salvation as determined by the Bible. Rather, God would seem to liberate people to a "salvation experience" in experiences ranging all the way from the traditionally accepted Christian experience of salvation to a purely temporal and secular salvation with such savior figures as Mao Tse Tung or Karl Marx or Che Guevara.

In the discussion of a paper prepared for a CWME meeting, various questions arose which gave opportunity to learn what the WCC staff had in mind in choosing the theme, "Salvation Today." For example: What is it that we are liberated from? And what are we liberated for? How does salvation for the individual relate to salvation for the community? How does our understanding of salvation relate to the development of peoples and societies in various countries? In other words, what is the meaning and task of mission in terms of development and how does mission relate to goals of world community? What is the nature and task of the Christian community today? That is, how does what God is doing in the world differ from what he is doing in the Church? Or, just how important is a visible baptized community to which people are joined?

It was claimed that there were two areas in which the Christian missionary community needed improvement: 1) In its activities—life-style and worship, in the structures of its missionary enterprise and its congregations, in its way of sending and receiving in mission as well as the extent to which its use of resources corresponded with what it proclaimed. 2) In its methods—the dated styles and content of education for mission and evangelism they used since these were not only out of date, but uncoordinated and inadequate.

A meeting of the Executive Committee of the CWME dealt with the theme, "The Good News of Salvation Today." Here priority status was given to four concerns. 1) The dialogue with men of other faiths, with Marxists and humanists had raised the question as to whether/how men were to be called to believe in Christ and be saved. 2) The Executive Committee of the CWME recognized the inconclusiveness of the discussion at Mexico City about whether or not people should be called to a visible, baptized discipleship. A broader issue involved the debate over whether God brings about salvation through secular history as well as through the believing Christian community. 3) The committee claimed discussion was needed about the nature and credibility of Christ as Savior. What does one do about modern secular man when he is said to have no need of a Savior in the traditional biblical sense? 4) In this same meeting the Executive Committee recognized that the question of salvation and damnation was of major concern to conservative evangelicals. How should we interpret the purpose of the proclamation of the Gospel of Jesus Christ—that "all men may believe in him and be saved"—in view of that concern?

A paper presented at that preparatory meeting for Bangkok served as the basis for discussion. It communicated a strong bias in favor of understanding salvation largely as secular salvation particularly since some understood it to mean freedom from all that hinders men from achieving their full humanity. To be saved was to be made free to enter the struggle for the salvation or freedom of others. A very strong pitch was made to decisively challenge the view that "personal salvation" and "social concern or participation in the struggle for social justice and meeting human need" were not equally integral to evangelism. The question of credibility was recognized, along with the need for the churches themselves to be liberated communities in order to participate in the ministries of liberation by both message and action.

By 1971 the discussion papers written by the WCC staff, and which formed the basis for Bangkok planning, indicate that salvation was to be defined very largely in secular terms and that the churches would be summoned to enter the struggle for liberation leading to a new society.*

Part of the preparations consisted of collecting texts to provide illustrative material especially from Third World countries which would show varieties of salvation experience. The bibli-

*Documentation can be seen in *Planning for Bangkok* '71/'72 files, and the CWME files, WCC Archives, Geneva.

cal model of the exodus would help answer the question, "What must I do to be saved?" Sub-headings could be "the cry for salvation," "liberation from bondage" and "towards a better world." This secular salvation could refer to biblical counterparts in such terms as "Let my people go" and "A land flowing with milk and honey." Phrases referring to biblical texts (cost of salvation, the suffering of the cross, good news being preached to the poor, signs of the kingdom and how one recognizes the signs of God's liberating mission to bring salvation) all were tied to improvements in this world rather than to eternal salvation.

It was obvious to me as I went over their materials and minutes of meetings that the CWME staff, in preparing for Bangkok, had by and large embraced the horizontal understandings that were set forth at Uppsala so far as their understanding of mission was concerned. The question, How is "salvation today" actualized through God's mission (*Missio Dei*) and how does the Christian community participate in God's mission, were to be answered by the Church's participation in the liberation struggles. This is the way salvation may be realized here and now. The goal is a more just socio-economic-political order. I found very, very little to suggest that a high priority in mission be given to communicating the Gospel message in such a manner that Jesus Christ is presented as the Savior who died for our sins. God's freely offered forgiveness to those who hear, repent and believe, based on what Christ accomplished in his sacrificial death, was scarcely mentioned. I found very little also to suggest that crossing cultural barriers and planting the church among peoples of every language and culture interested, or even concerned, the CWME staff in that pre-Bangkok period. There is little to suggest that the aim set forth for the CWME in New Delhi, or the promise given to the IMC, mattered very much for them.

Reorienting the Missionary Movement. Just what is the nature of the salvation God intends for modern man? This was only one of the aims for Bangkok. Therefore, mission had to be redefined so that it would harmonize with all of the WCC's understandings as set forth in Uppsala. In addition, all the planning for Bangkok pinpointed the great importance attached to radically redirecting the whole missionary enterprise. The CWME staff members wanted discussions and positions that led to action since they were convinced that the missionary movement the CWME had inherited from the IMC needed to be revamped and reshaped if it was to implement the goals for the new understanding of mission.

A memorandum from Steven G. Mackie to the CWME staff, shortly before the Bangkok meeting, specifically stated that in planning this World Conference they should keep in mind from the start that large-scale changes were needed in the missionary movement. He spoke of the need to review policies and programs of mission agencies and their relationship to churches—and perhaps their continued existence. The CWME needed a new role and it needed to be made up of a new constituency. He spoke of wanting the kind of decisions at Bangkok that would lead to action.

On numerous occasions discussions centered on the embarrassment of the continuing mission societies and the alleged outmoded methods and aims of the missionary movement. It was clearly recognized that in order to fully implement the new understanding about mission, the remnants of the missionary movement had to be "dealt with." Bangkok would lay the base for the sweeping changes that were deemed necessary. All these discussions had far-reaching implications. For example, some even questioned the continued existence of the CWME within the WCC; they would have been happy to see it phased out![*] The logic is there: If the whole church is mission, and if that mission is to join God in his mission of liberation by joining in that struggle, then a separate commission is hardly necessary to implement what is to be done by all, and which is already being implemented by appropriate units within the WCC.

Planning for Bangkok went even further. For its intent was to supply the basis for this radical redirection of the missionary movement among CWME constituent members at the grass roots. To do this, they needed to propose relevant subjects for the section reports. WCC staff planning would have to assure

---

[*]The future of the CWME and serious doubts as to whether the CWME was still needed were on the agenda of the WCC Geneva staff meetings on several occasions (Geneva WCC Archives).

that right issues were raised and that the approved final documents contained the references that would justify the actions contemplated.

If I may paraphrase one of the planning papers that touched on some of the changes which might be proposed, Section I.A would be expected to speak to one kind of missionary education, propaganda and training that might imply an acceptance of "dialogue"; Section II.D would deal with another kind in a way that minimized "domination" and "dependence" and maximized true self-hood.

The Bangkok meeting was supposed to result in providing guidelines for all subsequent CWME staff work. It was hoped that the various subsections of the conference would direct practical suggestions to those bodies most competent to act. The bodies affected would most certainly be the CWME itself, its constituency (i.e., councils, churches and mission agencies), and the WCC as a whole together with its various parts.

If the CWME through its staff was to accomplish this redirection—of how and where its constituents were engaged in mission—it was vital that there be a legitimacy and a sound basis for lending a hand and a good word of counsel. Great importance was attached to having all mission agencies moving in the same direction at the same time!

Any reading of the pre-Bangkok planning indicates the extreme care and thought that went into insuring, insofar as they were able, the end result. Attention was given to minutest details. This included not only choices of people needed for the various sections and workshops (drafters and counsellors) but also specific objectives for each section: what to accomplish and what to avoid. Interestingly, any attempts by the conference to formulate definitions or to produce a consensus were to be avoided. Incidentally, a post conference evaluation by the staff indicated they felt they had succeeded in those primary objectives. Records of WCC staff meetings and study working papers show clearly that a major concern in Geneva for the conference was the "Role of Mission Agencies" vis-a-vis New Mission.

I was surprised to learn that staff efforts went into ensuring that the right people were at the conference, and correspondingly, that certain people were *not* there. Great attention was given to proposed changes in the constitution which related to CWME. During this same time, the names of persons the staff wanted appointed to the CWME were made known to the appropriate people for nominations.

Plans for Bangkok and expectancies from Bangkok were worked out before the new director for the CWME was known (and he would not assume his duties until after the Bangkok meeting). It is both interesting and amusing to note the bit of apprehension and concern for the new CWME director to be clued in at an early date on what planners for Bangkok had in mind. There seemed to be a trace of uneasiness lest the new director not fully share the same enthusiasm for what was expected from Bangkok as did those who planned it so carefully. It was clear that they wanted the conference and the CWME to act in such a way that the new director would carry out the new directives. The gathering momentum preceding Bangkok needed to be maintained after Bangkok. And the new director of course would be a vital key.

BANGKOK'S SIGNIFICANCE

Success for Whom? The Bangkok Conference was at the same time both a success and a failure. It undoubtedly gave hope to those who wanted a speedy end to the missionary era so that the new forms for mission could inherit the vast resources and energy presently going into classical mission. The conference gave ample opportunity to the harsh critics of missionaries to point out their alleged failures. The missionary movement and the evils of colonialism and racism were linked together emotionally. If colonialism had been evil and needed to go, the same was true for missionaries and their respective missions. Statements made by Dr. Potter appeared to many as unkind and unfair observations about missionaries and missions. They seemed to be in bad taste, particularly in a conference entrusted with all that the IMC had held dear. The prominence given to the moratorium issue, for example, related directly to the efforts of those who wanted to bury the old mission in order to get on with the new.

The wide range of experiences to illustrate "salvation today" was expected to produce an openmindedness to the different ways one should see God in mission. The acceptance of these as valid "salvation today" experiences in the many cultures added a new category of authority alongside of Scripture. By avoiding sharp biblical definitions about the salvation God offers, the way was then clear for allowing an interpretation of mission with an emphasis on secular and liberating experiences.

Nevertheless, there was enough use of traditional words and concepts in the conference to provide comfort for those concerned about classical mission and its emphasis upon world evangelization. Statements adopted unanimously affirmed basic truths about God and mission which have always been held by Bible believing Christians:

> Each generation must evangelize its own generation. To work for church growth and renewal is the chief, abiding and irreplaceable task of Christian mission . . . .

> With gratitude and joy we affirm again our confidence in the sufficiency of our crucified and risen Lord. We know Him as the one who is, and who was, and who is to come, the sovereign Lord of all. To the individual He comes with power to liberate him from every evil and sin, from every power in heaven and earth, and from every threat of life or death.

> To the world He comes as the Lord of the universe, with deep compassion for the poor and the hungry, to liberate the powerless and the oppressed and to liberate the powerful and the oppressors in judgment and mercy.

> He calls His Church to be part of His saving activity both in calling men to decisive personal response to His Lordship, and in unequivocal commitment to movements and works by which all men may know justice and have opportunity to be fully human (WCC 1973a).

Despite these affirmations in the official conference documents, the conference itself seemed a failure for those burdened for the unfinished missionary task of worldwide cross-cultural evangelism. The CWME, as the specifically designated successor of the IMC, has the responsibility to assist the churches, its councils and its mission agencies in the task of biblical or Great Commission missions. It is sad to note that at the conference missions and missionaries were apparently deliberately attacked, and their motivation, their wisdom and the results of their obedience to Christ were called into question. Missions and missionaries were painstakingly, and in un-Christlike manner besmirched by unsubstantiated and blanket criticism—that because of their support base in capitalistic countries, they had therefore connived with colonializers in exploiting the poor. It seems incredible that leaders in the world's Christian community should seek to discredit the sacrificial work and witness of missionaries by attempting to associate them with such emotionally charged subjects as colonialism, capitalism and racism. A more careful judgment would seem to call for a doxology of praise to God for all he was pleased to accomplish through these humble servants. These seemed like cheap charges—unbecoming to people who were given the wonderful opportunity to know Christ because somewhere, sometime, someone had said, "Here am I, Lord, send me."

The conference failed to come to grips with the unfinished missionary task of taking the Gospel to the yet unreached with the news of God's provision for eternal salvation. New Mission concentrated on mission apart from evangelism, which seeks conversions and the resultant new churches.

The leadership at Bangkok had apparently decided against the historic understandings of classical mission. Dr. Potter had set the stage vis-a-vis the "unreached peoples" when he spoke disparagingly of these eschatological words of Christ, "This Gospel of the Kingdom will be preached throughout the whole world (oikumene) as a testimony to the nations" (Matt. 24:14). He acknowledged:

> This has created a lively debate in missionary circles as to whether the emphasis should be on proclaiming the Gospel to the two billion or more who have never heard it in the land which have lived for millenia by other faiths, or whether it should be preached literally to the whole

99

world, including the so-called Christian lands of Europe, North America, and Australasia. *The debate is totally futile* when we look closer at this one world in which we are living [emphasis mine] (WCC 1973a).

Dr. Potter's words about the futility of the debate and the doubt about whether the Gospel was intended to be proclaimed literally to the whole world, even what he said throughout his speech which discredited classical mission, clearly indicate the extent of his influence in his position as the first full-time director of the CWME following New Delhi. In pre-Bangkok planning papers there is the statement, "Philip has shown us the way."

When we recognize his many gifts and spiritual qualities, his gift for leadership and the many extraordinary and positive benefits that continue to accrue to the World Council of Churches through him, we can only deeply regret that Dr. Potter did not see fit to promote the historic aims of the movement for world evangelization as committed to the CWME by the IMC. In those crucial years when the CWME was finding its place within the life and work of the WCC, dynamic leadership was so badly needed. Continuity with the IMC traditions could have helped greatly. Unfortunately, both were in short supply. As a representative from the Third World, Dr. Potter could have helped ease tensions that developed between Third World churches and churches from the West with respect to missions and missionaries. In his key role, he could have kept the churches conscious of their primary task of communicating the Gospel to yet unreached peoples. He could have led the way in finding new patterns of relationships and new structures for this task.

Instead, during the period that climaxed with the Bangkok Conference the CWME progressively abandoned the historic aims of the IMC to steadily embrace the new emphasis produced at Uppsala which accented the horizontal and lifted up humanization as the goal of missions. The central thrust of carrying the Gospel to the ends of the earth, which was the earmark of the IMC, was no longer central to the CWME. Indeed, it was practically abandoned. While the IMC objectives still received lip service, the heart appeared to be in those kinds of mission that had potential for improving social conditions.

Mission defined as evangelism (sinners reconciled to God, true discipleship, conversion, baptism and membership in the Christian Church) was given token emphasis in the CWME in the Uppsala to Bangkok period. Programs supposedly designed to implement the IMC aims resulted in involvement of people in interchurch aid and church renewal more than involvement of people in cross-cultural evangelism—communicating the Gospel to new contacts and planting churches where they were not previously found.

In 1975 I asked the co-secretary for ESP (Ecumenical Sharing of Personnel) how many of the people in that program were actually engaged in cross-cultural evangelism among otherwise unreached peoples. He told me "not one" he could think of was so involved. Yet this is the very program that is often cited as an example of the new way in which the CWME is carrying forward the missionary movement in the spirit of the IMC.

A New Era for Mission. The CWME staff considered the Bangkok Conference a success. They had planned the meeting with meticulous care. It had even been postponed several times because the CWME staff thought neither they nor their constituents were ready for the new understandings about mission and its new directions. The primary objective was to adjust the CWME understandings and efforts to match the goals at Uppsala; the intended result was a reorientation and redirection of the missionary movement. If this could be accomplished, the whole church and all churches everywhere would be free to commit totally to the understandings about mission produced at Uppsala. That this objective for Bangkok was apparently attained is reflected in Emilio Castro's euphoric exclamation at the end of the conference: "The missionary era has ended and the era of world mission has just begun."

Their idea of portraying salvation as a many-sided experience helped the CWME realize its objective. It allowed for expressions which would appear to illustrate that God is active in mission in a variety of ways and among peoples of many different cultures. Wherever liberating experiences occur, or wherever the struggle against injustice results in gaining human

101

dignity and decency, there people experience salvation. These salvation ideas presented at Bangkok were entirely compatible with those produced at Uppsala. They were also compatible and supportive of a view that advocated "holistic evangelism." Some claimed that the prerequisite for communicating the Gospel verbally in a given place was the churches' need to first engage in the social struggle there.

Anthropocentric views like these were considered congenial with the world views of Third World Christians. It was assumed that Third World Christians found difficulty with the spirituality of the West where the accent was on the spiritual to the neglect of the temporal. The proposed new view of salvation emphasized that people experienced God's liberating help in a variety of cultural and social contexts. E.g., when people cried out for deliverance from oppressive situations and experienced help, they experienced salvation.

"*Doing Theology*." The formula for "doing theology" is to first be involved and to reflect later about the significance of that involvement experience. The conference at Bangkok fit neatly into this formula. What did all these salvific accounts and experiences from various places and cultures mean? The conclusion: God uses a wide variety of ways to bring his intended salvation to the world. The kinds of experiences and accounts shared at Bangkok accented strongly the liberating experience in the struggle against injustice. So God's salvation for today must be closely associated with this kind of secular experience. The idea of salvation advocated at Bangkok was actually conditioned by the experience at Bangkok.

The Bangkok experience fits neatly into the framework of thinking found in the pre-Uppsala study, *The Church for Others*. There one did not begin with the Bible. One began by participating in God's mission (defined as acts of liberation) in the world. Theological significance becomes apparent afterwards through reflection on the significance of what happened. The Bangkok experience fits that pattern. Paradoxically, *words* or *propositions* are required to interpret its meaning to those not present. But how does experience relate to the "evangel" and to verbalization? The great and historic truths of our faith are crucially affected by words and how they are put together.

102

It is not a question of saying nothing; for man will not be silent. The question is: What will we say and on whose authority? Salvation is a great biblical word. Was the use of the word salvation at Bangkok even close to biblical truth?

When is true salvation experienced? Are we to say that God liberates people (provides salvation) when terrible acts of violence are condoned? When millions may be slaughtered because of hopes for a promised better tomorrow? When individual rights are denied in favor of so-called "people's rights"? Is this the salvation brought by God? Without an authority—the authority of Scripture to test and evaluate liberating experiences (salvation)—whose view is to prevail? The overall spirit or mood at Bangkok left everything very open-ended. It allowed for new activities in mission which only remotely relate to the basic principles of mission that the IMC or their member churches had in mind.

"Reverse Flow." "Reverse Flow" meant moving missionaries in two directions. The missionary was regarded as essential in order to keep churches from becoming too much a part of their landscape. If this was true for Third World churches, it was equally true for the "sending churches." These sending churches needed a missionary presence from churches of other lands and cultures perhaps even more than churches of the Third World did. At least Western churches needed to hear what Third World churches with prophetic insight had to say. Such missionaries to the West, from the South and East, would rightfully have plenty to say about the exploitive, profligate waste of the world's resources by Western peoples! The missionary from the Third World was projected as sensitizing the conscience of the western people to the inhuman, destructive, powerless, exploitive relationships that kept too many poor while allowing others to be rich. Coming as they did from different cultural experiences of God in their lives and worship, these missionaries to the West would hopefully be a corrective to middle class ways of worshipping God and to life-styles of Christians that all too easily identified authentic Christian experience with Western cultural forms. All this was implied in "reverse flow."

At Bangkok the CWME was to take its place and fulfill its

role for harnessing the energies and resources of the churches in the social struggle to bring about a "just, sustainable and participatory society."* It was quite a challenge: churches and agencies needed to be reeducated as to what the mission of the Church in these times entailed. Churches needed to be renewed for mission; i.e., they needed to participate in the liberation struggle against oppression. New mission programs and people involved in them should focus on the goal of a new society. The IMC focus of past years on evangelism (taking the Gospel to the ends of the earth that people everywhere might hear, believe and be saved) seemed to the CWME staff planning Bangkok strangely anachronistic, irrelevant, old fashioned and simplistic—particularly in the context of the bold new visions for a brave new world with a new humanity. The utopia of a new world community occupied center stage. Injustices would be eliminated and people would unselfishly serve each other in a just, sustainable society where all shared in decisions for the larger common good.

Objectives Realized and Projected. The WCC staff, as well as those in the CWME, believed their objectives were realized. Specific definitions were avoided. Salvation was shown to be a multi-faceted experience. God appeared to be "saving" people here and now in socio-economic-political contexts. Other liberating, salvific experiences were shown to be part of God's larger mission—God was equally at work liberating people through non-church groups and movements. Criticisms and abuse of traditional missionaries and their goals somehow made redirection and reconstitution of the missionary movement less formidable. The moratorium issue also helped. By giving moratorium a high level of attention, other forms of mission which required no missionaries would appear less threatening. Moreover, a moratorium on missionaries would release funds, energies and people needed for the social struggle.

If the need could be established for all churches to have missionaries in their midst, this "reverse flow" would encourage Third World criticism of Western church life-styles. The classical-biblical and eternal goals of mission would then begin

*This is fully documented in the *Planning for Bangkok '71/'72* files, WCC Archives, Geneva.

to dissipate as churches responded to the urgent new social goals of mission. Perspectives derived from Bangkok would unmask complicity by Western Christians and their churches in those economic, political and social involvements, and in racist attitudes, that kept Third World peoples poor and powerless. In this "reverse flow," Third World missionaries would have a vital role to play in conscientizing Christians in Western churches to participate in the struggle. Bangkok pronouncements would legitimize concentration on CWME programs like UIM (Urban and Industrial Mission), URM (Urban and Rural Mission), TEF (Theological Education Fund), Dialogue, PCR (Program to Combat Racism) and others.

Since all of the other WCC programs were evaluated in terms of their contribution to the goals of social action mission, it follows that the CWME programs would be similarly appraised. This was how the "missionary era" ended and the "era of world mission" began. Evangelism was "out" and social action was "in." Evangelism and social action were fused—or was it "confused"?

POST-BANGKOK ENERGIES

Immediately following the Bangkok Conference, the CWME staff put concentrated effort into communicating the Bangkok experience to its constituency. High level visits were made to many parts of the world to share with WCC member churches the implications of the conference for the future involvement by both churches and agencies in mission. These meetings and consultations were expected to increase the momentum and expand the vision of the "era of world mission" just begun, catching up churches along the way.

Visions and proposals made at Bangkok would be unrealizable, however, unless those supporting the old missionary movement caught this new vision and poured their resources into the new directions for mission. There would be questions. These had to be answered. Suspicions had to be laid to rest. There were people in the churches who had not yet seen the vision or responded to the prophetic voice of Geneva. These needed to be reached. The Bangkok experience would no doubt help to persuade some of them.

The Bangkok meeting stressed the importance of inter-regional dialogue between Christians of the Third World and Christians from the West. There was need to explain "reverse flow" to Christians in the West who found it difficult to believe they needed missionaries among them when such quantities of literature, radio, television and a proliferation of churches existed to proclaim the Gospel to them. It was clear from post-Bangkok evaluations that Western Christians didn't fully appreciate the need for Third World Christian insights or "prophetic voices." The fact is, however, that affluent Western Christians do need to hear criticisms from poorer Christians of other parts of the world. Western church people need the keen, spiritual perceptions of Third World Christians.

But following Bangkok, beliefs of Western Christians about God and about living out their Christian commitment were increasingly challenged. Meanwhile, Third World Christians were encouraged to think for themselves. This would supposedly strengthen and enrich their Christian experience and understanding of God—the Gospel could then be effectively communicated and their Christian life be more culturally relevant and fully authentic in terms of their worldviews and their own culture. It was now legitimate for Christians to experience God in their lives and express themselves in forms they found culturally relevant, for those at Bangkok encouraged an awareness by the churches of their need to be culturally authentic and indigenous.

Plans included bringing authentic Christian spokesmen from the Third World churches to speak in the West about how Western culture might be redeemed. By this "reverse flow" dialogue could focus on how the (former) liberator himself can be liberated. Third World spokesmen were expected to call into question liberties, freedoms, power and affluence—lifestyles presumed to be responsible for exploiting others and keeping them powerless, while making luxuries possible at their expense.

Bangkok statements helped the churches to grasp the concept presented at Mexico City that the whole world is a mission field. The familiar expression was given a new twist, however. Third World churches at Bangkok began to talk about "how Western culture could be redeemed and Western Christians liberated from its/their cultural identification." And Christians from the West talked about "how the West can help the developing countries to be liberated from powerlessness and oppression."

"Holistic Evangelism." Discussions at Bangkok linked evangelistic and social concerns inextricably together in the term evangelism. Every genuine Christian act had its evangelistic dimension. In practice evangelism was relegated to social action. It was somehow deemed wrong to first talk about the Gospel before doing something about social injustice. Evangelizing apart from social involvement was considered an immoral act. Evangelism, it was said, should not be practiced without prior social involvement.

Bangkok is remembered for advocating "holistic evangelism." Evangelism as classically conceived and as practiced in the West was far too Western-culture oriented. There was too much emphasis upon the personal and spiritual. It was too other-worldly—too divorced from social concerns. Modern (secular) man presumably was no longer interested in a religious experience that was personal and private.

Post Bangkok reflections by the WCC staff anticipated dialogue between East and West where inter-regional conversations would eventuate in redefinitions of evangelism and conversion. Conversion would increasingly be understood as man turning to join his fellowmen in the liberation struggle rather than turning to God. It was believed that in solidarity with the oppressed one would meet Christ who himself identified with the poor and the powerless. Programs also increasingly reflected this basic assumption.

Holistic evangelism meant sharing the Gospel in the context of ministering to the total needs of a person. It connoted the idea that evangelistic efforts must be comprehensive. That is, the good news about Christ must not only be shared in a personal way in the context of doing something about social problems, but the scope of evangelism is larger than just meeting individual needs. The root problems of social injustice are then evangelistic concerns. One CWME fear however is that in this "holistic evangelism" the personal witness to

Christ (in WCC jargon, "the naming of the name") may become only marginally significant.* In other words, it is acknowledged that when everything becomes evangelism, the central motif itself is in danger of being lost. Social action at this point becomes an end in itself. That this sort of thing could develop by 1973 would have seemed utterly unbelievable to those in the IMC at the New Delhi Assembly!

A Dilemma. A feeling of helplessness and despair was in the air. The CWME/WCC member churches and mission agencies committed to classical mission wanted to be involved in evangelism. But what instrument of mission could they now use to participate with their finances and people? How could they be involved in world evangelization if their own CWME within the WCC lacked interest in evangelizing the three billion who are without saving knowledge of Christ? What should they do when there is no program within the WCC whose aim is to evangelize in terms of the Great Commission?

This question is particularly acute for Christians who are in churches committed to the ecumenical movement. These committed Christians within the ecumenical movement want to see their churches vigorously engaged in cross-cultural evangelism. They want imaginative and creative new programs. They want to see churches from six continents work together in new ways and with new methods. They want to be a part of those working together to evangelize the yet unreached everywhere in the world. So they are asking what they can do to help their organization, the WCC, find its way to a more biblical understanding of mission.

These Christians believe in much that the WCC says and does. Many are eager to support WCC programs of social action because they are convinced that churches need the renewal the WCC is advocating. Their problem—dilemma—is that they firmly believe that obedience to Christ means that the message of God's provision of eternal salvation must be proclaimed everywhere until Christ returns. They want opportunities to participate in that kind of classical mission. They know that the constitution of the WCC lists as one of its important functions: "to assist the member churches in their

*Emilio Castro has raised this concern with his staff on several occasions (WCC Archives, Geneva).

worldwide missionary and evangelistic tasks." These Christians prefer to stay within their ecumenical structures. But they are looking for WCC assistance and encouragement in their desire to support and participate in that kind of mission.

In the light of their commitment to this kind of evangelism, it is no wonder that Christians like these consider reports and pronouncements from both Bangkok and Uppsala a betrayal of sacred trust. When at Uppsala humanization was lifted up as *the* goal of mission and emphasis was put upon the horizontal rather than upon the vertical dimension of the Gospel, some who had previously supported the integration of the IMC into the WCC were deeply troubled about what the future might hold. Further confirmation of their fears came at Bangkok. The CWME had been entrusted to do within the WCC what the IMC had done previously outside this structure—only more effectively. Now it was deliberately discrediting the missionary movement and calling into question the wisdom, the motives and the accomplishments of the past. It was embracing the new, horizontal understanding of mission—the salvation God intended as described by New Mission. No wonder these loyal friends of the WCC felt betrayed! It was as if a duly signed will had been changed by the executor of the estate tampering with it. Or, to change the figure—a plane taking them to Jerusalem had been hijacked and was now bound for Moscow.

For them the key question became: How can we again be free to reach our intended destination? How could they participate with others of like mind in efforts intended to reach the three billion still without knowledge of Christ? Maybe, if their own churches carried out classical mission, they could at least support them.

But it might also mean that they would have to express their commitment through other missionary societies and agencies. For they are determined to get on with the unfinished missionary task.

SIX
NEW MISSION
RATIFIED
Nairobi: Prospect and Program

Following the assembly at Uppsala great efforts were made to involve the WCC and its member churches more completely in the social struggle. Events at Uppsala had signalled the direction. The Fifth General Assembly—to meet in Nairobi seven years later—was expected to intensify and consolidate what was begun at Uppsala. Programs to thrust the Church into the struggle for a just society and a new humanity began to take shape in those intervening years (1968–1975). It was a period increasingly influenced by ideology. In fact, the ideological and theological often blended. One couldn't be sure where one started and the other ended. Moreover, increasing attention was given to the Marxist analysis of history as an accepted basis upon which plans for action were predicated.*

Western capitalism and its institutions came under sharper and sharper attack. Injustices created by societal structures could not be adequately dealt with piecemeal. The only solution lay in a worldwide revolution in which the present capitalistic socio-economic-political institutions would be replaced. It would be a new world order in which ultimate power rested with the people.

Everywhere there was struggle between classes. The rich were seen as exploiters who gained their wealth, power and

*Documentation for these statements will be found in Appendices A, B and G. (Note particularly Appendix B, pp. 11–12).

comforts at the expense of others who by the same token were made poor, powerless and oppressed. Churches were roused to conscientize the poor and powerless to be aware of their exploited condition. Thus churches were to join in the whole liberation struggle to shape the new tomorrow. The chains of enslaving, oppressive structures must be broken. The rights of individuals must give way to the rights of the people* (Johnson 1975:135).

The Nairobi Assembly was being planned by the WCC staff to carry this struggle forward. Things seen only "through a glass darkly" at Uppsala were more apparent now. At Uppsala directions had only been identified and established. Now details were needed to achieve the utopian goal. Some lessons in the struggle had already been painfully learned by 1975. For imprisonment, torture and sometimes death were common experiences in many countries.

All along, WCC programs were evaluated in terms of their contribution to this ultimate objective of a new world order with a "just, sustainable and participatory society." The New Mission concept had replaced the classical mission concept. But not in the minds of all! Even within the WCC staff there were those who had serious reservations. In the CWME, for example, there were signs of new stirrings in the direction of classical-biblical mission. And the churches by no means all approved of the direction the WCC was taking. In fact, the great majority in many member churches did not accept these new definitions of mission. In many churches the prestige and reputation of the WCC and, indeed, of the entire ecumenical movement were at an all time low. Financial support for WCC programs was dwindling. Some even began to wonder if the WCC could survive.

Such anxiety however was perhaps premature. For the assembly at Nairobi would hopefully bring together the conflicting hopes and dreams of the WCC Geneva staff and the hopes and dreams of member churches. These hopes and dreams were by no means the same for everybody however. The WCC staff planners at Geneva appeared to presume that the assembly would approve an intensification of the social action direc-

*Documentation for these statements will be found in Appendices A, B and G.
(Note particularly Appendix B, p. 8).

tions, though there were also some in Geneva who hoped for a more balanced biblical perspective. The WCC's Commission on World Mission and Evangelism (CWME), for example, planned to sound a clarion call for evangelism to be restored to a place of importance. But first, let us look more closely at the planning that was underway.

AGENDA PLANNING

Normally, WCC assemblies are held every seven years. And preparations for the next assembly begin almost before the ink from the present one is dry. About midway between the two assemblies a theme is chosen, which means that the general direction of the forthcoming assembly is already established by that time.

Theme and Mood. The selection of a theme of course is a key aspect in planning any conference. Once a theme is selected, attention usually focuses on major presentations that will best bring out those aspects of the theme which are to predominate.

The theme chosen for the Fifth Assembly was "Jesus Christ Frees and Unites." And it was approved by the Central Committee. It was a theme admirably suited to New Mission. In the first place, it would allow the widely varying member churches to enter into discussion and dialogue with each other without at the same time threatening their unity. In the second place, it would provide enough leeway for interpretations to be catalytic, educational or inspirational. It also would allow theology and ideology to interact. A certain ambiguity would even be helpful. So consideration of this theme would permit the widest spread of interpretations of ways Jesus Christ frees and unites, and conversely of ways he may divide.

Another key aspect in planning an assembly is to set its mood. Nairobi planners relied heavily on the previous Bangkok experience. They hoped that the good things out of Bangkok could be repeated in Nairobi. Mistakes made at Uppsala were by all means to be avoided. For example, the Uppsala Assembly had been strongly influenced by guests and observers. Clapping, foot-stamping and shouting of non-delegates in order to communicate their views had been permitted at Uppsala. According to some, the mood or climate thus created influenced—even orchestrated—the debate, and certainly affected the decisions made.

The mood or climate at Nairobi therefore should be one in which the new understandings about mission could be consolidated and intensified. It could be created in several ways. Assembly planners actually have many options. Varying emphases can come from: the theme itself, the selection of speakers, the special plenary presentations, the worship, the use of the media, the daily assembly newspaper, the wall posters, etc. Press conferences may be scheduled for assembly actions considered significant for the waiting world to hear. These can throw the spotlight on certain actions and take it away from others. All these facets were to be taken into account.

Moreover, planning for each WCC assembly includes the writing of an official record to tell what happened since the previous meeting. There is also a workbook which sets forth the agenda. Dossiers of selected readings related to the assembly theme are packaged together and sent to member churches.*

Member church delegates are expected to study these prepared materials, drawing on the wisdom and insights of their fellow church members as they ponder the significance of these materials from Geneva.

In studying how the WCC staff prepared for Nairobi, I found little to indicate the kind of anxious concern that had gone into the preparations for the conference at Bangkok. There at Bangkok it was crucial that everything be planned in minutest detail. Nothing could be left to chance. The planners knew exactly what they wanted to accomplish in terms of the quest for reconceptualization of mission. Action at Bangkok had to result in capturing the CWME so as to put the whole WCC behind a common effort to implement New Mission. I detected little of this same frantic nervous anxiety in the Nairobi planning. There appeared to be a confidence that the Nairobi Assembly would confirm and consolidate the issue that had been settled at Uppsala.** Further application of the principles was all that was required. No real problems of policy were anticipated either.

*Appendix A and B.
**See Appendix A, pp. 7–8.

Materials Spark Alarm. The preparatory materials* sent by the WCC staff to delegates, however, aroused alarm among many of the member churches. There seemed to be an imbalance in Geneva's analysis of social problems. Problems of racism, sexism, youth, language and media—everything—seemed to be explained in terms of exploitation or oppression. And Marxism was the usual frame of reference in any evaluation made.

The WCC staff appeared to be proposing nothing less than the complete destruction of the capitalistic way of life, particularly its free institutions. For member churches, the alternative of a socialist society raised fears about Communism. Christians were especially alarmed by Geneva's apparent infatuation with the social experiments in China.** And they were troubled by violence that appeared to be too easily condoned.

Some churches met in denominational caucuses, others in regional meetings, some in councils and some in inter-confessional gatherings. But all met to consider the Geneva materials sent out under the theme "Jesus Christ Frees and Unites." Some churches pointedly instructed their delegates to express their misgivings when they went to Nairobi.

Such misgivings however could not have been entirely unanticipated in Geneva. Surely they had been forewarned by the diminishing financial contributions from member churches. Some wondered if the WCC's financial crisis might not be the "finger of God"—one of the "signs of the times" not to be ignored.

Delegates arrived in Nairobi knowledgeable, prepared to speak, and with confidence that their churches would be heard through them. Norwegian, Finnish and Swedish delegations came prepared to ask two fundamental questions: "Where is the WCC taking us?" and "What is the WCC going to do about evangelism?" They would tell their WCC leaders, "Your views are too shallow and your future utopias are unrealistic. Without the proclamation of the saving Gospel of Jesus Christ there can be no new humanity. 'Except a man be born again, he cannot enter the kingdom of God.' "

I received a personal letter from Gunnar Stalsett written in

*Appendix A and B.
**Appendix A, p. 8.

March 1977. (He is the General Secretary for the Foreign Council of the Church of Norway.) In it he shared the reasons behind the Norwegian Church's heightened concern about the WCC prior to Nairobi. In response to my question, he wrote:

> The general trend of the criticism has been one revolving around such items as: the mission concept of the WCC and the relation between mission and dialogue, and the assumed overemphasis on socio-ethical and political concerns.

> A permanent element in the criticism, which has been with us since the early fifties, has been a mistrust of the basis of the WCC, since the basis even after its change at New Delhi, does not exclude the possible reference to tradition alongside Scripture as the basis of faith and joint witness. The fact that the Orthodox churches obtained membership on this new basis is seen to prove that the foundation of the WCC is not "Scripture alone."

> The prevailing influence on the theological profile is understood to have been one of liberal and radical persuasion with less importance for a conservative-evangelical or confessional trend.

The preparatory materials served to confirm earlier suspicions about the WCC's intent. Delegates came concerned about what was being left undone, and about the implications of what they considered to be an excessive emphasis on the social implications of the Gospel.* In short, they were alarmed over New Mission.

Many delegates who did not accept the theological and ideological assumptions underlying New Mission were among the most articulate in speaking out on the floor of the Fifth Assembly as well as in the various sections and hearings.

There was of course wide agreement that churches, to be on the side of God, should stand squarely on the side of the poor

---

*Appendixes A and B detail significant portions of the extensive preparatory materials sent by Geneva WCC staff to help delegates prepare for the Fifth Assembly which met in Nairobi in 1975.

and the oppressed. Everyone believed that church people everywhere need to practice what they profess. Jesus Christ himself had set the example and had spoken clearly about the ethical dimension of being his disciples.

What many did not support was the method the WCC was adopting to tackle the social problems that needed change. Christians were alarmed that the institutions and the socio-economic-political order that had brought basic human rights and freedoms and a comfortable way of life to so many millions should now be under attack. They did not believe their way of life was made possible at the expense of others. It seemed simplistic to believe that the promised utopia of a just, sustainable and participatory society could come through the destruction of capitalism and its institutions. All they had seen or known about socialism and poverty and loss of freedoms were closely tied together. They wondered how the WCC could be so enamored with socialism when in country after country where either the socialists or Marxists seized power the churches suffered persecution; and the freedom to preach the Gospel and for churches to multiply and grow was restricted. It seemed to follow that wherever Communists seized power life became cheap. Tens of thousands and sometimes millions were "liquidated." And the promised utopia remained illusive. Nowhere in the world did they see that such slaughter and destruction had produced a land flowing with milk and honey. That is a strange kind of liberation indeed.

They were aware too that wherever Communists seized power the promises of joy resulted in hate or fear, and one's neighbor frequently became his enemy. More importantly, they knew that Communist takeovers inevitably meant that missionaries had to leave, thus depriving those who might respond to the Gospel of opportunities to hear it. Furthermore, prisons in Communist countries were filled with people who were being denied their basic fundamental human rights.

At the same time, they were also aware that all was not perfect in societies under capitalism either. Injustices kept many from having a chance to live in the full dignity of their humanness. But freedom of press, radio and TV did make it possible to expose and work to change at least some of those imperfections. Demonstrations, politicking, ballot boxes—

even with their limitations—were exceedingly precious rights enjoyed primarily in the so-called Christian countries.

Delegates at Nairobi were concerned also about what the WCC seemed to be neglecting. They remembered the promise at New Delhi that evangelism would henceforth be at the center of all that the WCC said and did. They asked why this objective had been totally eclipsed. They then asked the Fifth Assembly—their assembly—to correct this great imbalance. Some of those who spoke most passionately represented churches that were charter members of the WCC, and had faithfully supported programs for social action, including the controversial Program to Combat Racism (PCR). These now felt keenly that the WCC was failing in evangelism, and considered pulling out if no correctives were effected.

These representatives (particularly from the churches in Norway and other Scandinavian countries) articulated their concerns with a persistency and a graciousness that powerfully confirmed their sincere love for the WCC and their concern for what it should be doing. They came to Nairobi wondering if others held similar convictions. They found they were not alone. Nearly 80 percent of all delegates present registered to participate in the section, "Confessing Christ Today." For here their concern for evangelism could most readily find expression.

ASSEMBLY COMPONENTS

Let's take another look at the preparatory materials that had so aroused and alarmed the member churches.* The materials seem to indicate a smorgasbord type of approach. One can find beautiful affirmations of solid, biblical and theological positions. At the same time, the preponderance of materials convinced many that the WCC was preoccupied with an effort to bring in a new socio-economic-political order. Marxist categories were prominent, as was the Marxist analysis of history with its economic determinism. The material implied a lack of passion for evangelism and scarcely any interest in the unfinished missionary task of proclaiming the Gospel to those

*The reader will want to study carefully the material in Appendixes A and B with this in mind.

who have yet to have valid opportunities to hear and believe. Theological assumptions were mixed with ideological presuppositions. All of this combined to set the alarm bells ringing.

The Dossiers. Preparatory materials in six dossiers, under the general title "Jesus Christ Frees and Unites" make clear that the WCC staff plans aimed at assembly concentration on the struggles for liberation and creation of a new society. (The material in the dossiers sent out from Geneva is quoted at length in Appendix A. The reader is urged to read this carefully.)

Delegates were concerned about ideological and theological assumptions that had determined the selection of materials in the dossiers. And this led to concern about what to expect at Nairobi, particularly when conspicuously absent from the materials was any consideration of the three billion persons who remain without knowledge of Jesus Christ. Nowhere in the preparatory material was the slightest indication that this somber truth was even of concern to the WCC. For this reason many delegates were instructed to speak to this apparent omission.

We acknowledge that portions of the dossier materials were not meant to represent official WCC positions, but were included just to provoke discussion and stimulate thought. Nevertheless, the overall impression created was that the WCC was so preoccupied with the struggle to reshape society that it was neglecting evangelism.

More serious yet was the apparent acceptance by the WCC of the Marxist analysis.* The WCC seemed to find it so convenient to attack the evils of capitalism and the institutions of the West while at the same time seemed scarcely troubled by the evils of socialism and communism. Delegates were not convinced that the promised utopia of a classless society would ultimately emerge from struggles that pitted one against another and appraised everything in terms of an exploiter/exploited axis. An imbalance existed in associating the evils of colonialism and the rise of the industrial state (and the widening gap between rich and poor) with the spread of the Chris-

*Appendix B, pp. 6–8 make this apparent. Additionally, Appendix G, the Report on UIM makes this quite obvious.

tian religion through the work of the missionaries.

While it was good that the WCC had a legitimate concern in seeking to identify with the poor and powerless, it seemed to be naively joining hands with the Marxists by adopting their methods and goals. History had shown that this was too frequently an unholy alliance. Liberation struggles had not produced, at least to date, the promised utopia of freedom and equal rights for all. The testimony of Africa, alone, with its millions of refugees, is more effective evidence than mere words about what happens to liberation when Marxists seize ultimate power.

Idealists (including many Christians who have been in the forefront of such struggles because their commitment to Christ gives them a concern for their enslaved brothers and sisters) are being exterminated by the tens of thousands. To escape such prison, death and torture they need to flee for their lives. The performance by the post-colonial, post-capitalistic society has therefore not been a shining example of how the struggle for liberation really liberates. Many churchmen are not sure that this is the way to struggle for human rights and a new society—by cooperating with avowed Marxists or by using Marxist methods. Surely all this suggests that more is needed than simply commitment to struggle side by side with Marxists and revolutionaries of whatever kind!*

The member churches could endorse wholeheartedly the WCC call to renewal. They knew it was right to identify with the poor and powerless. What was in question was the method by which Christians could best unite to do this.

The Official Record (Uppsala to Nairobi). The official WCC account edited by David Johnson tells the story (Johnson:1975). The dossiers containing the preparatory materials for the Nairobi Assembly were designed to stimulate questions and provoke discussion about the future—beyond the assembly at Nairobi. The Uppsala to Nairobi account was prepared to detail the progress the WCC had made in carrying out the directives of the Uppsala Assembly. The record shows unmistakably that the WCC took seriously the mandate at Upp-

---

*The writer having lived in Ethiopia these past fourteen years has witnessed this first hand.

sala, to lift up humanization as the goal of mission. The direction was clear. "This is the way, walk ye in it." The WCC staff at Geneva was intent on moving swiftly.

New programs were examined and their worth determined by whether or not they contributed to the new understanding of mission. Each received a score or grade dependent upon the degree to which that program or project contributed to this objective. The inevitable question was, did it aid in the removal of oppressive structures and the replacement by new ones promoting a new society and a new humanity.

The Church had been challenged at Uppsala to join God in his mission of liberation. It was told to let the world provide the agenda and set the priorities for what it was to do. The Church was told to look with prophetic discernment at the signs of the times.* It was then to speak with a prophetic voice about what God was doing. Moreover, it was to hasten to join God in what he appeared to be doing in this matter of liberation. Act first and reflect later. Orthopraxis is more important than orthodoxy. It is the future that counts. All truth is not necessarily contained in repositories of past writings and experience. Believe that new prophets may be as equally sure of God's Word for today. Look out into the world. Recognize that God is also at work in other religions and ideologies. Join all persons of good will in the common struggle. These are only some of the many humanistic exhortations made to urge that through much suffering we must enter the kingdom!

What did the Uppsala mandate really mean? It had not followed a long period of agonizing evaluation. The signal from Uppsala may have been clear, but it was given in the context of churches striving for social relevance. The mandate was probably propelled to center stage there at Uppsala because of its historical moment. Boisterous, sometimes angry, and always revolutionary young people used shouts and catcalls to express approval or disapproval of any proposal that was before the Assembly. People and issues were immediately graded—and influenced—by such behavior.

When the sixties ended, calmer voices prevailed. And the churches returned to a degree of normalcy. God was not dead!

*See Appendix A, page 3.

Worship, Bible study, prayer and the joy of Christian fellowship and sharing were once again common and satisfying experiences.

Outside the church the search for meaning and for "God" was evidenced in spiritual pilgrimages and in the appeal of both the mystical and the spiritual in Eastern religions. In addition, Pentecostalism, charismatic experience and emphasis on gifts all combined to bring new vitality and increased awarenesses of God and his Holy Spirit.

But at Geneva the WCC planners held to the Uppsala mandate. Avant-garde voices from Third World churches rose in support. The center of gravity within the WCC was shifting. Leaders from the West no longer set the pace or determined the action. Third World leaders spoke out in behalf of their hurting people. They felt Christ crying out with them saying, "Let my people go." These cries of desperation, the imprisonment and the torture could be alleviated! This conviction influenced the WCC to plan programs of social action. WCC leaders believed that God was showing them what he was doing and how the churches could join him in his mission. They believed that this mission would require the thought, resources and will of the churches in their programs of social action.

They would therefore devise programs that would get at the root cause of everything that made life intolerable and would restore the dignity of human beings. Racism, sexism, multinational corporations, militarism, world hunger, population control, development, the environment—no area was left out. Each needed evaluation, study and a plan of action. Programs involving people and funds would follow. Church people together with others of good will everywhere could make this world what God intended it to be. The ultimate goal was a utopian world community with a new, "just, sustainable and participatory society." Amidst all this great good that was envisioned, it seemed inexplicably callous and indifferent on the part of the WCC to dismiss as futile the thoughts and plans spelled out in the New Delhi mandate for sharing the news of eternal salvation.

The Work Book–Annotated Agendas. In addition to receiving the dossiers as preparatory materials, the delegates also received instructions from the General Secretary, Philip Potter.

These instructions included the following paragraphs in reference to the Work Book:

> An Assembly of the World Council of Churches is, necessarily, a complicated affair. It demands careful advance preparation by all concerned, so that an extra-ordinarily diverse group of people may do a great deal of work in a very short space of time.
>
> Those who will be spending eighteen days and nights in Nairobi later this year planning the future of the WCC should devote at least an equivalent amount of time beforehand to studying the *Work Book* and other preparatory material, discussing the issues raised with their respective churches, reflecting on the theme, "Jesus Christ Frees and Unites": and readying themselves to contribute as fully as possible to the Fifth Assembly.
>
> The *Work Book* is an aid to preparation, as well as a reference guide to the daily activities and decision making procedures of the Assembly itself. It sets out the programme for Nairobi, explains how the various parts fit together, includes annotated agendas for the Sections and Hearings, and appends or refers to several other key documents. Please read it in conjunction with the *Pre-Assembly Booklet* of Bible studies, the six Section Dossiers and the retiring Central Committee's report *Uppsala to Nairobi*. More important, read it in the light of your own perception of where the ecumenical movement is and should be going, and of the obedience to which our Lord calls His Church in the years ahead.
>
> If I can be of any further help with your preparations please let me know. (Signed) Philip Potter, 1 June 1975 (WCC 1975j:V).

The *Work Book* dealt with the nuts and bolts of the Assembly (WCC 1975j). It explained how the Assembly would operate and where the delegates would plug in. It contained the agenda presented from the WCC staff point of view. It was an important, sophisticated piece of material. But it added unmistakably to the impression that the WCC Executive officers and staff believed that the primary task of the churches in mission was to work by every means possible to replace the existing, unjust structures of society with a new socio-economic-political order. It is assumed that only then will people be able to live together in peace and in a new human dignity.

By participating in this New Mission, the churches are joining with God in his mission of liberation. They are to work together with others from outside the churches as well as with those from other churches in this common liberation struggle. The appropriate manner for doing this was carefully outlined. The church is somewhat limited however by its assumed associations of guilt and complicity. And in some instances its privilege of engaging in such combined liberation struggles may even have to be forfeited because of past history or present associations. Nonetheless, however it participates, the envisioned result is a world community set free and united in some manner by Jesus Christ who alone is said to "free and unite."

Extensive extracts from the material in the *Work Book* are included in Appendix B. The reader is urged to read these carefully. They will clearly show that all the WCC programs chosen were evaluated on the basis of their contribution to the goals of New Mission, and that programs were conceived and conceptualized in terms of the ultimate issue of injustice and the need for an entirely new socio-economic-political system.

One notices that the vocabulary for New Mission was also affected. Familiar words like "salvation," "conversion," and "evangelism" were given secular connotations. Language was increasingly shaped to fit the New Mission concept. At Bangkok the term "humanization" (used first at Uppsala) gained religious overtones. Just as the meaning of *mission* had changed to connote new understandings, so now *evangelism* too was being redefined to serve the aims and secular goals of New Mission. For the unwary it became increasingly difficult to distinguish between New Mission and classical mission since so much of the vocabularly was the same. Confusion and obscurantism did not make truth more readily apparent.

The Work Book–Commitment to New Mission. The *Work Book* listed the priorities for the work to be done when delegates met in the Fifth Assembly. If we understand mission to be that which the churches should be doing, we find that "mission" for the WCC staff who prepared the *Work Book* material is regarded as "engaging the churches with others in the effort to achieve a new, just and sustainable society." The material in Appendix B shows conclusively that so far as the Geneva staff who prepared the *Work Book* were concerned the main work of the churches involved "the struggle." Delegates working in the Fifth Assembly were expected to accept the perspectives of the WCC staff. Over and over in all six sections the discussion of topics implied action by the churches in a common struggle to remove unjust structures and establish a just society. Marxist ideology is clearly reflected in many of the views which influenced questions raised and solutions suggested.

Delegates were however invited to bring their own agenda items and their own insights; and they were assured that they should not feel bound by the book's annotated agendas. They were told to feel entirely free to modify them. They were assured that their own insights, experiences and concerns were possibly even more important than the prepared agendas. Some of the delegates were therefore emboldened to ask about the apparent lack of opportunity to consider missions and the place of evangelism as they and their churches understood it.

In the end it was the assembly delegates who recognized this imbalance and tried to do something about it. The assembly did not criticize what had been done between Uppsala and Nairobi as unimportant or wrong. It just said, "It is not enough; we want classical mission and evangelism restored to a rightful, central place in the life and work of our WCC."

Major Addresses. As expected, the major addresses given at Nairobi reflect this same preoccupation with questions of liberation and justice. Speeches delivered by Robert McAfee Brown and the Honorable Michael N. Manley, Prime Minister of the Socialist Jamaican Republic, vigorously attacked the evils of the capitalistic system, appearing to turn a blind eye to injustices and failures of Communist and Marxist oriented societies.

But perhaps the clearest indication of the WCC leadership's total commitment to the liberation struggle came by way of the General Secretary's report. In it he acknowledged the WCC's acceptance of the new theological understandings of relations between the Church and the world; he approved the WCC's own report as to what had been accomplished in the interim between the Uppsala and Nairobi Assemblies, seeing it as indicative of understanding the implications of their action programs. He spoke with approval of the *Work Book*'s annotated agenda as a guide for the delegates. In so doing, the General Secretary clearly indicated what the WCC understood the task of churches in mission to be. He summarized the challenges facing the churches and the WCC at the time of Nairobi in terms of their inter-relationships—their mutual focus on one ultimate objective: a new kind of world order along socialist lines. He believed the Marxist understanding about economic and social forces would play a vital part in bringing about the new society.

Disappointingly, the secretary had nothing to say about evangelism aimed at reaching new peoples effectively with the Gospel. He used his opportunity solely to give a masterly report on the socio-economic-political forces operating in the modern world. He spoke of the challenge to refashion them so as to eliminate oppression and exploitation and thereby fashion a new society. Delegates clearly recognized the dehumanization of these forces present in every local situation, yet on a global scale. But we longed to hear also a recognition that God is eager for all people to have a valid opportunity to know his Christ and Savior.

The major addresses continued. There was no call to evangelism, no recognition that existing efforts of churches are inadequate to evangelize the multitudes yet unreached. The focus was on participation in the struggle against injustice. The vision was of a new *oikumene* where peoples of different religions and cultures learn to live and work together in a new community where all participate in determining the common good. The distinction between Church and world was clearly blurred. The new insights into Church/world relationships articulated at Uppsala had progressed to the point of being a theological assumption upon which to base our understandings of what God is doing in the world and of how the churches should join him in that part of his mission. Evangelism defined as bringing men and women to faith in Jesus Christ and into the fellowship of his Church may be of primary importance to God, but it obviously seemed of secondary importance for the Geneva staff leadership at the Nairobi Assembly.

"Behind the Mountain." A major presentation by the United Bible Societies also played a part in moving the churches to rethink concepts of liberation. The conflicts involved can aid one's understanding of what happens in the struggle, and Scripture can be used to justify the new understandings about God and his intent for mankind.

It was a free-wheeling use of Scripture that was displayed in the presentation "Behind the Mountain" about the prodigal son. Later, a keen African Christian leader from the Anglican Church said to me, "What I don't like is the way the WCC spokesmen twist Scripture to say what they want it to say."

The message many received from that presentation was that the younger son's revolt against the traditional ways of doing and understanding things should help us to learn to tolerate and appreciate his rebellious dissatisfaction. It will also help us to understand the older son who found some of the new insights and practices displeasing. We are to realize from this that God accepts both. We need to accept each other's conflicting views and presuppositions with a new degree of appreciation and tolerance. But one important factor was missing. There was no recognition that acceptance of the younger son was based upon his repentance and return—not on his rebellion!

"Muntu"—A Drama. In the play "Muntu" there was a hostility to the missionary movement that was offensive. To begin with, the play was written by a man who is reported to be anti-Church and anti-mission. The play itself leaves one with the impression that Africans were the recipients of many of their problems as a result of the intrusion of Christianity into their otherwise harmonious and peaceful relationships. Missionary efforts and colonialism are linked together—a charge

also commonly made by WCC related spokesmen. The anti-colonialism attitudes thus affect one's attitude toward the missionary movement. Just as the emotionally packed subject of racism is linked to economic exploitation and unjust economic and political structures, so the missionary movement was linked to the unjust, exploitive colonial movement (WCC 1975j:61). This overly general identification of missions (through the introduction of the Christian faith) with everything that is evil in colonialism can only hinder true understandings of the whole missionary movement and the truth of the Christian message.

One delegate from a large American denomination told me that if people from his church had seen the play "Muntu," they "wouldn't give a dime" to further support missions. One begins to realize that sentiments expressed in this play and other anti-missionary sentiments expressed by WCC spokesmen relate closely to the new understandings about mission and the goals of that mission.

Does the Geneva leadership perhaps consider that "old mission" and "new mission" are so basically incompatible in their essential understandings and goals that the former must disappear to make the latter possible? There have been, and not infrequently, instances when just grievances about missionaries and missions were exploited and given twists not congenial with the original intent. Furthermore, it apparently goes unrecognized that anti-missionary sentiments do *not* represent the views of the leaders most respected in Third World churches.

I was moved to weep quietly as I watched the play unfold. My thoughts were of a vast company of God's faithful missionaries who had gone out to distant places in response to their love for Jesus Christ. They knew that Jesus Christ wanted all men to experience God's love for them. There were those who braved an unknown and hostile world to live among strange people and killing diseases. Many had given their lives for the sake of the Gospel.

Suddenly I realized it was ironic, and tragic, that a World Council of Churches which owed its own existence to the missionary movement could sponsor a play besmirching the honor and motives of those faithful men and women of God. Without such sacrificial efforts of so many, there would not be—in 1975—a WCC Assembly in Nairobi with representatives from so many Third World churches. And now, in this play, these very representatives were being presented with a view of their origins that was degrading both to those who found life through Jesus Christ and to the servants he had called to share the Gospel with them. As I sat there, I was aware of mistakes missionaries had made. I was one of them. I had served among them and knew things from the "inside." Looking into my own mirror I saw an ordinary face. No halo there! But it was marvelously true that because we had gone there were those who had their opportunity to come to know Jesus Christ, the only appointed Savior for men everywhere. I knew too that there were many, now being depreciated en masse, who had long since heard from their master's lips, "Well done, my good and faithful servants. Enter into the joy of your Lord."

My tears were for the hundreds of millions still without knowledge of him. For there is no greater violation of human rights than to deny someone a valid opportunity to respond to the Gospel. Knowing God's Savior brings true liberation.

Yes, "Muntu" was an offense to Jesus Christ and to his missionaries. The WCC is to be censured for choosing to present such a play. No doubt the play was chosen and arranged for because of its message. There is no doubt either that its message hurt the cause of missions by aiming its barbs at the historic missionary movement. This was obvious in an interpretation of its significance in the WCC Fifth Assembly newspaper, *Target*. In the November 25th issue was an article written by Revelation Ntoula from South Africa. The large bold type read, MUNTU: SAD MEMORIES OF MISSIONARIES IN AFRICA. In the article he referred to the play's portrayal of the arrival of white missionaries in Africa. They "had the Bible in one hand and the gun in the other." He went on to state:

> ... the clear message was that the arrival of the missionaries had opened a sad chapter in their lives. None of the children seemed to have much time for the minister or missionary who had brought so much sorrow to the family ... to Africa still under white minority rule, the mil-

129

lion voiceless Africans still see the sources of their plight as the arrival of the missionary who carried a gun and a Bible . . . what, however, may not be rediscovered is the exploited wealth, which even decades after the re-awakening of parts of Africa, continue to be a monopoly of the same countries from which the missionaries came (WCC 1975r).

The play "Muntu" clearly associated the missionary movement with the hated colonial movement. Just as Africans had largely rid themselves of the colonizers, so now they must rid themselves of missionaries and their influence.

The presentation of "Muntu" does not help to allay the suspicions of those who see a correlation between such anti-missionary expressions as the call for moratorium, and the attack of the Barbados Declaration with the WCC's impatience to move beyond the missionary movement to new understandings of mission as social struggle. The reformulations or redefinitions of the basic concepts of the Christian faith and mission seem to be part of a pattern which only illustrates that classical mission and New Mission are by no means the same.

Press and Media Coverage. Besides the major addresses at the plenary sessions, there was the added impact of press and media. Press releases were carefully orchestrated. The WCC wanted the listening world to hear some things and not others. This was apparent. An organization publishes about itself only that which it considers to be of greatest significance as to its character and its intended accomplishments.

During the first few days of the assembly, WCC press releases highlighted news related to financial policies and to questions about nuclear policy with reference to South Africa and the banks there. As the days progressed, the accent fell on statements of speakers that attacked the capitalistic Western countries. More than a few commented that the assembly too frequently appeared to be a miniature United Nations Assembly. The press releases served to confirm this view.

The media walk, lined with the various posters and paintings was in many respects revolting and shocking. That presentation apparently was intended to shock. Ethical values that many held dear were held up to ridicule. Sex, morality (traditional) and relationships between otherwise cohesive elements in home and society were torn asunder. Much suggested that class struggle and polarization were desirable—suggesting that somehow, from the destruction of the traditional (assumed to be the exploitive and oppressive structures of society) a new day of a classless society with justice for all would be fashioned. No one could conclude from the wall posters, the works of "art" and the media presentations that the task was anything other than to smash the old and traditional and hasten its replacement by the new.

It was also apparent in the briefings with which each press conference began. Suggested questions and voiced concerns made it reasonably certain that news releases would highlight the matters the WCC press officer wanted the listening world to hear. In this way the hoped-for agenda was given publicity. Invariably, pre-question briefing dealt with some aspect of the struggle against unjust structures. References were made to a wide range of international socio-politico-economic matters ranging from WCC efforts to prevent further loans to South Africa, or efforts to prevent establishing nuclear reactors, to events in Angola and the Middle East. Questions fielded from press representatives were generally handled with equanimity—though there were exceptions. And, of course, permission to allow cameras to televise parts of press conferences gave even greater prominence to the planned agenda.

But all would not go as planned. Member churches, concerned and alarmed, would come asking where their WCC was taking them. And, they wanted to know, what had happened to evangelism? The WCC leadership would leave Nairobi facing the necessity of an "agonizing reappraisal." For, as we shall see, their member churches had spoken.

SEVEN
NEW MISSION
CHALLENGED
Nairobi as Process: Voices from the Churches

Bishop Arias's message stood out in marked contrast to the other major presentations. It carried the convictions that had given birth to and characterized the missionary movement. He well knew that the ecumenical movement itself had been born in the missionary movement. Without that movement there would be no churches. And without that movement continuing, though in differing structures and relationships, there would one day be no church to speak prophetically to the world—no church to engage in mission, even granting that the mission should be limited to restructuring society to eliminate its injustices.

A PLEA FOR EVANGELISM

Speaking with clarity and conviction on behalf of the CWME, the Bishop reminded the Assembly:

> The initial purpose behind the creation of the World Council of Churches was to "support the churches in their task of evangelism" on the basis of the conviction held at that time that "today more than ever before evangelism is the supreme task of the churches." The Amsterdam Assembly in 1948, after reviewing the situation of the world and the Church, declared: "The evident

demand of God in this situation is that the whole Church set itself to the total task of winning the whole world for Christ." And the Central Committee in 1951 reminded the churches that the word ecumenical "is properly used to describe everything that relates to the whole task of the whole Church to bring the Gospel to the whole world" (Arias 1976:13ff).

The Bishop went on to remind the Assembly that their decision at New Delhi to integrate the work of the International Missionary Council with the World Council of Churches was intended to give structural content to the theme: "The whole Church with one Gospel for the whole world." It was hoped that the missionary task of evangelism would not continue to be the specialized task of a few missionary organizations, but would become the responsibility of the whole Church— meaning all the churches.

Bishop Arias pleaded for a renewed commitment to evangelism by the WCC. The Holy Spirit seemed to be calling the churches of the whole world to once again take up their primary responsibility of evangelism. He cited particularly the International Congress of World Evangelization in Lausanne, the Synod of Bishops in Rome, the Jerusalem Conference, and other national and regional meetings. He quoted with approval the statement produced by the Orthodox churches who met in Bucharest in 1974. They had declared,

> We do not have the option of keeping the Good News to ourselves . . . (Romans 10:1). The uncommunicated Gospel (Good News) is a patent contradiction (WCC 1975s:87).

To show decisively that he was speaking in the best of current ecumenical understandings, Bishop Arias cited Philip Potter's dramatic conclusion to his message at the Synod of Rome: "Evangelization is the test of our ecumenical vocation." And he noted further:

> It will also be the test of our Assembly, called together to make the most daring missionary and evangelistic affir-

mation that can be made in the world today: "Jesus Christ Frees and Unites" (Arias 1976:13-16).

He declared evangelism to be the permanent task of the Church. Indeed, it was the primary task of the Church. It needed to be carried out no matter whether the society or culture were capitalistic or socialistic, or any other kind that might emerge in the years ahead.

He challenged the churches to find new ways of working together in evangelism. He made no sharp distinction between a cultural or evangelistic mandate. He just wanted the Gospel to be proclaimed in the context of participation in every social implication of that Gospel. He championed "holistic evangelism" while at the same time recognizing the potential danger that "holistic evangelism" could so intently concentrate on salvation here and now that the eternal dimension of life in God might be neglected. He quoted approvingly the comments of Emilio Castro, Director of the Commission on World Mission and Evangelism, that emphasized historical salvation:

> We surely cannot understand our participation in the history of mankind, in the search for social justice, as a manifestation of that salvation which God has promised us, without relating it to the eternal life which is promised to us, and that neither life nor death can take away from us. Social justice, personal salvation, cultural affirmation, church growth, are all seen as integral parts of God's saving acts (Castro, 1975b Document 3:5).

Bishop Arias clearly called for a restoration of evangelism as classically understood. He was speaking of that kind of evangelism that makes the Gospel credible because it is practiced in the context of life as experienced by human beings everywhere. It involved sharing Jesus explicitly in a manner that challenges those who hear to become his disciples and commit their lives to him as Savior and Lord.

As he was speaking, the Bishop seemed to be painfully aware of what had happened to evangelism within the WCC. The promise at New Delhi had not been kept. Evangelism had been relegated to a place of marginal importance, as a sub-unit within a larger unit. This was both symbolized and apparent in all the restructuring taking place. A single letter once a month from the Evangelism Secretary's office communicated matters of evangelism to the churches. It is little wonder that he said:

> . . . we must admit with shame that evangelism has been the Cinderella of the WCC, at least to judge by the extent to which it appears in its structure, where it figures by nothing more than one office with a single occupant, in a sub-structure which is itself merely part of a unit and with no more than a monthly letter by which to communicate with the churches of the whole world. . . (Arias 1976:13–26).

Bishop Arias challenged both older and younger churches to evangelize. He feared that the older churches, particularly, had lost the impetus to evangelize. He challenged these churches to move beyond their guilt complexes to recognize that true renewal comes only by active participation in evangelism.

With a passion characteristic of the great pioneers of the missionary movement, Bishop Arias summoned the WCC to engage in strategic evangelism in the full awareness that 2,700 million people know nothing of Christ. The motive for evangelism comes from Jesus Christ himself. He first found us The Gospel is not our private property. It is unthinkable that we not share it. Jesus himself had said, "I have other sheep that are not of this fold. I must bring them also." It had been prophesied that Jesus should "die for the nation; and not for the nation only, but to gather into one the children of God who are scattered abroad" (John 11:52–53).

Similarly, Christ's last commission is equally categorical and imperative. Each form of his last commission to his followers about the universal intent of the Gospel is emphatic and specific. Jesus wanted his people to know beyond the shadow of doubt his intent with respect to the Gospel. The universal intent of the Gospel was: "to all nations," "unto all the world," "to every creature," "to all the ends of the earth" (Matt. 28:20; Mark 16:15; John 20:21; Acts 1:8).

NAIROBI AS PROCESS: VOICES FROM THE CHURCHES

AN EVANGELICAL ANGLICAN RESPONDS

A clear challenge had come from within the WCC establishment itself. It somehow seemed so uncharacteristic of what usually came from the WCC that John Stott felt led to respond by asking,

> Would it be unfair to say that the Bishop's address is not typical of recent ecumenical utterances? The modern ecumenical movement was born of missionary passion, and an assurance was given at New Delhi that the work of the International Missionary Council would henceforth become central to the concerns of the whole WCC. Yet it seems to many of us that evangelism has now become largely eclipsed by the quest for social and political liberation (Stott 1976: Vol. 65:30-33).

He was heartened by Bishop Arias's call for a return to commitment to evangelism. At the same time, he implied a degree of skepticism about the possibility of words without confirming deeds. He implied a need for both programs and fund dispersements to implement any expression of renewed emphasis on evangelism that the Nairobi Assembly might make. He acknowledged the existence of a credibility gap between evangelical and ecumenical leaders as symbolized by Geneva and Lausanne. He challenged the Assembly to provide the evidence which would show a "heartfelt commitment to worldwide evangelization." Stott went on to say that the WCC needed to recover five essential theological convictions:

1. A recognition of the lostness of man.
2. Confidence in the Gospel of Christ.
3. Conviction about the uniqueness of Jesus Christ.
4. A sense of urgency about evangelism.
5. A personal experience of Jesus Christ (*ibid.* 1976:33ff.).

It is probably true that not all who are deeply concerned about restoring evangelism to a central place of emphasis in WCC life and work would express themselves in just that way. But the heart of evangelism has been and always will be the communication of the Gospel in a way that challenges those who hear to believe it as good news from God calling them to repentance and faith, and that challenges them to become disciples of Jesus Christ in the fellowship of his people, the Church. Who can doubt Stott is correct when he says:

> Universalism, fashionable as it is today, is incompatible with the teaching of Christ and His apostles, and is a deadly enemy of evangelism. The true universalism of the Bible is the call to universal evangelism in obedience to Christ's universal commission. It is the conviction not that all men will be saved in the end, but that all men must hear the gospel of salvation before the end, as Jesus said (Matt 24:14), in order that they may have a chance to believe and to be saved (Romans 10:13-15) (*ibid* 1976:33).

Or, who can question that a "major deterrent to evangelism today is the Church's loss of confidence in the truth, the relevance and the power of the Gospel."

Or again, if we are truly committed to evangelism as classically understood, how can we be intimidated to believe that "conviction about revealed truth" is arrogance? Rather, should we not affirm with Dr. Stott that the Church has been entrusted with a Gospel which is revealed truth that does not change? "To reject all syncretism in this way and to assert the uniqueness and finality of Jesus Christ is not 'doctrinal superiority' " (Stott 1976:30-33).

Who can doubt that "the primary factor in humanization is the knowledge of God revealed in Jesus Christ. No man is fully human until he has come to know God and himself in the searchlight of Jesus Christ" (Neill 1975:230). Is Stott not rendering the WCC a prophetic service when he says to those who make paramount the quest for justice, love, liberation, humanization, and the quality of life, that their concerns are absolutely right and urgent, but too narrow and even too superficial? (Stott 1976:30-33).

And who can fail to acknowledge with penitence and with a longing for a fresh visitation from his Holy Spirit that the greatest of all hindrances to evangelism is the poverty of his own spiritual experience? "He who is the object of the

Church's faith and adoration is both the historic Christ and the contemporary Christ, and never one without the other."

Both the call of the sinless Redeemer and the response of the forgiven sinner, who experiences forgiveness through the cleansing blood of Christ shed for him, are essential ingredients of true evangelism. We who have been to the cross for cleansing invite others to join us there. Without the shedding of blood there is no forgiveness of sin. To the penitent seeking the forgiving love of God, this comes close to the heart of the good news in Jesus Christ. He alone is appointed Savior. He alone can liberate all who turn to him from the power and guilt of sin. In him all can be restored to the position of sons of God. In him all things are made new. "Unto me who am the least of all saints is this Gospel given, that I should preach among the gentiles the unsearchable riches of Christ" (Eph. 3:8).

> I thank him who has given me strength for this, Christ Jesus our Lord, because he judged me faithful by appointing me to his service, though I formerly blasphemed and persecuted and insulted him; but I received mercy because I had acted ignorantly in unbelief, and the grace of our Lord overflowed for me with the faith and love that are in Christ Jesus. The saying is sure and worthy of full acceptance, that Christ Jesus came into the world to save sinners. And I am the foremost of sinners; but I received mercy for this reason, that in me, as the foremost, Jesus Christ might display his perfect patience for an example to those who were to believe in him for eternal life. To the King of ages, immortal, invisible, the only God, be honor and glory for ever and ever. Amen (I Tim. 1:12–17).

OTHER DELEGATE REACTIONS

Many delegates had been aroused by the preparatory materials to a variety of concerns about what the WCC was doing and proposing to do. But they were also passionately concerned about what the WCC was leaving undone. These believed that the Church had been entrusted with an evangelistic mission by its Lord. They believed the central task in that mission was to

139

make known everywhere the good news of God's intent for his world, through Jesus. These people influenced Nairobi in ways unanticipated by those who planned the Fifth Assembly.

Typical of their views is the statement they prepared in one of the sections where the subject was "Education for Liberation and Community."

> The approach in the documents and the first meeting of the unit seems to overstress the need to change structures and reject traditions. We felt a deep concern about the balance of the Church's concern for involvement in education and that insufficient attention had been given to nurturing people in Christ and the role of personal witness in social changes and too much emphasis placed on producing conflict and stimulating reaction to many situations [see Johnson 1975:193].

> It seems to us that in this Unit (and generally in the work of the WCC) an unbalanced over-emphasis has been placed on social and political concerns and insufficient attention given to the centrality of Christ, the present spiritual crisis, the presence of sin and the need of salvation. . . . We believe that the documents and introduction to this Unit (and indeed the whole work of the WCC) encourage an unexamined utopianism and messianism and that there has been some failure to take due account of the realities of human nature and the human situation in which we have to live.

> . . . We have been encouraged by the fact that our concerns and misgivings and suggestions have been supported by Christians from the Third World.

> We wish to have our submission recognized in whatever documents emerge from this hearing (from written statement given to the moderator of one of the hearings, copy of which was shared with some members of the press).

What impact, if any, could delegates from member churches actually have upon an Assembly so well-planned and directed?

140

Most of the time delegates felt they had little freedom or power. Much was said about the tyranny of unjust structures and the powerlessness of the exploited. Now they felt that they were the victims of their own unjust structures. They complained that things were not only determined long in advance, but that the work of the sections and hearings was dominated by people placed to insure a predetermined end product, even to the form statements should take to express the points the establishment wanted made. It was no small, isolated segment who felt this way as was apparent when the assembly burst into prolonged and repeated applause of support for one who courageously formed the words that were hidden in the hearts of so many others less articulate or less prepared to speak up.

THE NORWEGIAN RESPONSE

Among those delegates determined to speak up for a correction of perceived WCC imbalance with respect to social action and evangelism, the Norwegian delegation was especially active and vocal. These delegates shared with us how during the year representatives from member churches in Finland, Sweden and Norway had met to discuss the preparatory study materials. Out of such careful preparation arose a deep concern as to where the WCC was going. To underscore their concern they reminded the assembly that although the Church of Norway had been a charter member of the WCC and a supporter of the controversial Program to Combat Racism from the beginning, it had also appointed a commission to reexamine its membership in the WCC. This issue would come before the Norwegian Bishops' Conference in the autumn of 1976. Words such as these, from a Church that had not infrequently expressed gratitude for WCC leadership in the churches' struggle for social and economic justice, could not be overlooked.

Olga Dysthe, an articulate delegate speaking on behalf of the entire Norwegian delegation, responded to Philip Potter's address with words of genuine appreciation, acknowledging that he had expressed the historic Christian understanding of the significance of the "Crucified and risen Lord as alone the hope of the world." She went on to speak on behalf of many delegates who shared her concern—delegates who came from churches that had expressed doubts about their WCC, and not infrequently expressed those doubts by failing to support it with their finances.

> This was said fifty years ago, but it is to be regretted that this dimension has not been clearly spelled out in the assembly so far. It is not enough just to speak of the Cross of Jesus Christ and His resurrection as models for our struggle against evil and our overcoming of human obstacles. When we speak about freedom in Christ, the dimension of repentance, conversion and personal faith has hardly had the emphasis it deserves in this assembly (from speech delivered in plenary session in response to address by Philip Potter).

Other delegates began to share with each other in the corridors and hotel rooms, in the Bible studies and in the sections and hearings. Many of them identified with the Norwegian delegation's concerns that were so eloquently and forcefully articulated by their woman delegate. Some 80 percent of all delegates registered to participate in the section whose subject was "Confessing Christ Today." By common consent, the document this section produced (approved by the entire assembly without a dissenting vote) was the finest of all. The ten accredited conservative-evangelical advisors invited by the WCC to participate in the work of the assembly made a significant contribution to this document, as well as to other aspects of the work done by the Fifth Assembly.

There is little doubt that under the leading of the Holy Spirit, encouragement and hope has come for churches and individuals concerned about the future of the WCC and the cause of world evangelization. There is encouragement for those of the WCC staff who are concerned about evangelism—for those who long to see true, biblical evangelism have its rightful central place in all the WCC says and does.

BACKGROUND OF BISHOP ARIAS'S PLEA

How are we to account for Bishop Arias's address being given the prominence it received in the plenary session planning?

How should we account for its marked difference from the emphases in the preparatory materials and in the rest of the plenary sessions where social dimensions of the Gospel predominated? Was it merely part of an effort by the WCC to demonstrate to the Assembly that it is still concerned for evangelism? Or could it perhaps represent a voice or voices from within the WCC concerned to recover something lost in the post-Uppsala trends? My own view is that there is evidence to suggest the latter.

The full significance of Bishop Arias's plea which seemed so "untypical" must first of all be considered in the context of what was happening within the WCC in the period between the Uppsala and Nairobi Assemblies. And we must remember that Bishop Arias was speaking as an insider. He was chosen to speak on behalf of the CWME, representing those who were disquieted about the directions being taken by the WCC. His courageous, eloquent plea should give courage and hope to people and churches within the WCC membership who are concerned for evangelism.

Restructuring. New programs were mandated at Uppsala to implement the new understanding of mission. The accent was on the horizontal. Uppsala represented an endorsement of understandings already held by those in the WCC who had the power and influence to shape opinions and determine courses of action. The two main elements that had constituted the original WCC (Faith and Order, and Life and Work) presumably influenced the shape of these new understandings and goals.

Meanwhile, the CWME was trying to find its way in the integration process. In the WCC marketplace at Geneva, where heady new ideas were being bandied about, the CWME was the weak member. The old IMC leadership had left for various reasons. The new CWME leadership personnel had no historical roots in the missionary movement. Nor did they share with the IMC the same perspectives and convictions about the purpose and goals of that movement. Therefore, when humanization was lifted up as the goal of mission at Uppsala, this really represented the understandings of those in Geneva who were in a position to shape policy. As new post-

Uppsala programs were approved by the Central Committee, two of the most important were the Program to Combat Racism (PCR) and the Commission on the Church's Participation in Development (CCPD). Existing programs were reviewed and recast. Central to these efforts was the reeducation of the churches about the meaning and goals of New Mission. New terminology such as "conscientization" and frames of reference drawn from Marxist categories were employed to conceptualize the arena and methods of mission.

Restructuring of the WCC for its task was accomplished during the period between Uppsala and Nairobi. By the time the Nairobi Assembly approved the constitution legalizing the changes, the restructuring was an accomplished fact.

The way the WCC was restructured was greatly influenced by its leadership's understanding about mission. The quest for a reconceptualization of mission brought about a parallel quest. What sort of structure would enable the WCC to carry out most effectively its understanding about the Church and its mission? What functions should it have relative to its member churches? And how could it assist the churches in their task? The CWME itself was vitally affected. As a small subunit within a unit, how much influence would the CWME have?

In June of 1975, the Executive Committee of the CWME discussed in depth the problems facing the CWME that arose out of the restructuring. They appeared to be similar to the problems mission and evangelism faced within the churches. There, too, missions and evangelism were tucked into tiny slots in the larger mission of the Church. So a decision was made that the CWME was still needed; it should maintain its identity and not seek "to spread across the entire house." That it was an important part of the WCC and had certain specific contributions to make to the world Christian community is apparent from its stated aim: "to assist it to proclaim the Gospel of Jesus Christ, by word and deed, to the whole world to the end that all may believe in Him and be saved." It was also decided that:

1) The CWME would emphasize the evangelistic vocation of the Christian community—the name was to be named in such a way that those who heard it could

144

recognize it as a clear invitation to personal and community discipleship to Jesus Christ.

2) The CWME would seek to build up the Christian community and help it to sense its own missionary vocation to the world.

3) The CWME would continue to seek for the contemporary meaning of the missionary vocation and for the appropriate style of persons in mission today (WCC, CWME Minutes, Geneva 1975).

The International Review of Mission was the CWME magazine. Its validity and function frequently came into question. When the CWME was reduced to a tiny unit, the IRM had to struggle to maintain its identity. There were those who proposed that the IRM merge with the larger *Ecumenical Review*. They reasoned that if mission is one, and is the task of all the churches, then the CWME might not be needed after all; and it would follow that a single magazine for one overall mission would certainly be sufficient—and more economical as well.

There were those who sincerely believed that the restructuring would allow CWME concerns to filter through to all the units of the WCC. They felt a purposeful tension between the different traditional emphases within the various units of the WCC would be a healthy thing. But one could only be apprehensive as he watched a weakened CWME attempt to compete in the "big leagues" where advocates of New Mission were shaping the WCC perspectives. Since restructuring had eliminated its previous automatic visibility, freedom and flexibility, much would now have to depend upon the calibre of the people within the CWME.

We need to bear in mind that during this period of restructuring the new leaders of the CWME themselves no longer held to the classical understandings about mission that had so characterized the IMC. Its new director, Philip Potter, may not, in fairness, be suspected of being uninterested in evangelism. Friends and colleagues who know him well testify to his deep commitment to evangelism. Dr. Potter did however come from a different background. It is not surprising that he brought to the CWME a different emphasis and understanding about mission than it had before. He was from the Third World and he was black. He was to become both spokesman and symbol for certain avant-garde and Third World views. He would therefore be more strongly influenced by issues of racism and liberation. He was a part of a whole new way of looking at reality. He brought a tremendous understanding of the global nature of change taking place in the world. He recognized the revolutionary character of our times and the implications of secularization for communicating the Gospel. During this period the top executive of the CWME was found to be fully sympathetic with the horizontal emphasis at Uppsala. He believed that religious experience had to move away from the personal and private toward the social and corporate.

Seeds of Conflict. Between Uppsala and Nairobi, the CWME leaders were not only sympathetic to the understandings and directions from Uppsala, but they also nudged the CWME into fully supporting these new objectives. We have already seen how the Bangkok Conference was carefully conceived and planned to put the CWME effort fully behind the new understanding about mission as social action. Instead of passionately challenging the rest of the WCC about missions as classically understood, the CWME was becoming a fully integrated member of the WCC team in leading the churches to redouble their efforts in the struggle for justice. The CWME vocabulary matched its programs as it sought to implement mission horizontally. A one-sided emphasis developed. And unless corrected, the whole WCC was in danger of a serious imbalance in its neglect of an important, if not the most important, part of its work.

The new programs, the redirection of existing programs, the restructuring of the WCC and the acceptance by the CWME leadership of Uppsala's understanding of mission—plus Bangkok—all combined to form the background for the Fifth Assembly. But Marxist ideological influences upon WCC thought and programs were also becoming increasingly pronounced and transparent. Liberation theology had become the dominant theological perspective. The WCC was moving dangerously close to identifying God's intent for liberation and a new society with a call to churches to use Marxist methods to accomplish God's mission.

While WCC leaders looked ahead to Nairobi to endorse these new and more specific proposals for greater effectiveness in carrying forward the social revolution envisioned at Uppsala, the member churches were choosing delegates concerned about the Marxist ideological presuppositions behind these new proposals. The planners conceived of the Assembly as a prophetic voice sharing with the member churches its wisdom and its ability to discern where and how God was at work liberating people from injustices on many fronts. The member churches, on the other hand, would bring the prophetic insights of Christians who found their directions in the time honored Word of God, the Bible. These saw God at work gloriously liberating from sin and guilt those who believed on the Savior.

A collision course seemed inevitable.

New Leadership–New Hope? We began this section with a query about the significance of Bishop Arias's plea for the restoration of evangelism to its central place in the work of the WCC. To put that speech in its proper perspective, we analyzed the activities in the WCC between Uppsala and Nairobi. His CWME presentation appeared to be out of harmony with WCC expectations for the Assembly. Dr. Stott saw it as "untypical" in terms of what one normally hears from the WCC. From what we have seen, the pre-Nairobi activities would surely confirm the correctness of his observation. What had happened?

The explanation may lie in the changes that occurred in the CWME leadership following Bangkok. The new director of the CWME, Emilio Castro, brings to the CWME a perspective about missions, missionaries, and evangelism more nearly akin to the views that characterized the earlier IMC. This is not to say that Dr. Castro is less committed to the struggle for liberation. Just as we noted that Dr. Potter cannot be suspected of being uninterested in evangelism, so Dr. Castro cannot be suspected of being uninterested in liberation. The difference lies in their understanding of certain ultimate questions: about

God, the nature of man and his eternal destiny. Friends and colleagues of Dr. Castro told me that "at heart he is an evangelist and a preacher." I was told that he preaches a powerful evangelistic message calling men and women to repentance and to personal faith and commitment to Jesus Christ. Dr. Castro himself told me that for him the heart of evangelism is to make disciples of Christ.

Thus, the one entirely new factor between Bangkok and Nairobi was the new leadership of the CWME. Dr. Castro came with the highest credentials regarding his commitment both to liberation and to evangelism. It was doubtless this double commitment that commended him so highly to those charged with finding a new director for the CWME. Bishop Arias's role at Nairobi would seem to flow from this selection, and the shift of emphasis which it represents. Perhaps the question now is: In the restructured WCC where the CWME is only a sub-unit within a unit, can this concern for evangelism influence the rest of the WCC in its understanding of the central task of the WCC and its member churches?

The significance of the choice of Bishop Arias to represent the CWME in plenary session at Nairobi is perhaps best seen in Dr. Castro's first report as director of the CWME. The report was made in 1974 following the Bangkok meeting, and is itself a masterpiece of diplomacy. The emphases upon mission as both liberation and as evangelism are skillfully balanced and shown to be interrelated. Yet, Dr. Castro finds a place to call the attention of the Commission to a letter written by Patriarch Pimen of the Russian Orthodox Church which noted a weakness at Bangkok. There was inadequate emphasis upon the eternal dimension of salvation which is fulfilled in the life hereafter. In speaking specifically of his understanding of the nature and function of the CWME, Dr. Castro says:

> In the light of Bangkok and within the context of the totality of the WCC, we recognize that our Commission's cutting edge should be in the evangelistic outreach of the Church. You will receive a separate document on evangelism that will indicate the lines of thought and action that we are trying to follow. To us the challenge is clear—how can we create in the life of the churches an

atmosphere in which evangelism is a normal and permanent dimension? (1974:8).

There is no doubt that there is a resurgence of dynamic leadership under Dr. Castro that is more nearly in tune with the spirit at New Delhi that dreamed of evangelism becoming central to the WCC.

"OUTSIDE" VOICES

These developments heartened many, both inside and outside the WCC member churches, who had pled for some years with the WCC leadership to include effective world evangelization in its program. For example, in February 1968, when the preparatory materials for Uppsala reached the faculty of the School of World Missions at Fuller Seminary in Pasadena, they held repeated sessions to consider Section Two (on mission) which was full of revolutionary concepts which bypassed evangelism. In the May, 1968, *Church Growth Bulletin,* Professors McGavran, Winter and Tippett wrote articles pleading with the Geneva leaders.

> Section Two on Mission, prepared for the Division of World Mission and Evangelism "says nothing about the necessity of faith, nothing about the two billion, and nothing about sending messengers. . . . While the word mission is repeatedly used, its meaning is nowhere that of communicating the good news of Jesus Christ to unbelieving men in order that they might believe and live. . . . A deliberate purpose to direct men's attention *away from* men's need to hear about Christ, confess Him as Saviour and obey Him as Lord . . . marks all the critical passages. . . . The chief thrust of Section Two is . . . getting existing churches involved with all of life in points of tension, revolutionary movements, critical points of society and "the agenda of the world". . . . Section Two has apparently resolved to say nothing about . . . (men's) need to follow Jesus Christ and be found in Him. . . ,

Church Growth Bulletin cannot believe that Section Two represents . . . missionary thinking of the great Churches affiliated with the World Council of Churches. . . . We look forward with hope and support Uppsala with prayer, confident that Section Two is not the will of God and will be rejected, or revised . . . and brought . . . into harmony with the experience and understanding of the Universal Church, the clear intent of the Bible, and the express statements of Jesus Christ our Lord."

Before the Bangkok Conference, the *Church Growth Bulletin* for May, 1972, stated:

The issue at Bangkok is clear: does the word salvation according to the Bible mean eternal salvation or does it mean this-worldly improvements? It appears that the conciliar forces are set to maintain on the basis of the Old Testament that salvation means primarily if not exclusively this-worldly improvements.

Again, in the July, 1975, issue of the *Church Growth Bulletin,* prior to Nairobi, Wagner and McGavran wrote a lead article, "Will Nairobi Champion the Whole Man?"

Let the (Fifth) Assembly . . . reverse the Uppsala-Bangkok trend, which is tearing the Church apart. What is needed is a world program equally devoted a) to calling men from death to life through faith in Jesus Christ; and b) to calling Christians to practice social welfare, extend brotherhood, promote justice and liberate the oppressed. . . . Let the World Council put before Member Churches the main biblical options . . . and listen to what the Spirit is saying to and through the Churches (p. 516).

In the same issue, McGavran addressed a question to Canon Max Warren of the Anglican Church Missionary Society, asking if he agreed that "the Nairobi meeting of the World Council seemingly plans to say nothing about world evangelization?" Dr. Warren's answer: "Yes, I do see the omission." McGavran then asked, "Can evangelicals do anything to help their

150

WCC brothers and sisters back to a stand more compassionate as regards the eternal destiny of the three billion?" Dr. Warren had replied, "I do not think the WCC is prepared to listen to evangelical testimony."

In 1974, a published doctoral dissertation entitled *World Evangelism and the Word of God* made its appearance, written by Arthur P. Johnston, a missionary of The Evangelical Alliance Mission (TEAM) serving in France. Johnston's thesis was that because ecumenical leaders had gradually abandoned their belief in an authoritative, infallible Bible, during the period from 1910 to 1961, they deliberately reconceptualized their understanding of missions from evangelism to social action—stressed that the object of mission was not to concern itself with the eternal salvation of mankind, but with the improvement of the world. Reaction among evangelicals to Johnston's thesis was mixed. Many accepted his basic assumption unreservedly. Other competent evangelical scholars vigorously challenged what they saw to be a theological bias and a selective use of WCC documents. Our study demonstrates that additional complex factors are involved.

Replies from Eugene Smith and Philip Potter—published in the *Church Growth Bulletin*—showed that World Council leaders knew of the assessments the evangelicals were making about New Mission. But Geneva ignored them. Until the Fifth Assembly at Nairobi, the WCC staff appeared determined to press on all member churches the concepts of New Mission.

These few paragraphs scarcely do justice to the evangelical voices raised. For further study, see: *The Conciliar Evangelical Debate: The Crucial Documents 1964–1976* (McGavran 1977) and *World Evangelism and the Word of God* (Johnston 1974).

Interestingly, particularly in the light of the above, those who came to Nairobi concerned about what stance the Assembly might take on evangelism were heartened.

> Woven through the fabric of the Fifth Assembly was a fervent concern for the spiritual and evangelistic expressions of the Christian faith. Why this was so, I can only guess. Certainly the International Congress on World Evangelization held at Lausanne, Switzerland in 1974

151

was a factor. The call for the churches and para-church mission agencies to step up their commitment to evangelism on all continents has met with unexpected response, even among church men and women not represented at Lausanne. Surely the imposing presence of the world Orthodox community at Nairobi had a salutary effect, as the assembly was reminded time and time again of the importance of worship, prayer, and study for Christian discipleship. Many delegates remarked on the balance to Western political and social activism which the Orthodox theologians achieved (Hubbard 1975).

By the same token, those who came to Nairobi concerned about an over-emphasis upon social, economic and political matters to the neglect of evangelism saw the Fifth Assembly take steps to correct the imbalance.

. . . the long hard years of frustration with such meager results in the quest for economic justice, political equity, and racial understanding have led many Christians to reexamine the nature of the Christian message and the sources of spiritual power. Even where the call for political liberation was strong—as from certain African and Latin American spokesmen and spokeswomen—it was frequently coupled with a concern for the total needs of persons, including their need to know God personally through Jesus Christ (Hubbard 1975).

A NEW MOOD

Emilio Castro felt that the suffering, imprisonment, torture and death so integral to the liberation struggle, were driving those involved back to spiritual resources required for such a struggle.* Through their suffering many were personally experiencing the great affirmations about Jesus Christ to be true. And in the context of suffering for others, Jesus Christ's own suffering became part of their experience. Amidst the frustra-

*These views were expressed in personal conversations in taped interview, Geneva, March 1977.

tion and despair of those impossible situations of suffering, the hope of eternal salvation and all the Bible promised about heaven gave courage to endure. There was a dimension of spiritual reality in such a personal experience of the saving, powerful, presence of Jesus Christ, that made acts of evangelism logically inevitable and even irresistible.

The call to evangelism at Nairobi (see below) must also be seen against this backdrop of experience of Christians from within the wide sweep of churches from the Third World. They had placed more than half the delegates in that great Kenyatta Conference Center in Nairobi.

The Fifth Assembly laid a base for the WCC staff and Central Committee to respond with a new commitment, new programs and people to back up that commitment. It laid the base for Christian leaders and ordinary Christians in all WCC member churches to challenge their people to engage in evangelism. A climate was established at Nairobi which allows for discussions and plans by WCC member churches, and by the WCC staff and Central Committee, for new evangelistic programs in a context that is congenial to such considerations.

As a result, it has once again become fashionable to speak of evangelism in the churches. At a deeper level there is an awareness that God is at work in the Church summoning his people back to their glorious calling of sharing with people everywhere the news of the unsearchable riches of Christ. Christians are perhaps even more keenly conscious than ever before of the wonderful saving experience of Jesus Christ on a personal level; and they are challenged to share that experience and the marvel of what God intended for his world through him. Churches on six continents were challenged at Nairobi to live and work together in such a way as to effectively communicate the Gospel to people everywhere who, apart from new and creative programs, would otherwise have no valid opportunity to hear and respond to the Gospel.

In the document prepared by Section I, "Confessing Christ Today," which was approved unanimously and with commendation by the entire Assembly, WCC member churches through their representatives from churches all over the world said:

The world requires, and God demands, that we recognize the urgency to proclaim the saving word of God—today. God's acceptable time demands that we respond in all haste. "And how terrible it would be for me if I did not preach the Gospel!" (I Cor. 9:16) (Paton 1976:55).

It was not a choice of promoting evangelism at the expense of social action. Both social action and evangelism are considered urgent responsibilities for Christians. The best way to carry on evangelism is in the context of social action.

As the royal priesthood, Christians are called to engage in both evangelism and social action. We are commissioned to proclaim the Gospel of Christ to the ends of the earth. Simultaneously, we are commanded to struggle to realize God's will for peace, justice and freedom throughout society (1976:43).

This same concern was expressed in the context of what it means to confess Christ as disciples who acknowledge his Lordship.

Confessing Christ and being converted to His discipleship belong inseparably together. Those who confess Jesus Christ deny themselves, their selfishness and slavery to the godless "principalities and powers," take up their crosses and follow Him. Without clear confession of Christ our discipleship cannot be recognized; without costly discipleship people will hesitate to believe our confession. The costs of discipleship—e.g. becoming a stranger among one's own people, being despised because of the Gospel, persecuted because of resistance to oppressive powers, and imprisoned because of love for the poor and lost—are bearable in face of the costly love of God, revealed in the passion of Jesus (1976:44).

At Nairobi there was an attempt to set forth an understanding of what it really means to truly confess Jesus Christ today, recognizing at the same time there are barriers that make this confession more difficult. Confession was made that it is our

154

failure and our fears that stop us from confessing Christ. At the same time, the wonder of how Christ makes himself known in a variety of expressions among peoples of different backgrounds, experiences and cultures was joyfully acknowledged. Delegates at Nairobi agreed with those at Bangkok in saying,

> . . . we can say that Jesus Christ does not make copies; he makes originals. We have found this confession of Christ out of various cultural contexts to be not only a mutually inspiring, but also a mutually corrective exchange (1976:46).

What was confessed at so many previous ecumenical gatherings about not understanding how God reveals himself to people of other religions was repeated at Nairobi in these familiar phrases:

> While we cannot agree on whether or how Christ is present in other religions, we do believe that God has not left Himself without witness in any generation or any society. Nor can we exclude the possibility that God speaks to Christians from outside the Church. While we oppose any form of syncretism, we affirm the necessity for dialogue with men and women of other faiths and ideologies as a means of mutual understanding and practical co-operation (1976:46).

THE "CALL TO CONFESS AND PROCLAIM"

Nairobi's call is an encouragement to churches everywhere concerned for evangelism. The reader is urged to read the entire "call" in Appendix C. The churches through their World Council in Nairobi said:

> We do not have the option of keeping the good news to ourselves. The uncommunicated gospel is a patent contradiction. . . .

> The world requires, and God demands, that we recognize the urgency to proclaim the saving word of God—today.

155

God's acceptable time demands that we respond in all haste. "And how terrible it would be for me if I did not preach the gospel!" (I Cor. 9:16) (Paton 1976:53-55).

The assembly immediately followed this call with twenty-one specific recommendations for ways in which the WCC and its member churches may move ahead to implement this call. If these recommendations were to be faithfully implemented, the whole Christian community would more nearly become a credible people living under the Lordship of Christ.

There is, sadly, one real disappointment. The Fifth Assembly failed to recognize adequately the tragic fact of the nearly three billion people who remain unreached with the Gospel. Even if every recommendation were carried out faithfully, the great missionary task of the Church would remain unfinished. The recommendations fall short of indicating clearly what steps the WCC and its member churches should take to evangelize those three billion. This imprecision is in marked contrast to the specific recommendations the WCC does make, for example, as to how churches can participate effectively in the struggle for social justice. One cannot but wonder whether the WCC does in fact have a "heartfelt commitment" to that kind of evangelism needed among the yet unreached.

What was lacking at Nairobi was a most urgent and compelling recommendation calling upon the WCC itself to fulfill its constitutional function to "assist its member churches in their worldwide missionary and evangelistic task." Is it not God's intent that all persons everywhere shall hear the Gospel and be challenged to repentance and faith in Jesus Christ? Do the existing programs make it likely that current efforts will succeed, and unreached peoples will hear the Gospel in our time, or ever? If God's intent is that all shall hear, and if it is shown that existing programs, efforts and structures are not leading to that end, then there must be a group within the body of the WCC to recommend what steps need to be taken to make it a reality. The CWME is now challenged to put forth an extensive effort to explore how to reach the three billion who now have so little chance to hear the Gospel effectively—and, in most cases, not any at all.

New efforts must also be made by churches in each region to

assess the size and shape of their unfinished evangelistic task. They must first find out which peoples remain unreached. Then they must find which missionaries and evangelists from which churches will be the most effective communicators of the Gospel for such peoples. The churches in each region should rise to the challenge in the confidence that the resources, people and technology of the whole Church are just as available to them for their evangelistic work as for other churches elsewhere. They should be assured that just as funds from affluent Western churches are considered legitimate and available for hunger, development and disaster, funds are also legitimate and available for new evangelistic efforts. Missionaries and evangelists from within the churches on six continents should be sent across whatever cultural, linguistic or geographical barriers may exist in new efforts to evangelize those yet unreached.

The CWME can play a key role within the WCC in conscientizing the churches to this challenge—by catalyzing the churches to action in terms of its own passionate commitment to this kind of evangelism. In so doing it will fulfill its constitutional mandate to encourage and assist the churches in the worldwide missionary and evangelistic task.

The Fifth Assembly demonstrates what a combination of committed persons within an organization, together with the support of delegates from committed churches, can under the blessing of God accomplish. Nairobi illustrates the need which church leaders and church people have for one another. On the one hand, the complacent ones need to hear the prophetic voices calling them to participate in those activities intended to improve the quality of life. On the other, the WCC needs to hear from the people of God in the churches who learn from their Bibles that they are entrusted with the Gospel—and that God intends that through them this Gospel must be proclaimed to the ends of the earth until the end of time.

At Nairobi it was realized that the WCC staff must be representative as well as prophetic to fulfill its true function. Of course, the ultimate test of the significance of Nairobi to the WCC will be contingent upon how conscientiously the WCC leadership and staff respond to the signals from the member churches as expressed there. To that we now turn.

EIGHT
MY QUEST AT
GENEVA
The Response to Nairobi

The Fifth Assembly met during the last weeks of 1975. In an effort to ascertain what impact Nairobi was having upon Geneva, I spent six weeks there in March and April of 1977. I went to the WCC Ecumenical Center daily to comb the archives and interview the leaders.

I wanted to know: did Geneva get the message? This involved more than intellectual curiosity. I felt I represented a vast majority in the churches who wanted to know where their Council stood on evangelistic and missionary efforts to reach the nearly three billion people who remain without effective knowledge of Jesus Christ. I wanted to sense the "mood of the house" with respect to evangelism. I wanted to know in what ways the Nairobi Assembly had influenced Geneva.

I went mildly hopeful; I left six weeks later slightly more hopeful than when I arrived! I learned much. I came to appreciate more fully the complexity of the WCC operation. I realized more clearly and urgently the need for member churches to actively participate in shaping and determining what their Council is to do on their behalf. Nairobi was, in part, the voice of the member churches speaking.

Geneva represents the mind, feet and hands of the churches, carrying out their intent. The Central Committee deserves the best men and women of our churches to determine, direct and control the people *they* chose to carry out *their* decisions. In

Geneva I observed how far removed from the churches the WCC staff has become. Lines of accountability too easily become severed. In theory, the WCC Central Committee has enormous power; but I feel that it does not generally use that power to control its staff. Still, I looked for indications that Geneva was responding positively to the message of Nairobi with respect to evangelism.

INTERVIEWS

To gain my information and to assess the mood of the WCC staff in Geneva, I interviewed on tape some fifteen of the key leaders who have executive responsibility. I also circulated a questionnaire among some eighty persons with administrative or executive responsibilities. I spent long hours in the archives. Spare moments were spent visiting more informally. I was pleased to visit the Institute at Bossey and spend a profitable afternoon with John Mbiti, imbibing from his gracious spirit and gaining profound insights from the African point of view. I asked myself, what did it all add up to?

Alan Brash, Deputy Secretary of the WCC, assured me that the WCC was taking Nairobi very seriously indeed. He informed me that discussions and debates about its meaning were going on "throughout the house." He pointed to long discussions on evangelism by the Central Committee and to plans for its next meeting to center around evangelism. All this was evidence of the impact of Nairobi.

David Gill told me that the WCC staff had agonized over the meaning of the Nairobi message. He said he didn't remember any such agonizing following Uppsala.

I was told that the CWME had come alive again in the last couple of years. Nairobi's call for evangelism had been a great source of encouragement. Following Nairobi the continuous and persistent efforts by some to do away with the *International Review of Mission* were finally laid to rest. The magazine was assured that it was a necessary instrument of the CWME and its importance would not be questioned again. So events at Nairobi had an impact on that decision.

The director of the CWME shared with me his enthusiastic

expectations for evangelism following Nairobi. He pointed to plans being made for the 1980 meeting of the CWME when evangelism would be the main theme. He saw the impact of Nairobi on evangelism as felt in the regional conferences of churches. He shared with me Canon Burgess Carr's plan to lift up the cause of evangelism in Africa during the next several years. It was reported that Canon Carr said he now felt the liberation cause had sufficient momentum to move ahead without his having to devote so much energy to it. He wanted now to place the emphasis upon evangelism. Dr. Castro himself felt there was a direct connection between such indications of intention and the Nairobi call to confess and proclaim Christ.

Robbins Strong, veteran of many years in the ecumenical movement and deputy director of the CWME, told of the WCC plans to finance the proposed meeting of all Christian councils of churches in Africa this year to take up the challenge to evangelize. He said he understood the meeting arose out of an awareness of the need to alert the churches to the dangers of being diverted from their evangelistic tasks because of the availability of large amounts of money from many outside sources for development and other social concerns. He linked this new awareness to Nairobi.

I learned of continuing agonizing discussions about the significance of dialogue as it relates to evangelism. Some wanted to know more specifically about the purpose of it all. What is the end result? What is dialogue accomplishing? Nairobi discussions had a relationship. For at Nairobi the WCC's Dialogue Program was severely questioned. Dialogue was controversial.

Dr. Potter spoke of the WCC's keener awareness of the significance of the local congregation. For example, in the recent past there had been a tendency to concentrate on efforts to join with others outside the church in action-oriented projects. At Nairobi it was forcefully brought to the attention of the Central Committee once again that the local Christian congregation was of great importance. A renewed local congregation was vital to any thoughts about evangelism wherever such congregations were found. The Central Committee's plans to establish a program to meet the spiritual needs at the congregational level was also seen as an indication of the WCC's sensitivity to what the churches were saying at Nairobi.

Hans Rudi Weber cited the decision of the Central Committee to bring the Bible studies into the Unit on Education and Renewal as a direct response to Nairobi. It was recognized that the Bible has much of vital importance to say on issues discussed and planned by the Geneva staff. I recall that when we met, Dr. Weber had just finished an important paper on some biblical truths that related to a subject on the agenda of a forthcoming core group meeting. Nairobi had stimulated action that brought the relevance of the Bible to bear upon thought and action.

STAFF SURVEY

By way of a questionnaire (see Appendix I), I formulated a number of questions as to how Nairobi might be influencing Geneva. For example:

> To what extent would you agree that in the period since Nairobi, WCC staff is making a serious response to the intent for evangelism expressed at the Fifth Assembly . . . evident in continuing discussions and conferences . . . as well as in plans? . . .

Of 18 responses, 8 indicated there was substantial evidence of serious response, 3 indicated moderate evidence, 4 only marginal indication, 1 saw no indication at all, and 2 said they felt the question was irrelevant.

Another question dealt with prospects for changes in program:

> In the light of Nairobi's call to evangelism, to what extent do you anticipate changes being made in your program/project reflecting [this call]:
>
> —so that your program/project places more emphasis

162

upon encouraging and assisting the work of evangelism in local churches?

Of 15 responses, 5 were from CWME personnel. Two said they expected such changes to be forthcoming, 3 were reasonably hopeful about such changes, 2 said there was only a marginal likelihood and 7 felt the question was irrelevant to their program.

A second part of the same question was in terms of evangelism among "unreached peoples":

—so that your program/project places more emphasis upon encouraging and facilitating the participation of WCC member churches in "cross-cultural evangelism" among the "unreached peoples"?

Again there were 5 responses from the CWME people out of a total of 15. Only 1 indicated substantial hope for this to happen; 5 saw a moderate chance of this and 3 said it was only marginally likely. Seven claimed the question was irrelevant to their program.

I asked for a reaction to Bishop Arias's charge:

Recalling the lament of Bishop Arias that "evangelism has become the Cinderella of the WCC" and in the context of John R. Stott's challenge to the WCC to "provide evidence that it has a heartfelt commitment to evangelism," to what extent would you say the program/project in which you are working reflects such a commitment?

Here there were 17 responses of which 5 were from CWME people. Six persons indicated there was substantial evidence for such a commitment in their program/project, 2 said there was moderate evidence, and 3 felt it was only marginally evident. Two saw no evidence, and 1 felt the question was irrelevant for his program.

A further question dealt with what the WCC staff thinks about the prospects for developing new programs, or modifying existing programs to reflect a significant response to Nairobi's intent with respect to evangelism.

> During the period from Uppsala to Nairobi a number of new programs/projects were created by the WCC and existing programs/projects were modified to implement the emphasis given at Uppsala to the churches' responsibilities with reference to the social implications of the Gospel.

> To what extent do you anticipate in the period from Nairobi until the next full assembly of the WCC that its programs/projects will reflect a comparable response to the emphasis given to evangelism at Nairobi?

Again there were 16 responses, 5 from CWME people. Three felt there was substantial reason to hope this would happen, 8 were moderately hopeful, 2 only marginally so, and 2 felt the question irrelevant to their program.

One of the questions related to the theological convictions of those asked to respond:

> At Nairobi, J. R. Stott responding to Bishop Arias's address on evangelism said there were in his view five things the WCC needed to recover: 1. A recognition of the lostness of man. 2. Confidence in the truth, relevance, and power of the Gospel of God. 3. Conviction about the uniqueness of Jesus Christ. 4. A sense of urgency about evangelism. 5. A personal experience of Jesus Christ.

> Making due allowances for the fact that each of us might not view his assertions as of equal importance and that we might express ourselves in a slightly different manner, to what degree do you find yourself responding favorably to what Stott is trying to say?

Out of 16 responses (5 from the CWME), the answers were as follows: 6 in substantial agreement, 3 only marginally so, 2 disagreed completely and 1 said the question was irrelevant.

In all honesty, the questionnaire results should not be taken too seriously. This research device was far from a success. The response was even lower than the normally-anticipated low response to a questionnaire! Part of the blame is my own. I had not adequately established rapport and credibility with the WCC staff. There appeared to be some concern as to how the questionnaire might be used. This produced resistance to responding. In addition, heavy work schedules for all who were asked to respond contributed to the rather meager results. We should not take this small response as evidence that WCC staffers are uninterested in evangelism. While this could be true, the questionnaire results should not be used to say that. Some very dear friends were among those who responded. Their vital interest in the results suggest that there are those in Geneva who share a deep concern for how the WCC can assist its member churches in their worldwide missionary and evangelistic task.

PERSPECTIVES ON "THE UNFINISHED TASK"

In my conversations in Geneva I was rather surprised to find that when I spoke of an unfinished missionary task, most immediately assumed I wanted to restore the missionary movement of the 19th and early 20th centuries. It seemed to take a good bit of explaining to make it clear that I was no more interested in reviving that form of the missionary movement than they were. I found it difficult to make my point that an unfinished missionary task existed. And further, the WCC and its member churches needed to accept the challenge to find new ways for churches to join together in that task. Because they assumed that I represented a point of view they saw as inimical to WCC efforts to get beyond the missionary movement, they had difficulty in moving to the real question—the need for cross-cultural evangelism among unreached peoples. Aware of this hangup, I continued to deliberately pursue the subject of the unfinished missionary task to provoke discussion on these points which made them so uneasy. I did this purposely because in a very real sense it gets at the heart of the problem.

If there is an unfinished missionary task, and if the old missionary movement is ended, where do we go from here? To what extent are current programs, vaguely understood to carry forward the aims of the former missionary movement, actually doing so? How much of the remaining missionary work by WCC related churches can currently be called cross-cultural evangelism? To what extent do WCC programs encourage and assist member churches to take on and carry forward the unfinished task of a missionary movement that was aborted before the task was completed?

Prevailing Assumptions. In seeking answers to these kinds of questions, I ran into three assumptions that need to be recognized and renounced as erroneous if the WCC and its churches are to get on with the unfinished task of cross-cultural evangelism.

1) Mission/evangelism is carried on most effectively by each congregation in its local situation.

This assumption runs through all WCC thinking about the missionary congregation. I met it repeatedly in Geneva. This error, however, does represent a partial truth. Normally it is true that a local congregation *is* most qualified to reach its own people effectively with the Gospel. However, there may be historical, social, economic or other factors that alter this. Christians from such local congregations are normally best qualified to gossip the Gospel among their *like-culture* neighbors. Such churches need only the programs to equip and encourage their people to bear their witness to Christ in the most effective way possible. All of this is granted.

But suppose no church is present. Where there is no church—no one to witness to Christ among people of that culture using their language—there "the local congregation" is a weak reed indeed. What I found exceedingly difficult to get across was the hard fact that we live in a world where vast multitudes have no chance to hear the Gospel because there are *no* churches there to give their witness to Jesus Christ. To meet this situation we must find a way to send a witness across that cultural, linguistic and frequently geographical barrier involving distance so that such people may hear the Gospel. It is as simple as that!

The Apostle Paul of course was aware of this problem long

before *we* began to speak about "unreached peoples." How could we express it more succinctly?

> How can they call upon Him in whom they have not believed, and how can they believe in Him of whom they have not heard, and how can they hear without a preacher? And how can men preach unless they are sent? (Rom. 10:14-15a).

The essence of the unfinished missionary task demands a strategy for mission designed to take the saving Gospel effectively to the three billion who remain unreached. There must be new ways and new methods for the churches from six continents to pool their resources, people and technology for this task.

At Nairobi it was unmistakably clear that the churches do care whether or not the Gospel is preached. They said,

> The world requires, and God demands, that we recognize the urgency to proclaim the saving word of God—today. God's acceptable time demands that we respond in all haste (Paton 1976:54).

Where unreached peoples are concerned, it is irresponsible—a dodging of responsibility—to say that if the local congregation were to become a missionary congregation in its particular locality, then all those unevangelized will be reached. Unfortunately, this simplistic error is persistent and prevalent in Geneva. It is also, alas, similarly persistent and prevalent in churches at all levels!

2) Does God intend that *all* should hear?

There seems to be a prevailing skepticism in Geneva which questions whether it is God's intent that all people should literally hear the Gospel. One highly placed person spoke of the "rippling effect" of the Gospel. For example, the benefits God intends for the world through the Gospel are not necessarily tied to a hearing of that Gospel. The assumptions accompanying such statements do not foster an enthusiastic commitment to participate in an unfinished missionary task.

3) There are few really "unreached peoples" today.

Many question whether such large numbers of "unreached peoples" really exist. In my questionnaire and in my interviews I used the term, "unreached peoples." I spoke of the challenge to find effective ways to win them to discipleship and faith in Christ. I was surprised at the difficulty some people experienced with this term. I had spoken of unreached peoples who could not hear the Gospel because there was no one there to tell them the good news. And I had spoken of unreached peoples who did not hear the Gospel due to a failure somewhere in the communication process. The former are those who *cannot* hear the Gospel; the latter, those who *do not* hear the Gospel. By the former I referred to the nearly three billion persons of whom an estimated 85 percent cannot hear because no churches exist among them with Christians to give their witness to Christ. By the latter I meant those people within reach of churches but who, for a variety of reasons, actually do not hear the Gospel. They may choose not to hear. Or perhaps the churches fail to give a credible witness to Christ.

Some people find it difficult to draw this kind of distinction. To them it is much more congenial to talk about all those around us who do not hear because of our failure as Christians to act justly. It is harder to think about persons of other cultures, languages and places who cannot and will not hear the Gospel unless there is a clear-cut missionary effort from within the life of our churches to send someone there to communicate that message.

I readily acknowledge the evangelistic challenge to churches to become aware of peoples among whom they live and whom they must win to Christ. I can also recognize the need for "mission fields" in Western countries if people who are not hearing the Gospel are to hear it. Our churches need to wake up. They need to know they are not communicating the Gospel to pagans on the streets of our cities. I grant that this is an urgent and compelling task. Our people need to be trained equipped and led to communicate the Gospel with forms and language our pagan neighbors can understand.

Nevertheless, we need to distinguish sharply between unreached peoples who *cannot* hear the Gospel and like-culture neighbors of Christians who for various reasons *do not* hear the Gospel. Any failure to recognize this fundamental distinc tion leads to fuzziness in our understanding of the worldwide evangelistic task that challenges the churches. The WCC staff, and the CWME in particular, should work with member churches. This enormous unfinished task needs analysis and study to determine how the churches can best work together in faithful obedience to Christ who commanded his followers to "disciple *ta ethne*."

An Alternate View. The most incisive thinking I have come across on the nature of the unfinished evangelistic task, has been written by Ralph Winter of the U.S. Center for World Mission. Anyone concerned for a clearer understanding of the kinds of efforts required by churches to communicate the Gospel effectively to all who have yet to hear should make a careful study of Winter's concepts a basic assignment (Winter 1974).

Winter speaks of the evangelistic efforts of the churches in what he terms E^0, E^1, E^2 and E^3 evangelism. The numbers represent the different kinds of evangelistic efforts required if no one is to be missed.

E^0 is that evangelism carried on within the life of a local church. In this evangelism, nominal Christians who may be members of local congregations are brought to a saving knowledge of Christ and to true discipleship.

In E^1 evangelism, local Christians reach out into the community among people of like-culture to win them to Christ and bring them into the fellowship of their churches. It also includes those outreach efforts among people of the same language and culture aimed at winning converts to Jesus Christ and planting new congregations made up of those new believers.

In E^2 evangelism, churches send people from their midst to those of slightly different culture than is found in existing churches. The new converts are formed into congregations of their own kind of people. But more importantly, the communication of the Gospel requires that the evangelist cross a subcultural barrier.

In E^3 evangelism, the churches send out persons across cultural, linguistic, and frequently geographical barriers to communicate the Gospel. In E^3 evangelism the culture differential between the communicator and the hearer is much greater than in E^2 evangelism. E^3 evangelism is a recognizable missionary situation. Approximately 85 percent of the unreached peoples of the world have no valid chance to hear the Gospel apart from such E^3 efforts.

Here lies the great challenge for the WCC and its member churches. There is a need to recognize and respond with appropriate programs, people, resources, structures and relationships. Without such new, creative, joint efforts, our obedience to Jesus Christ remains sadly defective and deficient.

In Geneva I found it difficult to communicate the urgent nature of these new demands now pressing upon us. Yesterday's efforts are not only not enough, but present programs are totally inadequate. Our fuzzy thinking about current programs is related to our concept of the unfinished missionary task. We are ever so slow in coming to terms with this challenge. Will the concerns voiced at Nairobi affect this? Perhaps there should have been a specific recommendation vis-a-vis the unfinished missionary and evangelistic task there at Nairobi. But, it is not too late even now. The climate is favorable. Who will rise to the challenge?

The Role of Guilt. Those seeking new understandings about mission are sensitive and troubled by the failure of the Christian churches to evidence in their behavior the "new life" true evangelism should offer. With such a wide credibility gap between that professed and that performed in the social dimensions of the Gospel, it is hard for them to get excited about missionary or evangelistic efforts. This guilt complex, in effect, becomes a new excuse for apathy toward the Lord's command to disciple the nations.

This is not a new phenomenon. Reasons have never been lacking for arguing why the time to evangelize is not right. Even Jesus appears to have recognized this when he said, "Do you not say, 'There are yet four months, then comes the harvest?' I tell you, lift up your eyes, and see how the fields are already white for harvest" (John 4:35).

In their overwhelming sense of moral failure to expose and fight against the terrible evils of Nazism, the churches in

Europe, and particularly in Germany, felt they had forfeited the privilege to "preach to others." And church leaders in America were saying that until they had a better record with respect to racial discrimination, poverty and war, the numbers of missionaries from their churches should be reduced. Withdrawals, early retirements and phaseouts were the order of the day.

Ordinary people concerned for evangelism were told that this was a "time for silence," a "time for listening." There could be "presence" but not "proclamation"; "dialogue" but not "debate." We from the West were told that we needed to get over our compulsive urge to evangelize and export our theologies and our religion.

Moral failures in the West only made apparent successes in other systems more fascinating. The China experiment, and that which happened in Cuba, were held up as models of liberation and of secular salvation. Some even declared openly that China needed protection from those who dreamed about future evangelistic efforts—should existing barriers between East and West ever be lowered. This was really a time to learn; not a time to teach. But all of this was due to highly exaggerated guilt.

Strong guilt feelings were created also by those who amusingly linked the missionary movement and the spread of the Christian faith with the evil features of colonialism. It was as though they had taken unfair advantage of people by exposing them to the Gospel against their will. Some even gave the extraordinary impression that it would have been better had the missionaries and the Gospel never arrived. Riding "piggy back" on the colonial system was the exploitation and manipulation of the Christian missionary enterprise. Economic and political imperialism and religious imperialism had gone hand in hand.

In the post-colonial period, churches in the West were blamed for these assumed immoral relationships. Furthermore, churches increasingly believed what they were told—that they were part of a capitalistic system which enjoyed privilege, power and riches at the expense of the powerless and exploited of Third World countries who were becoming steadily poorer and were without hope.

The moral failures of the West and the alleged participation by the churches as accomplices in these failures, preclud-ed—so it was said—the possibility that such churches could speak with moral authority on socio-economic-political issues. It was also apparent that missionaries from such Western churches were then in no position to evangelize others.

Paradoxically, spokesmen from Western churches who reasoned in this way were also pointing out that "Christen-dom" in the West had ended. On the one hand, this kind of statement implied that the Church and Western culture and society were separate. It recognized the gulf between what the churches believed and proclaimed and the failure of the society in which the churches existed to reflect what the churches represented. At the same time, it was paradoxically implied that until Western culture adequately reflected the impact of the churches on society and its institutions, the churches should not think they could effectively communicate the Christian Gospel to peoples of other cultures.

This is a strange mixture of truth and error. The most paradoxical assertions are set forth to buttress the argument that churches in the West are not and cannot be effective communicators of the Gospel to peoples of other cultures though, curiously, they can be effective fighters for justice!

The entire subject and, indeed, the difficulties arising out of this guilt complex are directly related to the historical fact that a "committed few" are involved in the missionary and evangelistic outreach from within the Christian commun-ity—that the missionary movement has by and large been done by a "committed few." It was they who challenged the mem-bership of the churches to act on the missionary and evangelistic mandate. They spoke with prophetic voice within their own churches. And they spoke with prophetic voice to peoples of other cultures, calling them to repentance and faith.

Deep theological implications are involved for missions when we affirm that the entire Church is mission and then assume that the Church cannot speak until it has more per-fectly demonstrated in its own life and practices the fruits of the Gospel it is called to proclaim and profess. While it may be true that the whole community of God's people is called to declare the wonderful deeds of him who has called them out of darkness into his marvelous light (1 Peter 2:10), in fact the churches have never fully been sanctified to a degree that they could at any time say, "Now we will begin to share our good news about Jesus Christ." If the churches of any age, including the Apostolic, had waited until they were perfect before declaring the good news, we would all remain without knowledge of him.

A theological principle is at stake. Are we to preach our own goodness as a reason to follow Christ? Does not this whole elaborate configuration really result in preaching salvation by works? Is not the result of this concern, for "renewal in the churches *before* evangelism becomes credible," only—even if unintentionally—an excuse for silence? What about that large number within the churches who have experienced the transforming power of Christ in their own lives? Are these to remain silent until the whole Church is similarly saved and sanctified? Suppose the whole Church will not do missionary and evangelistic work. Should not then these within the churches find ways to get on with the task?

IMPLEMENTATION

The Fifth Assembly expressed a corrective. Many concerned for evangelism were greatly heartened. But the response of the WCC's Central Committee and Staff to Nairobi's intent would be crucial. Would the Central Committee exercise the needed control over the staff? Would the Central Committee assign substantial resources to this corrective? Until now the response has been negligible.

True, Nairobi produced no mandate. Nor was specific recommendation made. However, it clearly showed that the churches were ready to respond to new initiatives from Geneva—if the initiatives would zero in on this unfinished missionary and evangelistic task. There was no doubt how the assembly felt. Over the protestations of the leadership, the assembly insisted that the revised constitution retain the original wording which said the WCC was "to support the churches in their worldwide missionary and evangelistic task" (Paton 1976:318). The significance of that decision for retention should not escape the WCC leadership. The Assembly leaders had made three separate attempts to assure delegates that their concerns were already cared for in an existing provision which stated that the WCC was "to support the churches in the common witness of the churches in each place and in all places" (Paton 1976:318). But the delegates were not satisfied. They preferred a degree of duplication with overlap of allegedly similar ideas, rather than have their concern for the "worldwide missionary and evangelistic task" diluted.

The Fifth Assembly did not go so far as to spell out how the Central Committee and Staff should implement this function. But it had certainly established the mood and directed the Council to encourage and assist the member churches to take up once again the unfinished task of world evangelization. Unfortunately, there is little to suggest that the balance which the Assembly hoped for is being sought. WCC press releases and publications continue to concentrate on social issues and neglect evangelism. Anyone who reads WCC publications knows this is true.

Two recent issues of EPS (Ecumenical Press Service) confirm my observations. The July 7, 1977 issue notes plans being made for closer cooperation between the WCC-WSCF. It is an established fact that the World Student Christian Federation has for many years been dominated by radical, left-wing people with revolutionary and Marxist ideas. The WCC had tapped the WSCF reservoir for many of its leaders. And many of these had formulated their understanding about mission in this atmosphere.

> In the United States and Canada, the program of the Interseminary Movement, along with the World Student Federation, is the most promising seedbed of ecumenical leadership (Bristone 1963:204).

In recent years, however, the relationship between the WCC and the WSCF had broken off. It was at this time that the WCC turned directly to the churches for leaders and for the people needed in the administration. So this current move back to the WSCF does not give promise of a greater commitment on the part of the WCC to evangelism. It suggests rather an intensification of commitment to its struggle against injustice and the

THE RESPONSE TO NAIROBI

goal of a new socio-economic-political order—one in which the views of Marx and his methods will play a dominant part.

Further, the July 14th issue of EPS is equally disturbing. This issue contains the index for EPS issues for the first six months, January–June 1977. If the EPS was meant to inform the world what the WCC considers important—the news about what the WCC is thinking and doing—there is little comfort seen for those who had hoped for a significant shift in the post-Nairobi emphasis from Geneva. An examination of news items for that entire six-month period shows exactly *two* entries under the heading of Evangelism.

By way of contrast, the heading *Human Rights* had thirty-one entries, *Race Relations* had twenty, and *Social, Political, Economic and Legal Problems* and *Christian Action* listed ten. During this same period there was just *one* lonely article listed under *Mission*. Is this reappraisal—and implementation?

THE CENTRAL COMMITTEE'S ROLE

A heavy responsibility rests with the WCC Central Committee. It was they who were charged by the Fifth Assembly to correct the imbalance in WCC programs by giving evangelism a more central place. So far this has not happened. Where does the problem lie? Is the Central Committee perhaps failing to represent the assembly that appointed its members to their positions of responsibility? Or is it that the WCC staff is not adequately carrying out decisions made by the Central Committee? In its commissioned role, the Committee should consider the still-timely observation of the WCC's first Executive and continuing honorary President, W. A. Visser 't Hooft:

> The point is not whether the churches are too little or too much involved with the problems of the world. Basically they can never be involved deeply enough. But the question is whether they are involved in the right way (1974:95).

The Central Committee alone has the authority and power to determine that "right way." The Fifth Assembly represented the mind of the member churches. The Central Committee must translate that "intent" into programs with both people and funds. The staff is to find its direction from and be accountable to the Central Committee. Visser 't Hooft's query then is really addressed to the Central Committee. And it is worthy of a most careful answer.

One key is the reevaluation of existing programs. Earlier, the Central Committee insisted that all programs of the WCC be scrutinized and reevaluated as to their contribution to the struggle for a just society. Will they now, after Nairobi, similarly scrutinize and reevaluate all programs as to their contribution to evangelism? And will they approve and mandate new programs designed to implement the intent of the Nairobi Assembly with the same degree of enthusiasm that produced the new social action programs following Uppsala?

An examination of existing WCC programs makes it clear that the WCC to date has no programs that focus on the unfinished missionary task of evangelizing the three billion.* Programs that have been hailed as new, appropriate ways in which to carry forward the aims of the classic missionary movement do not in fact do so. Urban and Industrial Mission (UIM), for example, is presumably concerned with evangelization in the cities and towns. Instead of centering on evangelism, however, the program centers on social problems faced by urban people. Similarly, a new program, Rural Agriculture Mission (RAM) endeavors to help rural peoples achieve a higher standard of living. The claim is that both programs are concerned with evangelism. But in practice the major, or rather the only, emphasis falls on efforts to bring about the new society by removing injustices and helping people assert their rights.

The Report of the Advisory Group on Urban Industrial Mission given at the CWME 1975 meeting makes this emphasis on socio-economic and political matters evident:

> Mission . . . involves the church in penetrating all the diverse social milieux of mankind. It involves us in the process which we perceive more clearly in our own generation of the movement of mankind from old enslave-

---

*Abundant documentation for this startling statement has been provided by Appendixes D, E, F, G, H, I. Careful students will want to read them.

ments to new freedoms. . . . Mission is our participation in the action of God for the liberation of man. UIM believes that the church is renewed through participating in this action in solidarity with the oppressed. . . . Mission involves a process of movement back and forth between action and reflection or between context and text. . . . Action takes place in the sphere of politics but the motivation for action lies in the process of theological and sociological reflection. . . . There is a strong sense around the regions (where UIM has programmes) that we are all involved in a major movement of history. . . .

The UIM movement across the world is accompanied by a sense of togetherness in the pursuit of shared aims and often even by similar strategies . . . we might describe them as 'movement-oriented' projects.

Rural/Urban Nexus . . . There is a stronger sense that the lot of the urban poor and that of the rural poor are both part of one common situation . . . we recognize increasingly, the one mission which the church must undertake in the common liberation struggle of rural and urban poor (UIM Advisory Group Report, Appendix C, CWME 1975).

The program, Ecumenical Sharing of Personnel, (ESP) supposedly illustrates the modern way for churches to work together in mission. In practice the numbers involved are minuscule. Since the program began in 1970, the CWME has positioned less than twenty people in ESP. And not one of them is engaged in direct cross-cultural evangelism. Yet ESP is hailed as the successor to the "former missionary movement." Only in the remotest sense is ESP a missionary and evangelistic effort.

More accurately it is a program to facilitate an international exchange of religious workers involved in the inner life of the churches. In this respect it serves a useful purpose. But we must not think of ESP as a program through which member churches send missionaries or evangelists to proclaim the Gospel among otherwise unreached peoples.

Then there is the dialogue program. This, too, no longer focuses on evangelism in the sense of winning men and women to faith in Jesus Christ and bring such to baptism and into the fellowship of the Church. Dialogue has been discussed as far back as the Jerusalem conference in 1928. At that time it was considered as a method of evangelism through which misunderstandings could be overcome and the Gospel could be communicated more effectively. Today, dialogue has become controversial. Instead of being a method of evangelism, many suspect dialogue of betraying evangelism. It has become a program whose major goal is to enable the leaders of the Church and representatives of other living faiths and ideologies to share their concerns about world community. With this alteration of goal, the risk of syncretism is considerable. But in any case, like other WCC programs, it serves the ultimate goal of a new world order.

These are programs one would expect to focus on world evangelization. Ordinary Christians would understand these programs to connote evangelization. The fact that they do not means that the WCC has no effective programs for taking the Gospel to the three billion yet unreached. This being the case, how are member churches to receive from their WCC the assistance for "their worldwide missionary and evangelistic task" which the WCC constitution mandates? Something new must happen. Either existing programs must be refocused, or entirely new programs need to be fashioned. In either case, the result must be the sending of vast new numbers of missionaries and evangelists from churches on six continents across whatever barriers may exist—cultural, linguistic, geographical—to communicate the Gospel effectively among the yet unreached peoples of the world. Funds and technology must be released and directed for this new missionary and evangelistic venture.

Of course, WCC has many other programs. The Program to Combat Racism (PCR) concentrates on its thing. The Commission on the Church's Participation in Development (CCPD) focuses on efforts to improve the quality of life and other social issues. One does not expect these kinds of WCC programs to focus on evangelism as such, though the fact that they have a real bearing upon evangelism no one would deny.

My point is that no known existing WCC programs focus

specifically on assisting member churches to engage in world evangelization in the tradition of mission and evangelism as understood by the IMC. The seriousness of this becomes apparent when we realize that even those programs the WCC itself presumes are carrying forward the aims of the IMC are not in actuality doing so. Both the WCC and its member churches must squarely face this fact. And for the Central Committee, the question is inescapable: does it have a "heartfelt commitment to evangelism" or not? Mere protestations are not sufficient! A credible answer must be demonstrated through programs which involve people and money in world evangelization of those yet unreached.*

In a recent conversation I spoke with Sir Kenneth Grubb, now retired. He was a longtime responsible member of the WCC Central Committee and has a long record of distinguished service as co-chairman of the Commission of the Churches on International Affairs (CCIA). I asked him how much control the Central Committee has over what the WCC staff does in developing and administering WCC programs. He answered in these simple words, "A good bit, if they wish to exercise it."

Dr. Norman Goodall, now eighty years of age, in good health and with a continuing keen interest in the WCC also responded to a similar question. Earlier he had been active in the IMC, and served as chairman of the joint IMC-WCC committee in the period before integration. He was called out of retirement to become the Recording Secretary of the Fourth Assembly at Uppsala. In Geneva he had served as Deputy Secretary of the WCC, and had his office adjacent to the General Secretary himself. He shared with me his personal concern about where the WCC is heading. He mentioned there were others who were deeply involved in the work of the WCC from the beginning. They too loved this organization; they were deeply committed to it and believed that God intended it as one of his instruments to enable the churches to become and do what God had in mind for his people.

I asked Dr. Goodall how he thinks the imbalance that many of us see in WCC understandings, programs and declarations

*See Appendixes D through I for fuller study of certain WCC Programs.

might be corrected. In his answer he emphasized the importance of placing the kind of people in the key positions who
represent the viewpoint of the churches who spoke at Nairobi.
He acknowledged that this will take time. But he was confident
that by using existing channels people could be gotten on the
Central Committee and on other committees with influence
and authority. Every effort must be made to be fully informed
in order to be alert to opportunities to place the people who
truly represent the mind of the churches in these positions.

There was no hint from this ecumenical statesman that he
intended to pull out of the movement and its organization to
which he had given the best years of his life. He believes that
better times are ahead and that the churches can bring about
changes to make their Council more responsive to their wishes
and more representative of their understandings about God,
His Church, and the world.

We should not expect any changes to come about easily,
painlessly or quickly. This view was shared by a number of
persons with long records of experience with the system. Vig-
ilance, vision and insistence are required. Let no one assume
that the WCC is a polished model of the unity that churches
should represent. There are tensions in Geneva. The conglom-
erate of churches represents different cultural, geographical,
theological and ideological perspectives. Geneva is a marketplace of ideas. And many of the people in this marketplace
are refugees—refugees from their own people, their own
countries and, not infrequently, from their churches. Some of
them are inactive in the life of the churches they represent.
There are WCC leaders in Geneva who do not participate in
the life of a local congregation; they are absent from worship
and uninvolved in the life of the community. Yet, these are the
very men and women who are fashioning programs and
suggesting methods by which the churches may be renewed to
engage in mission.

The process of sanctification is not more advanced in
Geneva than elsewhere in the churches. Power struggles,
jealousies, ambition and pride are mixed with highest dedica-
tion and faithfulness to Christ and his Church. Let us not expect more from Geneva than we know to be true about our own
churches and their structures.

At the same time, we need to be realistic. Presently in control in the marketplace of Geneva are those who want to see the churches engage on all fronts in the struggle against all forms of injustice. Their aim is to seek a new, more just socio-economic-political order. They too should carefully ponder the words of wisdom from Visser 't Hooft. He is a sincere friend of the WCC. In fact, there is perhaps no one who is more informed or more qualified to speak.

> The ecumenical movement did not just exist to carry out common social tasks. The ecumenical movement is a specific manifestation of the Church, which is concerned with no more and no less than the rediscovery of the true task of the Church. This task consists in the proclamation of the presence of Christ in the world. It must be made clear to our society how Christ is our peace.

> . . . An ecumenical movement which is only concerned about action loses its identity as a Christ-centered movement and so becomes a tool of the forces which are drawn up against each other in the social and political field.

> It goes without saying that there must be social engagement. . . . But that is not an alternative to the gathering of the scattered children of God.

> . . . the ecumenical movement can only have a future if it avoids the temptation of choosing between the unity of the Church and the unity of mankind, and instead learns to realize more and more fully that the Lord gathers His people in order that they may be a light to the world. There is a future for the ecumenical movement provided it does not cease to reflect on its true *raison d'etre,* and draws its life from the heart of the Gospel (Visser 't Hooft 1974:97).

And, we would add, the ecumenical movement has a future only if, along with its concern for the unity of the Church and the unity of mankind, it lifts up the unfinished worldwide missionary and evangelistic task, making it central to all it says and does. The ecumenical movement has its roots deep within the missionary movement and its commitments. Its future holds promise only insofar as it gives priority to this missionary and evangelistic commitment to proclaim the Gospel.

NINE
EVIDENCE OF
CONCERN
Geneva Struggles over
Evangelism

At Nairobi John Stott challenged the WCC to prove it has a heartfelt commitment to evangelism: "You say that you do, but where is the evidence?" (1976:30–33).

I went to Geneva to gain some assurance on that very question. I was not surprised to find the strong advocates of New Mission are in the places of influence and power. They make the headlines; the press releases carry their stories. Their views are heard. But not entirely so.

A stronger evangelistic thrust from Geneva may come. But it is by no means certain. For it can happen only if those individuals and churches that influenced the Fifth Assembly will keep the pressure on those in Geneva. The churches must continue to insist that evangelism be implemented with adequate programs, budgets and personnel. We recall that a spokesman from within the WCC itself claimed that concern for evangelism was woefully lacking within its Geneva operations.

> . . . above all we must admit with shame that evangelism has been the Cinderella of the WCC, or at least to judge by the extent to which it appears in its structure, where it figures by nothing more than one office with a single occupant, in a sub-structure which is itself merely part of a unit and with no more than a monthly letter by which to

communicate with the churches of the whole world
. . . (Arias 1976:13–26).

AMONG WCC STAFF

There are within the WCC staff some deeply committed and
highly capable Christian leaders who are as concerned for
evangelism as were those whose voices were heard in Nairobi.
It would be great oversimplification to think that the WCC
represented a single point of view.

The CWME Secretary for Evangelism noted in his
November, 1973, communication to the CWME constituency
the interest in evangelism within the ecumenical movement.
He also referred to the problem of meaning.

> There is a current trend in the ecumenical movement to
> re-emphasize very strongly the importance of evan-
> gelism, but at the same time we realize that the word
> evangelism is overloaded with varying, often contradic-
> tory theological meanings and expectations (WCC
> 1973d).

These meanings and expectations are important aspects of the
problem. The WCC is composed of churches with widely different historical backgrounds. They have differing traditions
and ways of understanding the Church and its mission. These
range all the way from the most conservative Orthodox
churches steeped in tradition and deeply concerned for true
spirituality and separation from the world, to the most activis-
tic mainline denominations of the United States. Independent
African churches, charismatic Pentecostals, and militant, lib-
eration-theology-oriented churches, along with the others, are
combined in the WCC under the one common confession of
Jesus Christ. All this is stated clearly and succinctly in the
constitution:

> The World Council of Churches is a fellowship of
> churches which confess the Lord Jesus Christ as God and
> Saviour according to the Scriptures and therefore seek to

> fulfil together their common calling to the glory of the one
> God, Father, Son and Holy Spirit (Paton 1976:317).

That so many churches with such widely varying history, traditions and interests can co-exist in a single organization is in itself little short of a miracle. The fact of such a council is itself a witness to the uniting power of Jesus Christ who breaks down barriers and is our peace. In the words of the Nairobi theme, Jesus Christ frees and unites.

But, in recognizing this fact, we hardly expect to hear a united voice. The voices that predominate in speeches, literature, in the press and the media are those advocating New Mission. This fact should not however blind us to the truth that not everyone in the WCC, or even in Geneva, feels the same way. Strange paradoxical combinations of churches and views unite on some issues and divide on others. So the problem remains. Let me illustrate.

In Nairobi the Orthodox and the conservative evangelicals not infrequently spoke as one voice in calling for a stronger emphasis upon the spiritual aspects of the Church's true nature. They appeared to be united in seeking a greater recognition of the spiritual and vertical relationships between man and God. They hoped to bring a more balanced perspective into the WCC's understanding of itself. They advocated change in certain activistic-oriented social programs.

At the same time, these Orthodox and evangelicals were poles apart in their outlook on mission and evangelism. The Orthodox have a built-in hesitancy and suspicion when it comes to any suggestion that missionaries be sent to cross frontiers. They fear missionary and evangelistic activity that might result in their people becoming Methodists, Baptists, Presbyterians or Pentecostals. The evangelicals, on the other hand, desire a new missionary outreach by all the churches; the Gospel must be taken to the unreached no matter where they live.

And, while the Orthodox and the evangelicals mistrust one another in this area, the activists within the WCC take another view. To them, any suggestion of aggressive missionary thrust accompanied by high evangelistic components are triumphalistic. Incidentally, if aggressive evangelism is triumphalistic, what about aggressive participation in the struggle against injustice? Why is this regarded as merely joining God in his liberating mission? Obviously, one's views about evangelism are colored by numerous and often subtle conditioning factors rooted in tradition, in theological and ideological assumptions and in varying culturally-determined experiences.

Those within the WCC in Geneva who are concerned for evangelism and the unfinished missionary task need not only encouragement but counsel from individuals and churches within the WCC who are of like mind. Our challenge is to seek every opportunity to communicate our concerns to influence the decisions. The process may be slow. There will frequently be the temptation to give up. Nevertheless, influence may properly come through properly nominated and positioned officers within the system. The WCC can be no better than her member churches make her. We must use the ballot box. We must let our voices be heard in determining where monies are spent. Both are legitimate ways to work from within. But we need to find additional ways to articulate our views.

IN THE CENTRAL COMMITTEE

I found several indications that the Central Committee is taking a new look at evangelism in the light of events at Nairobi. At its first full meeting following Nairobi the WCC Central Committee adopted as its theme for their upcoming (1977) meeting, "Mission and Evangelism." I was told in Geneva that this meeting was being planned to include sharing by members of the Committee from their own personal experience of what they and their churches have been doing in evangelism since their previous meeting.

(It must be said, however, that if by "Evangelism" the Central Committee means "social action," this paragraph would need to be rewritten. I assume that the Committee will shoot square with its churches; that it means the classical "believe on the Lord Jesus Christ and you will be saved" kind of evangelism.)

In that 1976 meeting in Geneva, (the first following Nairobi), the Central Committee approved studies in the field of evangelism with high priority to be given to clarification of how dialogue relates to evangelism in a program called Dialogue with Peoples of Other Faiths. The Committee asked for further information on the Urban and Industrial Mission program preparatory to a careful review and appraisal of this program at the forthcoming 1977 meeting.

Probably the Central Committee's most significant and far-reaching response to the Fifth Assembly's action was its mandating of a new program on Congregational Life. This shows recognition of the assembly's emphasis on congregational life within churches at the local level. Staff was reassigned to this new sub-unit. Although the aims of this new sub-unit do not relate directly to Nairobi's call to evangelism, they do focus on the needs of congregations. If local churches are renewed and living as the true people of Jesus Christ, the result just might be a desire to cross new frontiers in evangelism. At the same time, of course, there is always the danger that renewal efforts do not always end in evangelism.

A good deal has been said about "Renewal in Mission" in recent years. Unfortunately, such renewal generally meant churches being conscientized to participate in efforts to renew society through social action. As far back as 1969, Dr. Potter spoke on the subject: "Towards Renewal in Mission."

> Only as God's People go out boldly into those fields of mission where men are struggling for a truly human life shall churches be renewed. And only as they do this together in joint action shall they receive mutual correction, be enabled to share their varied gifts and begin to manifest the contours of a renewed humanity (Beyerhaus 1969:253).

Such "renewal in mission" is not apt to issue in evangelism as classically defined.

Nonetheless, the Central Committee's action in regard to the controversial and radical program of the Unit on Education and Renewal may prove extremely significant. The official WCC 1975 account of what happened between Uppsala and Nairobi states that conscientization has become central to all WCC programs to bring about greater justice in society.

187

Conscientization poses radical political and ideological questions about education which cannot be neutral with regard to the political and economic systems of a society. From the first consultation held by the Office of Education in Gergen (see "The Record," no. 13), the prophetic challenge of conscientization has been a factor in the WCC's work in education, and indeed the prophetic challenge of this emphasis has *become central** to the work of the Unit of Education and Renewal as well as of the programmes in other Units of the WCC (Johnson 1975:193).

Because many in the churches were deeply troubled by this one-sided emphasis, the Central Committee's action in 1976 appears to be an effort to respond. This is their statement:

> The Review Committee is convinced therefore that the present emphases of the World Council require a modification of the programme thrusts developed in this Unit in the post-Uppsala period (WCC 1976a:103).

A further decision to place the Portfolio for Biblical Studies as a sub-unit under Education gives additional encouragement that this unit will more adequately serve to build up the congregational life within the churches. Many of the concerns expressed in Nairobi stemmed from information contained in the preparatory materials describing the activities of this unit. There was alarm over its radical orientation and its conscientization, its exploiter/exploited and oppressor/oppressed concepts. Concerns that the Marxist views of Paulo Freire exert undue influence, and that a real need exists for growth in the Christian faith within the churches are possibly being met. It remains to be seen whether or not at Geneva the Bible is allowed to speak clearly about eternal salvation through faith in Jesus Christ. But anyone who is aware of the high quality of biblical scholarship and spiritual perception of Hans Rudi Weber—the man in charge of the Biblical Studies Portfolio—

---

*Italics mine

can be deeply appreciative of the Central Committee's action which placed the Bible Studies in this sub-unit.

These are positive evidences of the Central Committee's response to Nairobi's action. And for them we can be most grateful. Granted, it is only a small beginning. But it is a step in the right direction.

Limitations. At the same time, the Central Committee has limitations that need to be recognized and appreciated. Financial restrictions severely limit the Committee's control over WCC programs. Then, too, the financial contributions from member churches and donor agencies are not only grossly inadequate, but the funds received are, for the most part, already designated as to how and where they may be used. Approximately 80 percent of all WCC funds received have been designated by donor churches and agencies*—much of it raised by groups through public appeals. Since these funds come from the larger secular community, they are not available for programs of evangelism. More than 60 percent of the funds received are earmarked for service and justice projects. In a very real sense, staff positions and programs are determined by the realities of these financial limitations.

Potential. But the Central Committee could do a good bit to alter this situation. For one thing, it could stimulate giving for evangelism. Think of the veritable flood of appeals we receive constantly with respect to world hunger and other disaster or development needs. When have we had an appeal from either the WCC or leaders of ecumenically related churches for funds for evangelism that would be remotely comparable?

Third World churches could be encouraged to propose bold and far reaching evangelistic projects for which the WCC would seek financial support among its affluent member churches. If the Central Committee evidenced a "truly heartfelt commitment to evangelism," and if it involved its member churches in programs to demonstrate that profession,

---

*Information given me in March, 1977, by Willem Schott, WCC chief finance officer.

189

the WCC would receive additional millions of funds that would benefit its many worthwhile activities. And the credibility of the WCC would be enhanced in the process. It would be favored and blessed by God; and it would contribute to a better world. What challenge could be more compelling and more exciting?

IN THE COMMISSION
ON WORLD MISSION AND EVANGELISM

I found abundant evidence among CWME people of a deep commitment to evangelism. Probably most indicative is the evangelistic passion of the director of the CWME, Emilio Castro. Friends and colleagues say he is really a pastor and evangelist at heart. I was told of powerful, moving messages he delivered during his pastoral days as he called people in his church to full discipleship and commitment to Jesus Christ. Still, he is deeply and totally committed to the need for Christians to participate in the social struggle.

When I read in the Geneva files his first report as director, I wrote in bold red letters across my copy: TREMENDOUS! It was like a breath of fresh air. I felt I was again in a familiar world. His perspectives were more nearly akin to the biblical-classical understanding of mission I've been writing about. True, his basis seems to reflect other assumptions and has its paradoxes. But the commitment to what is classically understood by missionary and evangelism was abundantly evident. For example, it was refreshing to read, for the first time in years, a call to a new Christian missionary activity in response to the challenge of missionaries from other faiths.

An examination of the director's first report provides us with important clues as to possible future directions of the CWME:

> . . . we must look at the need for a permanent conversation on the subject of evangelism and dialogue.

> There is no such thing as evangelism without a dialogical attitude coming from respect for one's neighbor. And there is no possibility for a Christian to engage in dialogue without bringing with him the good news of the Gospel,

unless he betrays his very being as a Christian and in that way prevents himself from honest participation in a human dialogue.

We recognize that our Commission's cutting edge should be in the evangelistic outreach of the church.

To us the challenge is clear—how can we create in the life of the churches an atmosphere in which evangelism is a normal and permanent dimension?

Recently, twenty-five Asian leaders met in Korea for several days without any Western participation to discuss among themselves the evangelization of Asia. Later they asked for the help of Western missionaries for the spreading of the Gospel in particular regions.

Over the weekend, there will be a joint meeting of the CWME and the CICARWS Executives on the Project List System. We want to be sure that the projects convey a total missionary vision and try to incorporate the local Christian communities into the fulfilment of the Christian mission.

. . . the integration of the IMC into the body of the WCC has been completed. This state of affairs is full of promise in the sense that we are now in a position to influence the churches from inside and to try to carry on our missionary emphasis and our evangelistic commitment not only through CWME programmes but through all the other programmes of the WCC. Of course, this will finally depend on the quality of our work because from the structural point of view we are now one department among many others in the house. . . . We are called to learn the meaning of powerlessness and to trust in the quality of our work for our effectiveness rather than count on any actual constitutional rights that we might have.

As you know, voices in missionary circles have repeatedly said that this integration will mean the death of mission and that the traditional patterns of missionary societies parallel to the church structures should be kept both at the local level and world level. It is now our chance to prove that precisely the contrary is the case: that integration holds the promise of permeating the everyday life of the Church in its manifold expression with a missionary dimension and an evangelistic reality.

. . . to discuss moratorium should *not* mean *fewer* missionary vocations *but more,** and more intelligently used. Ecumenical Sharing of Personnel should not be a way to substitute one group of persons for another, but a way to bring forward into the missionary adventure new life, new visions, new possibilities.

The magnitude of the problems that the missionary enterprise faces today should not restrain our missionary zeal nor our call to young people challenging them to commit themselves with Jesus Christ in the world. For this reason we hope to enlarge our missionary discussion (Castro 1974).

I have quoted at length from that first detailed and wide-ranging report of CWME's new director. I do so to show that his interest in and concern for the unfinished missionary and evangelistic task are clearly not incidental to his understanding of the work of the CWME and of the WCC as a whole. His subsequent reports (both to the CWME and those included in the Geneva files among the minutes and discussions of meetings) all indicate his deep and passionate commitment to evangelism.

A few further examples will help to illustrate. From the 1975 director's report to the CWME, in the context of the discussion about the churches participating in the struggle of the poor, he states:

But the evangelistic question remains. Can we deprive the poor of the earth of the joy of consciously knowing

*Italics mine

Jesus Christ? We know that Jesus is for them, is with them, is one of them. But we know that there is a joy, a new experience of life, a new consciousness of forgiveness and our eternal life when we come to know Jesus Christ in a personal way. How can we struggle for justice with the mass of poor people in the world and withhold from them the right to be the Church of Jesus Christ on earth? (Castro 1975a).

From the director's report, 1976, to the CWME Core Group Meeting:

The Nairobi Assembly wanted to underline the missionary vocation of the ecumenical movement. So, when discussing the Constitution of the World Council of Churches, it decided to preserve one phrase of the former one in order to affirm the importance for the whole WCC of helping the churches in the fulfillment of their worldwide missionary task.

To understand the World Council of Churches as a missionary movement, we should look at the whole programme of the Council and not only to the programme of our Commission. It is our particular responsibility . . . that will keep alive the conscious missionary vocation.

. . . historically, we have seen and still see corporate and individual manifestations of specific vocations: religious orders, missionary societies, lay associations, action groups, etc. A holistic understanding of the mission of the church demands a permanent integration of the Church and mission. The Church cannot delegate its mission to any specialized group unless that group is recognized as an integral part of the Church and is fully supported and responded to by the rest of the community. It seems that there is a permanent process of creation of new voluntary groups for specific missionary action.

We must be aware of the tension between integration and

193

separation and try to keep it as a creative relation. The search for the unity of the Church should incorporate the richness of the diverse manifestations of Christian obedience (Castro 1976).

We found a live interest in the subject of evangelism and the missionary task within the CWME. Much of that interest is currently focused in plans for the CWME sponsored meeting in 1980 where the central theme is evangelism, based on the words "Thy Kingdom Come."

In its various meetings, the CWME has frequently considered the role of mission societies within an integrated view which sees the entire Church in mission. Among other discussion topics were: "mission in six continents," "ecumenical sharing of personnel," "reverse flow," "moratorium," "contextuality," "cultural relevance," and "naming the Name." These may however remain but a profusion of empty words and phrases if social struggles continue to be substituted as concerns in place of evangelism.

The CWME has avoided precise definitions by using the umbrella term, "holistic evangelism." But what does this term mean to the CWME? Does everything have an evangelistic dimension? Are we to think that since everything is seen to be "mission" so now all mission should be seen as "evangelism"? There has been an overemphasis on the non-verbal side of witness—a certain reluctance to insist on a verbal proclamation of the Gospel. Are we no longer certain as to what the Gospel is, and therefore unable to verbalize it? Or is there nothing to say? To what degree have our frantic efforts to renew society even related to evangelism? Was our spiritual poverty only confirmed by this? Why is it so easily affirmed that mission (or authentic evangelism) includes social action, development and struggle for justice, and yet so rarely claimed that social action, etc., should include mission or evangelism?*

It remains to be seen how Geneva will respond to Nairobi. The churches are hopeful and expectant. They want programs that will allocate new funds for evangelism, enabling mis-

*This question was raised by Gerhard Hoffman in a letter to all Core Group Members and Consultants of CWME 1/14/77.

sionaries and evangelists from all the churches on six continents to go out with a new effort to take the Gospel to the unreached peoples of the world. They want that Gospel to be so presented that all who hear may believe the good news from God about Jesus Christ—that those who hear may believe and be saved, and become his disciples and members of his Church. When such programs are fashioned the churches will know that the CWME and the whole WCC does indeed have a "heartfelt commitment to evangelism." This is the kind of evangelism of which the Nairobi delegates were speaking.

I recall a few personal encounters which to me were heartwarming indications of interest in such evangelism there in Geneva.

A staff member whom I had not previously met stopped to share a concern with me. He had received a copy of my questionnaire and feared that somehow his response did not make evident his deep, passionate concern for evangelism. (His work was in the program of Dialogue with special reference to Muslims.)

Later, on my last morning in Geneva, I was finishing reading microfilm and was alone in that tiny room when the door opened quietly. A secretary had walked 100 yards across the courtyard in the rain to tell me how thrilled she was about our work in cassette evangelism. She was from a church in Spain. From her I also learned of a weekly Bible study attended by a group of WCC staff members.

The Assembly at Nairobi underlined the missionary commitment of the ecumenical movement. It happened because this was God's timing. It happened because alert member churches spoke out. But, it happened also because some of the WCC staff at Geneva had like concerns. These mutual and urgent concerns found expression in the following words:

> We need to recover the sense of urgency. Questions about theological definitions there may be. Problems of precise implementation will arise. But neither theoretical nor practical differences must be allowed to dampen the fires of evangelism.
>
> . . . The world requires, and God demands, that we rec-

ognize the urgency to proclaim the saving word of God today. God's acceptable time demands that we respond in all haste. "And how terrible it would be for me if I did not preach the Gospel!" (I Cor. 9:16) (Paton 1976:55).

It would be unthinkable to leave this unfinished missionary task solely to churches outside of the World Council of Churches—as if they alone were commissioned by our Lord to proclaim the Gospel to the ends of the earth. Many WCC member churches have had a long history of missionary sending. And the member churches throughout the Third World are in large measure the result of such missionary labors. The challenge is to join together to continue the unfinished missionary task with new structures and in new relationships. We must move swiftly to insist that the WCC establish whatever programs are needed.

A mood and a climate for evangelism exists in many churches now. And it is gratifying to know there are more than a few in the WCC leadership who are also deeply committed to a stronger emphasis upon evangelism.

TEN
REFLECTIONS AND
RECOMMENDATIONS

The International Missionary Council was preeminently concerned with the unfinished task of carrying the Gospel to the ends of the earth (IMC 1961b:3). When it was integrated into the World Council of Churches, the Commission on World Mission and Evangelism was formed to carry forward, on behalf of the churches and mission agencies, this same vital concern. This was not only intended, but promised.

But this has not been the result. Restructuring greatly impaired the CWME's ability to encourage and assist the churches. And the fate of the CWME (within the WCC) through restructuring paralleled the fate of missions and evangelism at all levels in the life of member churches.

Over the years a common pattern emerged. Initially, the "committed few" organized themselves apart from existing church structures. They enjoyed freedom, flexibility and visibility as they banded together to carry the Gospel to the ends of the earth. Without the pioneering efforts of these "missionary minded" bands within the churches, there would be no missionary movement. In fact, a large proportion of Third World churches within the World Council and the CWME owe their existence to such mission activity.

Yet today these churches born of mission have relegated the mission task to a Cinderella-like insignificance in both life and structure. Mission has become a plant root-bound in the ecclesiastical pots to which it is now confined—denominational and ecumenical structures which frown upon spontaneous action and establishment of direct relationships which they do not initiate or administer (Beaver 1968:203).

MISSIONARY TASK ECLIPSED

The pattern in Western mainline denominations belonging to the WCC is well known. Mission bands, agencies and societies were gradually domesticated and regularized. These semi-independent mission agencies became subordinate to and replaced by denominational boards of foreign and world missions. Gradually their budgets were restricted and then subjected to the limitations of a unified budget. In a restructuring process, the cause of "missions" was assigned to a committee among other committees within a program agency or program council. These councils shaped programs to reflect the concept that the entire Church is Mission. The result was the eclipse of the unfinished worldwide missionary and evangelistic task.

The "committed few" lost freedom, flexibility and visibility. Greatly frustrated, disillusioned and skeptical about their church's interest in "missions," they turned in increasing numbers to participate in and support missionary societies which were involved in worldwide, cross-cultural evangelism. As support for "missions" within the mainline denominations continued to decline, the number of missionaries in these denominations was progressively reduced—in some cases by as much as three fourths to a half.

For all practical purposes, mainline denomination efforts became insignificant in the worldwide efforts to cross frontiers with the Gospel. There was even little concern for those vast unreached multitudes who remain beyond existing evangelistic efforts of churches anywhere in the world.

Meanwhile, at the international level, these mission agencies and/or boards were deprived of their structure which related them to the younger churches in an organization and forum where their missionary and evangelistic task was of mutual concern. Almost immediately after the IMC was integrated into the WCC in 1961, the focus of both the younger churches and the mainline denominations began to shift away from concern for the unfinished task to focus on church-to-church relationships. Efforts increasingly engaged churches in struggles for social justice. The cause of "missions" and "outreach" to those untouched by the Gospel became only one concern among many. And attention was diverted away from the missionary task. The pattern was common at all levels—denominational, national, regional as well as international. Inevitably, even the burning conviction that had so characterized the "committed few" in their vision for worldwide evangelization became less compelling, and even indistinct.

As time went on, persons less committed to the cause of classical mission gained influential positions in the new denominational, national and international structures. These new structures promoted the new understandings about mission in the life of the churches. New priorities and goals were established. At the international level, efforts to establish the pattern of church-to-church relationships worked to the disadvantage of missions and evangelism. What remained of the missionary effort tended to become a gigantic program of inter-church aid (Beaver 1970:9). Remaining missionaries were often little more than ecumenical deacons, and were tolerated only because of the funds they brought with them. In their new church-to-church relationships, the younger churches were bogged down with problems they inherited from the missionaries—the problems of dismantling the mission apparatus and of finding scholarships to educate and train people to operate the ecclesiastical machine. All these concerns took precedence.

Funds provided for evangelism were often redirected to enhance the positions of persons within the system. Not infrequently, church leaders were motivated by ambition for advancement and prestige within the ecclesiastical organization. Church-to-church relations included so many concerns that the subject of evangelism was a low-priority item on an agenda, if it even appeared at all.

Affluent churches made funds available for many good and legitimate causes. But somehow the use of these funds for world evangelization among unreached peoples was not considered, or such use of funds was dismissed as not being in the best interests of new churches if they were to become fully authentic or independent.

With its complex and widely ranging concerns, the WCC and its CWME could manage only marginal interest in the nearly three billion people who had no valid opportunity to know Jesus Christ. Some said it was simply futile to think along these lines (e.g. Philip Potter at Bangkok).

So the question arises: is it even possible for the CWME to yet be the structure through which such concerns are made central to the life of the members? Are existing structures capable of being revamped to care for that task? Or should those concerned for world evangelization create new structures within their churches in order to be effectively involved?

Alternately, their frustration and disillusionment will only lead them outside of their own churches as they seek to find opportunity to take part in and to make real their obedience to Christ.

No questions are fraught with greater consequences for the churches concerned—and for the unreached millions who wait to hear the Gospel. The crucial challenge for the WCC and its member churches is to find ways within their system by which their people can share in this unfinished task of cross-cultural evangelism. God's purpose to bring the nations to faith and obedience (Rom 16:25) will not fail. The question is whether or not the WCC and its member churches can be God's instruments. Churches that fail to be concerned with the unfinished missionary and evangelistic task become little more than religious clubs or political and social action groups. Such churches soon dwindle and shrivel.

At Nairobi, concerned member churches spoke to their organization, the WCC. They asked the WCC to support them in their obedience to the evangelistic task. But they need support from every level: from the Central Committee, the Geneva Staff and from leaders within the churches.

Do our leaders have the theological convictions, the spiritual depth of relationship to Christ and imaginative obedience necessary to help us get on with the unfinished task? Do our leaders have the will to make it so?

Even if they do, this new effort will need concerned and

informed people in the churches who continue to speak out and act. Results do not come automatically or spontaneously. We need facts and we need to be realistic. Actions at Geneva and actions in member churches intersect at various levels. Courageous men and women must hold firm and not allow the cause of world evangelization to be dismissed by either the WCC or its member churches. We must not abandon lightly this one ecumenical organization and structure which brings Third World churches and ecumenically related churches from the rest of the world together. Third World churches in particular need the encouragement and support of people from within the WCC member churches who are committed to classical mission. Such support will not only help the evangelization task itself, but will also help prevent diversion to other tasks.

FACTORS TO CONSIDER

What can WCC member churches do? May structures be reshaped? Or must new ones be created? Consideration of these questions must take into account at least these four minimal factors:

1) God's intention for world evangelization is based on his self-disclosure found in Scripture.
2) Unreached multitudes remain beyond the evangelistic and missionary efforts of churches anywhere.
3) Historically, the missionary movement was carried forward largely by a "committed few" within the churches. Churches, as such, have had a notoriously bad record in terms of their commitment to worldwide evangelization. So much so that the question must be faced: can churches be trusted to carry out programs of worldwide evangelization? (Perhaps Christians within WCC member churches—those who feel deeply about this unfinished missionary and evangelistic task—must continue to create and rely upon para-church structures to assure their participation in missionary efforts among the unreached.
4) Existing WCC programs are grossly inadequate. Current programs focus primarily on social action. And those pre-

sumed to carry out tasks formerly belonging to the missionary movement do not, in fact, include efforts to evangelize unreached peoples.

RECOMMENDATIONS

What then is needed? How can the focus be realigned so that those without the opportunities may be reached? I will list seven areas that need attention. These are not exhaustive, but may bring to mind others.

1) New or revamped structures are needed at every level of church life if cross-cultural evangelism is to be effective.
2) A new missionary movement is required. Missionaries from the West need to be joined increasingly by missionaries from Third World churches in efforts to evangelize those peoples remaining on six continents without knowledge of the Gospel of Christ. "Inter-church aid" in terms of personnel and funds can and should play a key role here.
3) Projects for evangelism should have just as legitimate a claim upon the financial resources of the churches as do those for service and justice.
4) Third World churches in particular should be encouraged to plan evangelistic efforts and projects with the assurance that such projects may be commended to donor churches and organizations of affluent Western churches through the CWME. (At present, the projects sponsored by the WCC are limited almost entirely to areas of service, justice and development.)
5) Donors who wish to emphasize evangelism through the WCC should specifically designate these funds for the evangelization of those yet unreached. The WCC could show its commitment to evangelism and the missionary task by publicizing widely that at least 50 percent of all undesignated gifts received will be used for world evangelization.
6) Let the WCC urge its member churches to designate funds to support evangelistic efforts among peoples previously unreached. At every level, existing programs or

new programs should focus on various aspects of the un-finished task.

How can this happen? Able advocates plus a majority vote within the system is all that is required. God uses both.

7) Appropriate ways must be found to channel the financial resources of affluent churches into projects for new evangelism in ways that do not impede efforts of receiving churches to be truly independent under God and fully authentic.

There are four options available to WCC member churches vis-à-vis the unfinished worldwide missionary and evangelistic task: a) Content themselves to be of non-significance in this task. b) Participate through non-WCC structures. c) Insist on refocusing existing WCC programs (and programs at all levels within the churches). d) Create the new programs and structures required to enable them to participate with significance in this unfinished missionary and evangelistic task.

We do not have the option of keeping the good news to ourselves. The uncommunicated Gospel is a patent contradiction. We are called to preach Christ crucified, the power of God and the wisdom of God (1 Cor. 1:23,24).

Confessing Christ must be done *today*. "Behold, now is the acceptable time; behold, now is the day of salvation" (2 Cor. 6:2). It cannot wait for a time that is comfortable to us. We must be prepared to proclaim the Gospel when human beings need to hear it. . . . The world requires, and God demands, that we recognize the urgency to proclaim the saving word of God-today. God's acceptable time demands that we respond in all haste. "And how terrible it would be for me if I did not preach the Gospel!" (1 Cor. 9:16) (Paton 1976:55).

Appendix A
Preparatory Materials
Fifth Assembly

Preparatory materials were provided for the delegates prior to the Fifth Assembly held in Nairobi, 1975. The following extracts are taken from the Dossiers (six Sections) on the theme, "Jesus Christ Frees and Unites."

SECTION I, "Confessing Christ Today"

Questions: As we face a polarization between Christians who emphasize faithfulness to an everlasting deposit of revealed truth, and others who see faithfulness to Christ expressed in meeting the needs of today's world how do we relate doctrine and experience? How do we relate the basic historical apostolic witness to Christ to the ongoing apostolate of the Church?

To confess Christ is to confess the heart of the Gospel; to affirm the total Scriptural revelation of God. It is to acknowledge that through our experience of history, we, together with our forefathers in the faith, have come to recognize God as the Almighty and Everlasting moment in history; as the Holy Spirit, the Advocate ever present in the life of every believer. It is to assert the totality of Christ's nature; to accept fully the paradox of both His divinity and His humanity, and His consequent concern for nothing less than the total life of the world, both physical and spiritual (Introduction).

APPENDIX

The WCC staff group which had the task of preparing this dossier also offers a kind of theological statement about "confessing Christ today." This should not be regarded as a "WCC doctrine"; we were merely trying to "rationalize" faithfully the experiences of "confessing Christ today" which were available to this particular staff group—slightly edited by the Assembly preparatory group of the WCC Central Committee (WCC Dossier 1975:4).

They went on beating me, but I learned to pray while the screams issued mechanically from my ill-used body wordless prayers to a universe that could be a person, a being, a multitude or something utterly strange, who could say? We say "Thou" to it, as though to a man or animal, but this is because of our own imperfection: we may no less say "Thou" to the universe and hear its voiceless answer in our hearts as though it were a person and had heard us. But it is He who prays with us and answers the prayer which is His gift. *Salvation Today and Contemporary Experience* (WCC 19751:28/29).

The American problem is not so simple that it can be attributed to a few—or even many—evil men in high places, any more than it can be blamed on long-haired youth or on a handfull of black revolutionaries. Besides, our men in high places are not exceptionally immoral; they are, on the contrary, quite ordinarily moral. In truth, the conspicuous moral fact about our generals, our industrialists, our scientists, our commercial and political leaders is that they are the most obvious and pathetic prisoners in American society. There is unleashed among the principalities in this society a ruthless, self-proliferating, all-consuming institutional process which assaults, dispirits, defeats, and destroys human life even among, and *primarily* among those persons in positions of institutional leadership. They are left with titles but without effectual authority; with the trappings of power, but without control over the institutions they head; in nominal command, but bereft of dominion. These same principalities, as has been mentioned, threaten and defy and enslave human beings of other status in diverse ways, but

206

the most poignant victim of the demonic in America is the so-called leader.

It is not surprising, thus, to find—in addition to the ranks of those whose conformity to and idolatry of the principalities means that they are automatons or puppets—some persons, reputed leaders attended by the trappings of high office, who are enthralled by their own enslavement and consider themselves rewarded for it, and who conceive of their own dehumanization as justification or moral superiority (Stringfellow 1973:87–89).

The moment the "agents of salvation" are even equivocally on the side of the oppressor, the Christian message is distorted and Christian message is in jeopardy. This happens when those who are seen as being in a position of power, economic, political or spiritual, attempt to preach the Gospel. The converts are then enticed to embrace a religion which not only alienates them from the deepest aspirations of their cultures but also presents them with a Christ whom they identify with those who have power over them. This is evil. We are greatly concerned that in the unliberated areas of Southern Africa churches and missions still think of fully fulfilling their mission out of a position of power and privilege. In order to identify ourselves with the oppressed who resist this annihilating power, we believe that concrete action is required (Bangkok Report 1973:72–75).

On The Theology of the Signs of the Times
The Church is not to decide for itself—"independently" of God—what it must do at any given moment of history. Rather, it is the task of the Church to find out what God is doing in the world and to lend all its mind and all its will and all its effort to second the movement of God's doing. One privileged way the Church can find out what its task is then in this given moment of history is to listen attentively to the aspirations of men. Within the voice of the aspirations of men the Church can discern the voice of God. But if the Church refuses to make the effort at keeping its ear close to the hearts of men, then it is failing its essential duty.

To reiterate: the theology of the signs of the times has an anthropological dimension in the great aspirations of men, as indicators of the purpose of history.

The first task is to listen to the aspirations of men, to listen to what men are longing for so that it may hear where God is calling it.

. . . it is a theology that leads immediately to action.

[This theology] cannot accept the findings of fifty years ago simply as findings which can be applied today. Every day it must renew its hermeneutic in prayer, in contemplation, in dialogue so that it can constantly move forward where God Himself is moving among men (Arevalo 1972:51-60).

SECTION II, "What Unity Requires"

Ever since the Fourth Assembly of the World Council of Churches in Uppsala, attention has been directed to the "unity of mankind."

Many are of the opinion that a more just order can only be established by the struggle against the power of injustice and oppression. It is significant that in the beginnings of Marxism the slogan, "All men are brothers" was replaced by the call "Workers of the world, unite." Behind this change stands the conviction that the unity of mankind can only be achieved by class struggle. Unity is not the object of a development to be awaited, but the goal of a struggle that has to be led consciously (Faith and Order Commission, "Unity of the Church," 1973).

Traditional language continues to be used with little change but with widely divergent meanings. It can no longer be assumed that such words as "atonement," "redemption" and "reconciliation" are being employed in their primary and familiar Biblical meaning. To one Christian "reconciliation" is a precious word, full of deepest spiritual meaning assuring the believer that he is at peace with God, that the estrangement of sin has been ended through the work of Christ, and that he is received into full fellowship with the Heavenly Father. As used by another, the word has little of such content and refers mainly to human relations, the breaking down of those barriers of class, nationality, culture, language and race that separate men and engender misunderstandings between them. . . . Is the Bible the authentic and infallible Word of God, or is it a mixture of wisdom and error from which the truth must be separated by careful rational examinations? Is the essence of the Gospel soteriology or sociology? . . . In all these, the differences are overwhelming.

The real "scandal" is not in the plurality of churches. Rather, it is in the disaffections in faith and doctrine that have made divisions inevitable (Fulton, *Christianity Today,* Nov. 5, 1965).

There is no possibility of being "Church"—or of being anything, for that matter—in today's world without making an option concerning the struggle for a post-capitalist, post-neocolonial society. It is only natural that a discussion of unity which refuses to face this fact can excite no interest and inspire no lasting determination (WCC *What Kind of Unity* (1974:52ff.).

The innumerable ecumenical studies of the last twenty years have shown only too clearly that contemporary churches usually more or less mirror the values, assumptions, world-views and prejudices of the societies, cultures and ethnic groups within which they exist, with their only "distinctive" marks the historical inheritance of theologies, traditions, buildings and resources from their particular denominational/national histories. They are not free. They are not themselves "liberated." And the salutary acts of Christian Aid and the Programme to Combat Racism only serve to repeat the deception that middle-class institutions can proclaim freedom by generous external acts rather than by radical internal conversions (Vincent 1974:SE55).

SECTION III, "Seeking Community: the Common Search of People of Various Faiths, Cultures, and Ideologies"

Any exploration of the religions is an exploration into Christ. When grace visits a Brahmin, a Buddhist or a

Muslim reading his scriptures it is Christ alone who is received as light. Whoever dies as a martyr for truth or is persecuted for what he believes to be right is in community with Christ (Kodr 1971:105).

I am a North American Indian and a victim of Christian missionary schools. . . . Missionaries. Christians. Anthropologists. White people. Listen. If you would know the rage that is in me, surely you would wither like the summer grass, from the force of it.

There is no doubt that missionary work is the *raison d'etre* of the Church, yet from my place I find that to be ugly and directly against Jesus' teachings. As long as the Church sees as its duty propagation instead of liberation it cannot be more than another self-aggrandizing corporation.

You use discussion to drown out prophetic voices and to avoid prophetic action. Now I give you a prophecy: soon there will come Indians from the wilderness, like John the Baptist, and say, "You viper's blood! Who warned you?"

Missionaries, listen. You should go home, or you should help us fight. We do not live for your curiosity or your exploitation. We are suffering not to entertain you or to give you an opportunity to get glory in your heaven or to preach your religion.

You are those whom Jesus spoke of as people who do things in His name but know Him not. I ask that you think on what I say until the sun rises (Durham, in *International Review of Mission* 1973:487ff).

On the one hand I might say paradoxically that I think China is the only truly Christian country in the world in the present day, in spite of its absolute rejection of all religion.

. . . the Chinese, because of this freedom from supernatural sanctions, have an enormous amount to teach the rest of the world. If you go there today, you can really see the ethical character of their civilization.

My ideal is a practical socialism, and in the end, communism, if you like, but nevertheless not one which is basically atheistic and agnostic, and one which at any rate allows for the practice of liturgical worship in the temple (Needham in *Anticipation* 1973).

In Asia and Africa the traditional style mission is increasingly felt to be paternalistic and a by-product of colonialism. This is why the younger churches in these continents turn to dialogue (Berlin Ecumenical Institute, Report of working party 1973).

Thus today I do not quite know how Scripture is to be understood, and its capacity for my nourishment appears subverted.

Erosion of confidence in both systematics and Scripture, two major foundations of the Christian Church in which many of us were formed, seems to me to have led to nearly total breakdown of consensus over the meaning of the word "God" and over the nature of mission of "God's" Church (Institutes of Religion and Health 1973).

For us, to be "drunk with the message of Christ's liberating power" means staying very close to the people and living the risen Christ with the men of the people so as to put an end to their different faces. If we are to be a sign of liberation, then private ownership has to be brought to an end so that the land and the factories can belong to those who work them (from *Letter from Taize* Oct. 1973).

SECTION IV, "Education for Liberation and Community"

At the Fifth Assembly members of Section IV must concentrate on certain questions in order to discover lines of action for the future. For groups working with this topic a first step must be careful investigation of the meaning of "education," "liberation," and "community" in their particular language, culture and political situation.

We need to build awareness about what oppresses people through these processes of socialization, identify the forces behind the oppression, and then act to liberate ourselves and others.

This topic offers an opportunity for Christians and

others to pinpoint the various styles and results of socialization in their own societies, to search for ways to change harmful conditioning practices and the structures that support them, and to experiment with and develop styles of relationships and community that can better equip us to become liberating agents of the Church and society (WCC, Notes for Sections 1974).

The elitist, meritorcratic system of education inherited from the colonial era serves these purposes very well. Education, rather than being regarded as a process of development and liberation for the individual and society, is seen as a scheme of training whereby the student is manipulated into a product suited to the demands of a technocratic, capitalistic society. The student is discouraged from any basic questioning of structures and institutions of society (Chong-Carino).

We are becoming incapable of imagining any other course than the feverish pursuit of Western productivity, constant increases in profits, and a rapid growth in consumption. Here we come upon a *second* symptom of a profound *alienation* and *loss of freedom* in the Western world. Is this state of unfreedom an inalternable fate? We believe not. It is tied up with the principles and contradictions of a capitalistic economic system (Study Encounter 1974:SE59).

We discover that all those new developments we have learned and are learning to see as *gains* were *imposed on us*—and did *not* arise from our Bible reading or from our theological reflection. They were initiated (often in spite of our strong resistance) by non-Christians, Marxists, who seem to be today the more genuine interpreters of a tradition, which we used to recognize as our exclusive Christian private property (Skladny 1973:64–65).

This analysis clearly revealed the socio-political and religious implications of the class struggle.

We have to make clear that the struggle for liberation is already a reality in our world. It is not a privilege of the Church to begin thinking about this. Christians themselves should not initiate efforts for liberation; it is much better to become involved in liberation projects that are already going on. In their involvement, Christians will discover that in most cases the Marxist analysis has been chosen as an instrument to work out ways of confronting concrete situations (from working papers for Education and Theology in the Context of the Struggle for Liberation 1973).

Our concern for humanity throughout the world demands that justice be realized in the development of people and nations. And justice in turn demands a major redistribution of economic resources and decision-making power throughout the globe today (from "Some Reflections on Canada's Relationship with the Third World").

The educational system introduced into China during the years of China's encounter with the West was on the Anglo-American model. . . . As props of both the Kuomintang and the imperialists, this class was part of the concomitant denigration and humiliation of the Chinese in their own cities, and of that system of excessive exploitation whose roots ran deep into the countryside and whose impact was felt by virtually every peasant. . . . Mao understands the difference between "schooling" and "learning." Schooling, regardless of its many permutations around the world is functionally a system of privilege. . . . China's experiment in education has helped to bring home the lesson that the ordinary, common peasant is capable of both learning and teaching, if only education can be charged with cultural and political meaning. The fundamental aim of education has been to provide people with a political language and a revolutionary consciousness thus preparing them for a permanent personal and cultural revolution.

In the Third World, educational reforms have been directed to the same ends of structural change and technological progress. Here, education has been considered mainly an administrative problem and therefore educationalists have concentrated their energies on providing better administration while leaving essentially intact the colonial educational systems implanted by their former imperial masters (Barkat and Jones article to be published in 1974).

SECTION V
"Structures of Injustice and Struggles for Liberation"

As a partisan of the poor, the Church is called to clearer thinking and more courageous action in solidarity with those who struggle to change unjust and oppressive structures.

Successive World Council Assemblies have all confirmed the churches' prophetic role in understanding the will of God for all men.

In response to these situations, churches have become less statement-minded, more action-oriented, less individualistic, more focused on combating structural and institutional injustice.

Are the churches moving to liberate themselves from their captivity to the prevailing power structures?

The extent to which the decision-making bodies of the churches are themselves structures of injustice, as symbolized by the largely marginal position of the majority of church members: women, laity and youth.

What glimpses can be discerned of the more just social order towards which God calls His people? How significant are ideological perspectives in giving shape to the Church's social engagement?

The continuing debate about strategies and forms of action appropriate to churches and individual Christians, as they seek to become more fully engaged in the world's struggles for justice and peace.

What recommendations for action can be offered to church groups, congregations, member churches and the Council of Churches so that each may assist the liberation struggles going on in many parts of the world? (notes for Sections, WCC).

What we have tried to do is to gather together theological reflections related to the concern for social justice and the struggle for liberation. Many of the writers are deeply involved in particular struggles and their comments relate principally to these. Others are seeking to formulate guidelines for Christian churches in relation to structures of injustice and to the complexity of political and economic life. Different stands are taken, and different strategies advocated. All alike would affirm that the concern for justice and for liberation of the oppressed is central to the Gospel (introductory remarks).

It is emphasized as well that the task of sensitization and conscientization cannot be reduced to verbal teachings or to the written press, but that it acquires particular significance through concrete actions and decisions (e.g., the Program to Combat Racism).

In this same line, the need to intensify the conscientization of churches who financially support projects and programs in our continent is also affirmed. . . .

In other words, in the effort to sensitize and conscienticize the Christian community divisions are created when, upon perceiving the socio-politico-economic implications of the Gospel, some accept to serve it at any price and others resist doing so because in the depth of their beings they want only to be served by it (from report of a consultation on Human Rights and the Churches in Latin America 1973).

It is vital, therefore, that the widespread concern about violence and nonviolence should not obscure but rather highlight the larger challenge to which the ecumenical movement in recent years has given increasingly clear expression. This is the challenge to all Christians to become wiser and more courageous in translating their commitment to Jesus Christ into specific social and political engagement for social justice; and in this sphere to find their place as servants of the servant Lord with people of other beliefs concerned with human freedom and fulfillment (from "Violence, Nonviolence and the Struggle for Social Justice" 1973).

As a result of this analysis we conclude that the suspension of all missionary activity is the most appropriate policy for the good of Indian society and for the moral integrity of the churches involved.

. . . the denunciation of the historical failure of the missionary task is now a common conclusion of such critical analyses (*International Review of Mission* 1971).

SECTION VI, "Human Development: the Ambiguities of Power, Technology and Quality of Life"

Rapid economic growth for many of the poorer developing countries has become a deception and there is little real hope for the future.

. . . the gap between the rich and the poor within countries is widening day by day.

What can the churches do to promote new international structures of economic and political cooperation for global justice?

The lack of a clear distinction between what is needed and what is superfluous has resulted in consumerism, one of the diseases of affluent societies. What elements of modern economic life contribute to this acquisitive greed and what might the churches do to define a life style which would help societies and individuals control their appetites for goods? How can this be combined in a positive way with the concern to reduce the consumption of the rich countries in the interests of world justice? How can the churches educate Christians to see this as their fundamental task in developing solidarity consciousness (Notes for Sections).

In the interim our economies will continue to receive the familiar contaminated technology. According to one line of thinking in developing countries the establishment of branches and auxiliaries in the Third World by some big Western concerns is a way of shifting pollution from their countries to ours, at the same time exploiting the cheaper inputs of men and material available in developing countries. No amount of optimism can remove our misgivings about technology. . . (Parmar 1974:44–45,47).

The promotion of the various Asian quests for self-identity is the Church's task.

Imperialism is understood as a disproportionate influence by one nation or group of nations upon the

216

economic, social, cultural, or political processes of another people (*Theology in Action* 1973).

Can the ambiguities be transcended? The pedagogy of the oppressed, as a humanist and libertarian pedagogy, has two distinct stages. In the first, the oppressed unveil the world of oppression and through the praxis commit themselves to its transformation. In the second stage, in which the reality of oppression has already been transformed, this pedagogy ceases to belong to the oppressed and becomes a pedagogy of all men in the process of permanent liberation. . . . It is therefore essential that the oppressed wage the struggle to resolve the contradiction in which they are caught and the contradiction will be resolved by the appearance of the new man; neither oppressor nor oppressed, but in the process of liberation. . . . Resolution of the oppressor oppressed contradiction indeed implies the disappearance of the oppressors as the dominant class (Freire 1970:40,42).

It is morally imperative that the industrialized countries stand ready to share in the advancement of indigenous solutions as requested, and to minimize their technological frivolity and overproduction resulting from Western consumer attitudes. Besides being a pragmatic response to a real situation, such an attitude of technological restraint reflects the basic Christian attitude of the stewardship of material creation (WCC Consultation in Cardiff, Wales 1972).

. . . that humane decisions require expert scientific knowledge, but that scientific knowledge does not itself constitute moral wisdom or sensitivity to human values (from "Genetics and the Quality of Life" 1974:SE/53 pp. 5-6).

Appendix B
The Work Book,
Fifth Assembly

The *Work Book* dealt with the nuts and bolts of the Fifth Assembly. It explained how the Assembly would operate and where the delegates plugged in. It presented the agenda and the WCC staff point of view. It is an important, unsophisticated piece of material. The following excerpts add unmistakably to the evidence that the WCC executive officers and staff believe the primary task of the churches in mission is to work by all means to replace the existing, unjust structures of society by a new socio-economic-political order in which people may live in the dignity of their humanity—and the WCC programs have been evaluated on the basis of their contribution to realizing this new understanding of mission.

Section I, "Confessing Christ Today"

The foundation of the ecumenical movement is the common confession of Jesus Christ:

The World Council of Churches is a fellowship of churches which confess the Lord Jesus Christ as God and Saviour according to the Scriptures and therefore seek to fulfill together their common calling to the glory of the one God, Father, Son and Holy Spirit (WCC 1975j:15).

Today, as in every age, the Church is caught up in the joyful, dynamizing confession "that Jesus Christ is Lord,

219

to the glory of God the Father" (Phil. 2:11). But how can Christians bear more faithful witness to His liberating, reconciling power in this shackled, divided world? This section's task is to help the Church make confession of its Lord, not only through worship and teaching but in every dimension of human life (*ibid*:16).

Further, we must look at certain situations of oppression, discrimination, injustice and human suffering where Christians, tired of void pious words, hardly confess Christ verbally at all, but are deeply committed to human liberation in the name of Christ (*ibid*:16).

. . . the search for cultural identity in our divided world implies a struggle against political, economic and cultural imperialism. When Christians question the legitimacy of Western power structures, they also question images of Christ influenced or determined by Western culture. Christians living under political or economic oppression will question the spiritualized and a-political image of Christ that seems to sanctify the *status quo* (*ibid*:19).

Which Christ do we really confess? The question requires that we reflect on the power structures and vested interests which distort and obscure the image of Christ in today's world. Prophetic criticism of corrupting structures and false loyalties must certainly include self-critical sensitivity, as individuals and as churches, to our own involvement in oppressive and dehumanizing structures (*ibid*:20).

We also need to listen to what other people of other faiths say about Jesus Christ, whether with approval or in disagreement. For we cannot exclude possibilities of God speaking to Christians from outside the Church. We need therefore to discuss whether our quest for one Christ must take place within a much wider context (*ibid*:20).

For many Christians in very diverse situations, confessing Christ amounts almost to the same thing as involvement in struggles for justice and freedom (*ibid*:21).

In this way, confessing Christ is liberated from mere verbalism which renders the life and ministry of the Church stagnant, introverted and contentious (*ibid*:22).

What is the relation between "Christian action" and "signs of the Kingdom"? Should we strive to create signs, or should human action "follow" divine signs? If the latter is true, how do we recognize and discern the signs of the times? (*ibid*:23).

Section II, "What Unity Requires"

The task of the Section, within the total work of the Assembly is to reflect afresh on the nature of the "unity we seek"; and on the responsibility of the churches to "manifest visible unity among all Christians" (*ibid*:23).

The importance and relevance of the quest for visible unity is being called into question today (*ibid*:25).

The question is being asked: Does the search for unity really contribute to the renewal and the mission of the Church? The Church is called to be a sign of God's presence in the world; sign of the redemption accomplished in Jesus Christ; sign of the world God will finally bring into being. What is the relevance of visible unity in the context of this calling? . . . (*ibid*:26)

Many hold the conviction that the primary obligation of the churches is the common struggle for social justice. Unity is to be realized around the common commitment to this task. The quest for visible unity detracts attention from this primary task and contributes to maintaining the *status quo* (*ibid*:26).

Christians have a vocation to be the fellowship of reconciliation. But Christians involved in the struggle for liberation in fact often find themselves closer to others who share the struggle with them, Christian or not, than to other Christians who are not committed to it (*ibid*:27).

The struggle for unity among the churches in Asia, Africa, and Latin America is also intimately connected with the painful attempts of many of these churches to free themselves from what they regard as the bondage of superimposed Western patterns of theological thinking and method (*ibid*:28).

Section III, "Seeking Community: the Common Search of People of Various Faiths, Cultures and Ideologies"

Men and women everywhere are coming to recognize common human aspirations and responsibilities in the search for justice, peace and a hopeful future (*ibid*:32).

Should it not be said that Jesus Christ unites those who believe in Him and frees them to break the bonds of cultural isolation and so to recognize their solidarity with all human beings? (*ibid*:33).

Does Jesus Christ want the Church to remain a group of believers called away from the wide human community just to be in communion with each other, or does He rather want the Church to be a group of disciples seeking community with their neighbors in order to serve humanity and promote its unity and so carry out the original purpose of God the creator of all? (*ibid*:34).

Christians believe that Jesus Christ has assumed humanity on behalf of all people of all ages and cultures and answers the basic human need for community (*ibid*:34).

The Church is a provisional sign of the eschatological community. Her understanding of its fullness is tentative, her forms to express this in history are preliminary. Sharing her vision of the eschatological reality in joy with neighbors of other faiths and ideologies, Christians are committed to break down walls of separation and to work for reconciliation, trust and love (*ibid*:35).

(With respect to making a critical evaluation of dialogue efforts) One way of raising a basic question would be to ask how Christians can discern the work of Jesus Christ not just within the structure of Christianity, but in the context of faiths, cultures and ideologies, not just within the Christian community but in the larger community of people of other faiths and convictions with whom Christians share a common human life and destiny (*ibid*:37).

It would be helpful therefore to discover what if any are the ideological elements in ecumenical thinking today and how these are understood in relation to the ultimate demands of the Gospel (*ibid*:39).

What are the ways in which Christians can cooperate

with people of other faiths and certain ideologies committed to the same struggle for justice without transforming the Christian faith itself into an ideology?
(*ibid*:39).

Section IV, "Education for Liberation and Community"

Section IV has the double task of *analysing* issues in the
area of education which the Church needs to confront
during the next several years, and proposing future directions for the work of the churches in this field
(*ibid*:40).

This agenda presupposes Christian faith in the God
who is creating, judging, redeeming and sustaining His
world. Theological undergirding for this Section must develop from a very close relation to the Assembly theme,
the Bible studies, the work of other Sections, the Assembly's prayers and worship, and the input of Christians
who bring to the discussions their reflection upon their
Christian experience in many situations (*ibid*:40).

To educate is not so much to teach as it is to become
committed to a reality in and with the people, it is to learn
to live, to encourage creativity in ourselves and others;
and under God and His power, to liberate mankind from
the bonds that prevent the development of God's image
(Final Assembly of the World Council of Christian Education, Lima, 1971 (*ibid*:40).

The threats to human survival now looming call for
changes in the world far beyond minor reforms in present
systems. Those who are committed to work for such
changes often come from the "educated" groups, but
they have to work against their fellow alumni for those
changes. This agenda reflects the view that education,
though important, is dependent upon and serves the more
powerful economic, political and social structures of
society. Major changes in education cannot occur therefore until there are similar changes in the context of society (*ibid*:41).

"Know your place," these structures say to people.
All structures tend to perpetuate the system they serve

and thus maintain the *status quo*. They tend to give people only those opportunities for development that will maintain the system. If a system is oppressive, its structures will perpetuate various forms of social injustice by conditioning people to accept them. The structures of a society usually serve its *elite,* controlling the system on their behalf rather than for the good of the people (*ibid*:42).

Many churches have agencies which study social issues, but still too few recognize that the best strategy to overcome social injustice is to enable the oppressed to gain consciousness of their plight to do something to change it (*ibid*:43).

Today, church-sponsored schools, institutions and colleges are under fire: often they serve an elite of rich people who pay. They are diploma-oriented, and they do not provide the community with the kind of people needed for its full development (*ibid*:46).

Hence a wider concept of ministry calls for radical rethinking of Church education. Education for mission today calls for "theological education of the whole people of God" (*ibid*:47).

But above all else: if the Church's members are to grow towards the maturity of being God's co-partners in creation, they can be adequately fitted for their task only by engaging in mission (*ibid*:47).

But "the fight is the best teacher": learning rather than teaching must be the central focus of education, and concrete action the core of the curriculum. . . . as they work together to transform their world and themselves (*ibid*:49).

Churches can learn much about how to educate for liberation and community from people's movements all over the world (*ibid*:50).

Section V, "Structures of Injustice and Struggles for Liberation"

. . . Uppsala Assembly was a turning point in helping the churches move from affirmation to action in combating structures of injustice and in support of struggles for liberation. The message of the assembly stated: "Especially we shall seek to overcome racism wherever it appears. We Christians want to ensure human rights in a just world community" (*ibid*:50–51).

This commitment was translated into ecumenical action-oriented programs by the WCC in the fields of racial and social justice, economic development and human rights. The ecumenical movement's participation in the liberation struggle began to take more concrete forms.

Since 1968 several historic changes have taken place which need to be analysed by this Section. Some of these are:

a) dramatic progress in the struggle for liberation in Guinea Bissao, Mozambique and Angola and its bearing upon liberation of Zimbabwe, Namibia, South Africa and Portugal itself;

b) attempts by economically underdeveloped nations to secure control of their natural resources, as part of the struggle against exploitation by the dominating powers;

c) the growing movement for women's liberation;

d) the epidemic growth of human rights violations (including torture and political repression);

e) the upsurge of youth and students searching for education, employment and political and cultural rights (*ibid*:51).

The task of this Section is, first of all, to examine present patterns of domination (especially economic exploitation) as they are revealed in various struggles for liberation (*ibid*:51).

The following issues are highlighted because they appear to be of particular concern at this time to many churches:

—the struggle for human rights;

—the struggle of women;

—the struggle against racism (*ibid*:52).

This Section may wish to discuss other examples that it feels are equally pressing for the churches (for example, injustice in "traditional societies," the international armaments trade, and so on). The examination should include an account of the churches' past and present involvement in both the patterns of domination and the struggles for liberation. Perhaps it can identify particular churches or related groups, which are engaged in these struggles in specific ways (*ibid*:52).

The ecumenical movement from its early years has maintained that the Biblical view of love must be translated into a vital concern for justice; and this means an obligation to work for "the best possible social structures for the ordering of human life" (Oxford Conference 1973). This in turn makes political action inescapable (*ibid*:52).

... the churches have only started to examine questions of racism in theology and how theology can make its contribution to combat racism (*ibid*:52).

Christians have discovered that in the struggle for human liberation the problem of power cannot be avoided. The structures of injustice are maintained through dominating power(s). The struggles for liberation are struggles against such power but at the same time struggles for the sake of acquiring power—liberating power. This Section must therefore seek to clarify the Christian understanding of power in relation to oppression and liberation. What is the Church's responsibility to the oppressed in their struggle to gain power—and its message to those who hold power and are endeavoring to retain it? What is *legitimate* power in the Christian view? How can the negative effects of power be controlled?

A vision of a liberated world community? Many ecumenical statements have maintained that the essential element in the various struggles for liberation is the search for new liberating structures of society, a society in which "all the people participate in the fruits and the decision-making process, in which the centres of power are limited and accountable, in which human rights are truly affirmed for all, and which acts responsibly toward the whole human community and toward coming generations" (*ibid*:52).

The Fourth Assembly (1968) reviewed WCC involvement in the field of human rights since 1948 and called for a reassessment of the ecumenical approach based on contemporary socio-political realities. Since then, considerable re-thinking has gone on in the churches, and this found expression in the consultation on "Human Rights and Christian Responsibility" held in October at St. Polten, Austria. *The Consultation called for a shift* [emphasis by the author].

—away from a partial approach where protection of any specific right can be considered in isolation, to an understanding of the inter-related and inter-dependent character of social, economic, cultural, civil political and religious rights;

—away from excessive preoccupation with violations of human rights as symptoms of deeper social ills, to action to remove their root causes;

—away from an individualistic approach to more socially or community oriented strategies capable of confronting massive violations (*ibid*:54).

In what ways do transnational corporations erode these rights? . . . Groups and individuals are excluded from the decision-making processes in our societies—and in our churches. How is the peoples' participation blocked? (*ibid*:55).

Racism is linked with economic and political exploitation. The churches must be actively concerned for the economic and political wellbeing of exploited groups so that their statements and actions may be relevant. . . . they should also withdraw investments from institutions that perpetuate racism (*ibid*:60).

Racism has shown itself to be a tool of economic, political and military power structures which use it in their own interests and to obstruct the liberation process of racially oppressed peoples. For this reason, the WCC Central Committee decided to work for a withdrawal of investments from southern Africa (1972), and for an end to loans to the South African Government (1974). What are the theological implications of such actions (for instance the Christian understanding of stewardship)? (*ibid*:60).

Combating racism has important implications for the way the Church pursues its missionary activity. For example, Indians in the Americas and Aborigines in Australia have been and are being deprived of their lands and subjected to cultural imperialism, which increasingly robs them of their cultural identity (ethnocide) if not of their lives (genocide). In such situations, how have missionary enterprises aided and abetted this process? How have they sought to work for the genuine liberation of deprived peoples? (*ibid*:61).

Section VI, "Human Development: the Ambiguities of Power, Technology, and Quality of Life"

The mid-1970s is a historical moment of deep crisis for both affluent and poor countries. The optimism that prevailed in the 1960s—and the belief that development would be a relatively easy task for the world—has now collapsed. The fundamental hindrances to development became clearer, as one crisis followed another caused by food shortages, the oil issue, monetary instability, contagious national inflation, unemployment, and depression. The poorest sectors within each country and, among the countries, those with the least developed structures, are suffering the most. The gap between the rich and the poor—nations and peoples—continues to widen. Poverty, both in relative and absolute terms, is spreading and increasing; and in recent years the concentration of wealth in the hands of a minority has become more evident than ever before (*ibid*:62).

Technology had promised increasing material progress, greater control over the vicissitudes of nature, and economic security. Yet societies which put all their hopes in technological achievement are experiencing great confusion about their aims for the future. There may be a divine irony in the fact that the very technological victories which once supported the vision of affluence, now—by their contributions to increasing consumption of resources, growing population, and pollution—are

228

bringing an end to the dream of a carefree and affluent future (*ibid*:62).

This present world economic, social, and political crisis has at least three dimensions:

a) the struggle for social justice, involving new structures of political and economic life;
b) the struggle for a society in harmony with nature;
c) the struggle for human purpose and identity in a world increasingly dominated by a science-based technology.

Salvation in the Christian Scriptures is a promise to the whole of creation. The Christian hope is that God is working for the good of creation. The Christian hope is that God is working for the good of all through all things and that He will bring the new for the benefit of all. Therefore justice, more than ever before, must be justice for all humanity. And justice includes nature as well as humanity (*ibid*:63).

Ambiguity does not mean lack of conviction about the fundamental struggle for justice, but acceptance of a limited certainty about what are the best short-run goals and policies to achieve that aim. One of the objectives of Section VI will be to define as precisely as possible the criteria for establishing these short-term or approximate policies. The concern must be to see ambiguity as the motivation for a constant renewal of discernment (*ibid*:63).

How can we as churches understand and accept this dialectical relationship between absolute commitment to social justice and the limited certainty about particular policies and actions to achieve it? Have the churches today a satisfactory theological way of interpreting and explaining this creative understanding of ambiguity in the struggle for human development? (*ibid*:63).

In recent ecumenical thought, development has been understood as an inter-related process of economic growth, social justice and self-reliance. In the context described above and with this understanding of development, new perceptions and courageous action are required to destroy present-day patterns and mechanism of domination and dependence (*ibid*:63).

Real development can no longer be conceived apart from a people's movement for liberation and social justice. Such a movement will result from the efforts of those who are victims of present trends of unequal or uneven growth. By this means the dispossessed and exploited groups can fully participate in the accumulation of wealth, knowledge, techniques, and political power. The churches should support them at the local, national and international level, in their struggle for ultimate systemic transformation, and the formulation of new values and new patterns for a superior quality of life. Learning how to identify with the poor people, how to work with them, how to learn from them should be a primary task of the churches in promoting development (*ibid*:65).

. . . improvement of development processes requires more than a transfer of resources. It requires a deeper commitment with the poor and a realignment with the oppressed, expressed in attitudes, beliefs and action in solidarity. The churches must not become so co-opted by their intimate existence with the powerful that they underestimate the vested interest and intransigence of those who hold power. They should recognize the real capacity of the masses to achieve their own development when they are enabled to express and act with their own power (*ibid*:65).

Since power is a fundamental factor in the establishing of a just and sustainable society, what elements should be taken into account in efforts to achieve acceptable structures of power in the centres of decision-making? How can the churches contribute to this? (*ibid*:69).

How can the churches witness to the power of the incarnate, crucified and resurrected Christ, who liberates and unites, amidst contemporary power struggles? (*ibid*:70).

Restriction on consumption, the "new asceticism," advocated also in the churches, has to be examined in the context of global economic and power patterns. The risk of individual action, divorced from the political, is not only that it may be an escape from the struggle for social justice, but also that it may reinforce the very unjust structures themselves. Can a simpler life style express and promote solidarity? What political action must accompany the search for change in life styles if justice is to be achieved? (*ibid*:71).

Appendix C
"A Call To Confess and Proclaim"
WCC Fifth Assembly Nairobi, 1975

We do not have the option of keeping the good news to ourselves. The uncommunicated gospel is a patent contradiction.

We are called to preach Christ crucified, the power of God and the wisdom of God (1 Cor. 1:23, 24).

Evangelism, therefore, is rooted in gratitude for God's self-sacrificing love, in obedience to the risen Lord.

Evangelism is like a beggar telling another beggar where they both can find bread.

The Whole Gospel. The gospel is good news from God, our Creator and Redeemer. On its way from Jerusalem to Galilee and to the ends of the earth, the Spirit discloses ever new aspects and dimensions of God's decisive revelation in Jesus Christ. The gospel always includes: the announcement of God's Kingdom and love through Jesus Christ, the offer of grace and forgiveness of sins, the invitation to repentance and faith in him, the summons to fellowship in God's Church, the command to witness to God's saving words and deeds, the responsibility to participate in the struggle for justice and human dignity, the obligation to denounce all that hinders human wholeness and a commitment to risk life itself. In our time, to the oppressed the gospel may be new as a message of courage to persevere in the struggle for liberation in this world as a sign of hope for God's inbreaking Kingdom. To women the gospel may bring news of a Christ who empowered women to be bold in the midst of cultural expectations of submissiveness. To children the gospel may be a call of love for the "little ones" and to the rich and powerful it may reveal the responsibility to share the poverty of the poor.

While we rejoice hearing the gospel speak to our particular situations and while we must try to communicate the gospel to particular contexts, we must remain faithful to the historical apostolic witness as we find it in the holy Scriptures and tradition as it is centered in Jesus Christ—lest we accommodate them to our own desires and interests.

The Whole Person. The gospel, through the power of the Holy Spirit, speaks to all human needs, transforms our lives. In bringing forgiveness, it reconciles us to our Creator, sparks within us the true joy of knowing God, and promises eternal life. In uniting us as God's people, it answers our need for community and fellowship. In revealing God's love for all persons, it makes us responsible, critical, and creative members of the societies in which we live. The good news of Jesus' resurrection assures us that God's righteous purpose in history will be fulfilled and frees us to work for that fulfilment with hope and courage.

The Whole World. The world is not only God's creation; it is also the arena of God's mission. Because God loved the whole world, the Church cannot neglect any part of it—neither those who have heard the saving Name nor the vast majority who have not yet heard it. Our obedience to God and our solidarity with the human family demand that we obey Christ's command to proclaim and demonstrate God's love to every person, of every class and race, on every continent, in every culture, in every setting and historical context.

The Whole Church. Evangelism cannot be delegated to either gifted individuals or specialized agencies. It is entrusted to the "whole Church," the body of Christ, in which the particular gifts and functions of all members are but expressions of the life of the whole body.

The wholeness must take expression in every particular cultural, social, and political context. Therefore, the evangelization of the world starts at the level of the congregation, in the local and ecumenical dimensions of its life: worship, sacrament, preaching, teaching and healing, fellowship and service, witnessing in life and in death.

Too often we as churches and congregations stand in the way of the gospel—because of our lack of missionary zeal and missionary structures, because of our divisions, our self-complacency, our lack of catholicity and ecumenical spirit.

The call to evangelism, therefore, implies a call to repentance, renewal, and commitment for visible unity. We also deplore proselytism of any sort which further divides the Church.

Yet, even imperfect and broken, we are called to put ourselves humbly and gladly at the service of the unfinished mission. We are commissioned to carry the gospel to the whole world and to allow it to permeate all realms of human life. We recognize the signs that the Holy Spirit is in these days calling the Church to a new commitment to evangelism, as evidenced by his voice to the Bangkok Conference on "Salvation Today" (1973), the Accra conference on "Giving account of the hope that is within us" (1974), the Lausanne Congress on "The Evangelization of the World" (1974), and the Synod of Bishops of the Roman Catholic Church on "Evangelization in the Modern World" (1974). Clearly this is a common mandate which deserves common support.

On Methodology. In our times many churches, Christian individuals, and groups find themselves under pressures and challenges which demand a clear choice between confessing or denying Christ. Others, however, face ambiguous situations in which the question arises: When is the appropriate time to confess and how should we do it? This leads to the question of education for mission. Programs of lay training ought to be encouraged in order to equip lay workers for communicating the gospel at their particular place in everyday life, including those who, for professional reasons, cross cultural frontiers.

Never before has the Church universal had at its disposal such a comprehensive set of means of communication as we have today—literature, audiovisuals, electronic media. While we need to improve our use of such media, nothing can replace the living witness in words and deeds of Christian persons, groups, and congregations, who participate in the sufferings and joys, in the struggles and celebrations, in the frustrations and hopes of the people with whom they want to share the gospel. Whatever "methodologies" of communication may seem to be appropriate in different situations, they should be directed by a humble spirit of sensitivity and participation.

Careful listening is an essential part of our witness. Only as we are sensitive to the needs and aspirations of others will we know what Christ is saying through our dialogue. What we should like to call "holistic methodology" or "methodology in wholeness" transcends mere techniques or tactics. It is rooted in God's own "strategy of love" which liberates us to respond freely to his call to union with him and our fellow human beings.

Sense of Urgency. We need to recover the sense of urgency. Questions about theological definitions there may be. Problems of precise implementation will arise. But neither theoretical nor practical differences must be allowed to dampen the fires of evangelism.

Confessing Christ must be done *today*. "Behold, now is the acceptable time; behold, now is the day of salvation" (2 Cor. 6:2). It cannot wait for a time that is comfortable for us. We must be prepared to proclaim the gospel when human beings need to hear it. But in our zeal to spread the good news, we must guard against fanaticism which disrupts the hearing of the gospel and breaks the community of God. The world requires, and God demands, that we recognize the urgency to proclaim the saving word of God—today. God's acceptable time demands that we respond in all haste. "And how terrible it would be for me if I did not preach the gospel!" (1 Cor. 9:16) (Paton 1976:53–55).

Appendix D
Program to Combat Racism (PCR)

The World Council of Churches, in numerous ecumenical statements, recognized the increasing urgency for the Church to participate actively in the struggle for racial equality, the dignity and self-respect of all persons. From the earliest beginnings in Stockholm, warnings were sounded in ecumenical gatherings about the impending crisis in race relations. The concern for potential conflict arising out of the unjust structures based on race were expressed in almost every responsible ecumenical gathering both within the WCC and in the IMC before it was integrated.

But the Uppsala delegates recognized that the time for mere words had passed; the time for action had arrived. That Assembly called for a crash program to make clear to the world what the Church believed about racism and what it was prepared to do about it. The language spelled it out with precision:

1. the development of comprehensive and up-to-date reports on the racial situation in various regions of the world. The prototype for this might well be the comprehensive PEP (Political and Economic Planning) report from the United Kingdom. Immediate studies are needed from Southern Africa, USA, and Australia;

2. consultations on racism on a regional and international level;

3. creation of a consultant service to make available the counsel of experts to various secular and church agencies;

4. relating the view and experience of the Church to various international agencies, especially the United Nations;

5. research on the areas of potential crisis and alerting the churches and secular agencies in helping to prevent the growth of tensions arising from racism;

6. action-coalition projects, particularly for developing models for action (e.g. in some of the joint action for mission projects);

7. mass educational materials on racial issues;

8. establishing within the General Secretariat a coordinated secretariat on the elimination of racism, and the appointment of an ecumenical commission to supervise this program (WCC 1968d:242).

The Uppsala documents recognized the existence of many forms of racism, but felt that because of the special historical significance of *white* racism, the focus should be on exposing and eradicating it. For some this would be controversial and questionable, but the compelling reasons to adopt this approach cannot be denied. The documents also recognized the close inter-relatedness of racism and economic, social and political questions.

We believe, however, that white racism has special historical significance because its roots lie in powerful, highly developed countries, the stability of which is crucial to any hope for international peace and development. The racial crisis in these countries is to be taken *as seriously as the threat of nuclear war* [emphasis by the author]. The revolt against racism is one of the most inflammatory elements of the social revolution now sweeping the earth; it is fought at the level of mankind's deepest and most vulnerable emotions—the universal passion for human dignity. The threatened internal chaos of those countries in which racial conflict is most intense has immediate world-wide impact, for racism under attack tends to generate and to spread counter-racism. We submit that this crisis will grow worse unless we understand the historical phenomenon of white racism, what has distinguished it from other forms of intergroup conflict, and what must be done to resolve the crisis on the basis of racial justice (1968:242).

In calling for a program to expose and eradicate racism, the Fourth Assembly carefully defined its understanding of this phenomenon and knew what it was up against.

By racism we mean ethnocentric pride in one's own racial group and preference for the distinctive characteristics of that group; belief that these characteristics are fundamentally biological in nature and are thus transmitted to succeeding generations; strong negative feelings towards other groups who do not share these characteristics coupled with the thrust to discriminate against and exclude the out-group from full participation in the life of the community (ibid:243).

The theological convictions and Christian compassion underlying Uppsala's mandate had been expressed more than fifty years earlier by J. H. Oldham when he started the ecumenical discussion on racism in his book, *Christianity and the Race Problem*, 1924.

Christianity is not primarily a philosophy but a crusade. As Christ was sent by the Father, so He sends His disciples to set up in the world the Kingdom of God. His coming was a declaration of war—war to the death against the powers of darkness. He was manifested to destroy the works of the devil. Hence when Christians find in the world a state of things that is not in accord with the truth which they have learned from Christ, their concern is not that it should be explained but that it should be ended. In that temper we must approach everything in the relations between races that cannot be reconciled with the Christian ideal (Adler 1974:V).

239

The Uppsala call for a crash program was heard by the Central Committee. It approved in its Canterbury meeting in 1969 a comprehensive program to combat racism with the focus on combating white racism. It was clearly recognized that the problems of racism and the struggle against unjust social, economic and political institutions were enmeshed and inter-related. To tackle one without dealing with the other is futile. Further, the fact and effect of racism in an ecumenical community whose membership was composed of churches that practiced racism, and that were victims of racism, made such a program inescapable. The program was intended to cover a wide range of concerns whose roots in one way or another were the results of racism. This Program to Combat Racism was charged to carry out the intent of Uppsala for five years, after which the program would be reviewed.

Unfortunately, many of the excellent and necessary aspects of the program have not been sufficiently recognized by member churches, churches outside the WCC and by the world community—particularly the Western world community. The suspicions, concerns and misunderstandings that have surrounded this program were triggered by the decision in Canterbury to create a special fund to assist groups engaged in struggles for liberation. This special fund was only a small aspect of the entire PCR, but in the minds of many it was *the* program. The WCC staff, in many respects, has only itself to blame for this unfortunate misconception.

During my research in Geneva, WCC staff members related how, immediately after the decision by the Central Committee at Canterbury, certain persons rushed out and gave a press release which highlighted the Special Fund. For all practical purposes, the impression received by the waiting world was that the heart of the program was the Special Fund to assist liberation groups, including those using violent means to achieve their objectives. People in the churches were alarmed and a continuing atmosphere of distrust and misinformation has plagued the entire program.

At its next meeting the Executive Committee was so disturbed and angered over the bad publicity created by these staff "zealots" that they had a mind to fire some people high in the system. The whole affair gives insight into the inner dynamics of the WCC, and how good programs can be manipulated, and the direction shifted, to implement ideologies quite different from the original intentions of well-meaning people.

The Central Committee knew that the new Program to Combat Racism would be controversial and threatening to some. Even now, many in the churches are unaware of the distinction between the larger PCR program and the Special Fund to assist oppressed racial groups. This aspect of the program, more than any other single activity of the WCC, has raised doubts in the member churches, particularly in the West, about where the WCC is heading. As indicated, the WCC staff itself is not without blame. Knowing that the press picks up and emphasizes the controversial, those who prepare the releases cannot escape responsibility for unduly accenting this single aspect of an otherwise commendable program.

While this program has turned many of the Western churches off and raised doubts about the whole fabric of the WCC, for people in Third World countries the PCR program has been looked upon generally with enthusiasm and appreciation. Dr. Kenneth Kaunda, who heads the Zambian government, credits PCR with having restored in Africa the credibility of the Gospel. David Gill of the Geneva staff says that PCR, more than any other WCC program, has aroused the conscience of the whole Church to the evils of racism and other forms of repression and exploitation. There is no doubt that for many within the WCC and its churches, particularly those of the Third World, the Program to Combat Racism is the "darling" of the ecumenical movement. Who can deny that no new social order is possible without the elimination of racism?

> The Programme to Combat Racism pre-supposes the vision of a world community in which not only all races but also all nations have their adequate share; and international, responsible society in which each part is enabled to be itself and to develop its own identity. The struggle against racism must be understood as a contribution towards this goal. If this is made evident, PCR will be shown to be part of a much larger struggle. It, like all other WCC programmes, is conceived and executed as

part of a total effort to eliminate structures of injustice and the creation of a just, sustainable, and participatory society. All is mission, and the mission is to bring about a new socio-economic-political order where people are free to determine their own lives (Johnson 1975:161).

Appendix E
Commission on the
Church's Participation
in Development
(CCPD)

Development was a major theme of the Fourth Assembly at Uppsala. Speakers asked the churches to launch a war on mass poverty and economic and social injustice. The Section on "World Economic and Social Development" stated:

> We live in a world where men exploit men. . . . The political and economic structures groan under the burden of grave injustice. It urged Christians everywhere "to be on the forefront of the battle" and "to participate in the struggle of millions of people for greater social justice and for world development." At the same time the report warned that "to be complacent in the face of the world's need is to be guilty of practical heresy." . . . "The ever-widening gap between the rich and the poor . . . is the crucial point of decision today" (Johnson 1975:139).

Guidelines for the new program were hammered out in a WCC-sponsored consultation at Montreux in 1970. The consultation spoke of development as aimed at three interrelated objectives: justice, self-reliance, and economic growth. The task of the churches was seen primarily as participation with the poor and the oppressed in their struggle for development. It also involved efforts to change socio-economic and political structures which continue to enslave, impoverish, and dehumanize the poor population. The task of the WCC was to assist the churches in their concern for reflection, development education and political action, as well as provision of technical and financial assistance to development programs.

The importance the WCC attached to both Uppsala-mandated programs (PCR and CCPD) is indicated by the restructuring of the WCC to link these two programs in the same unit. Because the WCC had no structure to accommodate the new emphasis represented by these programs, a new unit was created. The new programs were linked together with CICARWS and CCIA in the new Program Unit on Justice and Service. Increasingly all these programs of this new unit have directed their efforts to the root causes of injustice and have assessed the value of the WCC's work in terms of their contribution or relationship to social, economic and political justice.

Appendix F
Ecumenical Sharing
of Personnel (ESP)

The Third Assembly at New Delhi coined the term Joint Action for Mission (JAM). The goal was to create a climate in which churches and mission agencies would look at a mission task together and pool their resources and people according to the need. In practice, JAM represented an ecumenical era of good will rather than a program.

Mexico City popularized an awareness about mission that was capsulized in the term "mission in six continents." And earlier Whitby had called for a new "partnership in obedience." These expressions represented a growing realization that whatever was done in mission could best be done together.

Uppsala saw the need to move beyond slogans to a program. It recognized that old bilateral ties did not loosen easily. While it was easy to subscribe to a slogan and to see the reasonableness and correctness of the ultimate objectives, the direct planning of two at a table proved more practical and efficient. The Uppsala delegates wanted a breakthrough and it was seen that a new program was needed to give a new mix of people, churches and missions working in a common task.

We therefore urge
    a) that any new undertaking in the field of mission be started in the pattern of JAM;

b) that churches, Christian councils and mission agencies be constantly reminded of the importance of JAM as a way in which the churches in any given area—geographical or sociological—can make a common response to Christ present and active in the world—a real partnership in mission;

. . . In such ways as these the theme of this Assembly, "Behold, I make all things new," may find some practical expression through the action of churches and councils on the basis of the divine promise that all things are being made anew (WCC 1968d:234).

In the context of this awareness that JAM needed more than good intentions and a congenial ecumenical atmosphere, Uppsala urged the DWME to do something practical about it:

The Committee urges the DWME to develop procedures for facilitating the international exchange of personnel. It is expected that the DWME should work closely with DICARWS (Division Inter-Church Aid and Refugee World Service) and regional conferences in pursuing this concern (1968d:237).

The Central Committee in its first meeting after Uppsala, in Canterbury, 1969, hoped that the work of ESP would go forward rapidly. In February, 1970, the ad hoc committee was reconstituted as the Committee on the Ecumenical Sharing of Personnel. The program was the joint responsibility of DWME and DICARWS, with co-personnel secretaries. Both divisions made staff available. The committee was given $10,000 to do its work.

Mr. Gerhard Hennes has been a co-personnel secretary of ESP for CWME from the beginning. In a report dated February 4–9, 1977, he shares his understandings about ESP:

Conceived in Uppsala as an "ecumenical plan for the churches' manpower" and an "international exchange of personnel. . . ."

ESP was to stimulate thought, action, and attitude toward more multi-lateral, multi-directional, and more ecumenical patterns in the deployment of people in and across churches. The bonds between people and money were to be loosened. The ideology was to challenge structures and to reform ways; the experimental and the operational were to try new models and to test new relationships. ESP was to advise the Personnel Desk of CICARWS on policy governing the coordination and recruitment of "overseas" workers for programmes of relief, rehabilitation and development—a traditional North-South brokerage which places some seventy "technicians" a year against a demand of about one hundred. A hybrid task, with hybrid methods; not surprisingly, then mixed results (Hennes 1977a).

Dr. Hennes, in a further paper dated April 26, 1977, answers the question, "What has ESP done?" With his characteristic, straightforward style, Dr. Hennes reports:

Although, to the possible frustration of some mission and service agencies, ESP fell far short of becoming a viable alternative to bilateral personnel patterns, it did prosper in what might be called its ideological task—contrasted with its operational involvement (1977b).

In other words the total number of people involved in an ecumenical exchange of personnel was relatively small. In response to requests received from the DICARWS side from 1970 through 1976, ESP facilitated the placement of 395 persons. These were people asked for by churches and missions to work in agricultural, administrative, community/social, medical, technical and teaching areas. The highest number in any given year was 73. In 1976 the total was 60, most of them from Europe and most of them placed in Africa. Only 4 came from the Third World. These people came from that part of ESP which has recruiting facilities to locate the personnel requested.

Turning to the other half of ESP—that part related to the

CWME—the statistics are sobering indeed. From 1970 to March, 1977, 19 persons had been placed, of whom 2 were still pending: 8 did the work of clergy/theology; 7 were involved in teaching; 1 was in community/social work; and 1 was in administration. The terms of service requested varied from a few months to three and one-half years. At least 3 people extended their terms of service beyond the initial term.

However, the direction of movement of personnel is interesting and significant. (The personnel from USA member churches does not show.)

Country Requesting	Country Responding
Australia	Uruguay
Barbados	Sierra Leone
Bolivia	Japan
Bolivia	Japan
Bolivia	Japan
Botswana	Switzerland
Canada	?
Costa Rica	?
Germany (W)	?
Japan	Korea
Japan	Philippines
Kenya	Hungary
New Zealand	Sri Lanka
South Africa	USA
Thailand	Philippines
UK	Korea
USA	South Africa

It is important and significant to recognize that ESP has a very limited budget which is for operational costs, not for program. That budget in 1970 was $10,000 and the budget for 1978 is $53,000. On the DICARWS side, funds are more readily available; DICARWS can recruit personnel and finance them, but CWME is not set up to operate in that manner.

ESP leadership had said from the beginning that one of its aims was to bring into mission/church-to-mission/church relationships a new mix of peoples and monies. Of the cases handled this mix of monies was achieved in just a few instances, but in three instances at least three partners shared in the support budget. The Hennes report on ESP's accomplishments continues:

> It tackled or handled thirty-two cases in some five years. Nineteen persons were eventually placed. Two-thirds of the requests were for clergymen. No fewer than twenty-two requesting and twelve responding countries shared in the demand-and-supply pattern.

> In spite of ESP's 1974 "mandate" and its subsequent efforts to generate exchanges within and across Third-World continents, there were only eight such cases, or 25 percent of the caseload. This fact would confirm what seasoned international personnel people have long known: nothing is more difficult—and more necessary—than exchanging Third World people in and across their own continents! Requests from the First World to the Third—"mission in reverse"—accounted for 44 percent of the caseload; those from the Third to First, for 33 percent.

> As a general rule, jobs needed people and money. But the number of cases in which people were looking for jobs and even money and turned to ESP for both, has been uncomfortably high, at least for this reporter. Indeed, one gains the feeling as if too often ESP was incidental rather than causal to new relationships, exchanges and experiences.

> On the other hand and perhaps because of its own resources, however limited, ESP did contribute to a wider and more diverse sharing of financial resources in support of jobs and people. This strength in raising flexible funds should be matched more fully by ESP's determination and competence in planning for and mobilizing human resources and resourcefulness. Here the task remains tall; and the struggle uphill.

In general terms, ESP's follow-up on personnel requests

made and candidates placed was intermittent at best. To find out where obstacles lay and opportunities beckoned; how persons and relationships actually fared in ESP's experimentation; and to what extent experiences gained, good and bad, was instructively shared among those affected and concerned: here, too, much more profound evaluation and more systematic information-gathering and disseminating are called for.

This sober assessment may lack spiritual quality and human touch. A customary flourish of challenge and exhortation may well be expected—and proper. But I will stick to the record and stand by it.

Indeed, far be it from me to suggest that in these thirty-two cases and nineteen actual encounters churches, institutions, and people were not enriched or blessed. For all of them to meet and to be together in mission and service is no small achievement (Hennes 1977b).

No one is in a better position to tell us what ESP has done or failed to do. The report is rich in detail, instructive, informative and sobering. It has many implications for future considerations about the task of world-wide evangelization of unreached peoples.

When the CWME Executive Committee met in 1975 and considered its programs for the years 1973–1975, ESP was said to be more than theory: it was seen as a manifestation of the missionary vocation which corresponded to the Committee's understanding of world mission. These men spoke of the need for the program to include the training of personnel to cross frontiers, and acknowledged that while the entire Christian community is engaged in mission, there remains a need for missionary personnel and training. In the wide-ranging discussions, the Committee considered ESP one of the important programs to help make real a true internationalization of the missionary witness to Christ.

Again the following year, when the important WCC Core Group meeting was held in Geneva with people involved who were deeply committed to evangelism (including some of the top people in Geneva) ESP was discussed at length. It was recognized that this program faced administrative problems because of its hybrid nature, relating to two commissions, but it still affirmed that ESP was the program for the basic thrust of the work: it was seen as an enabler and facilitator that would make it possible for Third World churches to share their personnel with one another. ESP was asked to give major attention in the future to the growing network of relationships developing between Third World and First World churches, and to promote and facilitate the "reverse flow of personnel" since this missionary presence from non-Western churches was needed by the former sending churches. ESP was seen as the program that could make it happen.

ESP was also asked to lift up the subject of moratorium and explore ways to move beyond the moratorium debate to a more deeply committed mutual relationship of churches involved. ESP was felt to have a pastoral ministry to personnel involved in the exchanges envisaged. At the end of the discussion the unanimous judgment of the group was that the CWME considered ESP as a vital part of its total program and recommended that ESP be continued. Steps were taken to have a smaller group from both CWME and CICARWS study the ESP program and make recommendations as to the future shape that ESP should take.

Mr. Robbins Strong, Deputy Secretary of the CWME, a veteran of many years in the WCC and knowledgeable beyond many of the later newcomers, in his report to the Affiliated Bodies of CWME, members and consultants of the CWME, dated March 1, 1977, describes the ESP program for which they are budgeting $53,000 for 1978 as follows:

> While some aspects of this programme are now part of the CICARWS study on the "Ecumenical Sharing of Resources" the basic concern of the CWME for the movement of persons in mission remains. The issues facing this movement of persons are vital to the development of mature relationships between churches. CWME is also concerned to see that new experiments are made. While the basic exchange is a matter between the churches involved, CWME has tried to serve as an honest broker. It

has facilitated recently a teacher from Korea serving in a women's college in Japan; a secretary from the Philippines helping NCC Japan; a Swiss pastor to minister, on terms equitable with those of nationals, to a congregation of the Methodist Church in Bolivia; the Department missionaire in Lausanne a new partner for that church; a Filipino Baptist clergyman to conscientize an affluent West German congregation; a Hungarian professor teaching theology in Kenya; and a Uruguayan pastor exploring with Australian churches the situation of Latin American migrants in that continent (Strong 1977:3).

In its first regularly scheduled meetings after Nairobi, the WCC Central Committee (August, 1976) expressed its views on the importance with which it views this program:

The demand for mature relationships between churches in mission is a pressing ecumenical issue. CWME's involvement through the ESP has been and should be that of an enabler and a catalyst in all possible situations to stimulate and integrate the new emerging pattern of relationships. CWME should concentrate its work on "relationships in mission," keeping close cooperation with the CICARWS based on sharing resources (WCC 1976e:27).

Personal Evaluation. One question remains: has the ESP been in any vital sense involved with member churches and agencies in a missionary and evangelistic effort through which otherwise unreached peoples are enabled to hear the Gospel? I asked the co-personnel secretary how many of the people that ESP had a share in placing were directly engaged in such missionary activity. His considered reply was, "I would have to say, not one."

This is not to say that ESP is not an important and necessary program. It is to say as strongly as possible that ESP, as presently conceived and functioning, does not meet the need for a program that will bring WCC and its member churches together in a new internationalization of personnel engaged in cross-cultural evangelism among unreached peoples. For that

to happen ESP must be sharply refocused and its aims redefined—or a new program must be fashioned to do what ESP is
not now doing—in the content of the intent of the Nairobi
delegates with respect to evangelism.

Appendix G
Urban and Industrial
Mission (UIM)

The UIM is a program of the CWME. Because of UIM's dramatic expansion and the volume of work entailed, the CWME has not been able to supervise the program directly. An advisory board supervises the UIM work, which board is in turn ultimately accountable to CWME.

UIM began as the vision of Dr. Paul Loeffler who, on his own, made two world-circling trips in 1964 to discover what groups or churches were engaged in social action. Regional meetings in different parts of the world brought together people having similar interests. Out of such meetings, UIM gradually took shape and eventually was represented in church structures at various levels. East Asia Christian Conference, with offices in Tokyo, has been particularly active and recently held its 9th annual UIM meeting. These regional UIM offices are independent of the Geneva office, but the WCC finances a large part of their activities.

The UIM office was established in Geneva in 1964 with Dr. Paul Loeffler as its first director and a $15,000 budget. Today it is a million dollar operation. The UIM has increasingly been involved in funding social action projects of churches and groups in all parts of the world. Although popularly presented as involved in over 500 such projects, a recent, more careful investigation done by UIM showed that they were involved in some 1200 projects in over 60 countries. It is a big operation!

What is meant by Urban and Industrial Mission was spelled out in a carefully prepared document, *Becoming Operational in a World of Cities,* prepared for the Fourth Assembly of the World Council of Churches by the DWME Advisory Group on Urban and Industrial Mission. This study showed what humanization meant in a secular, urbanized society; it recognized the dehumanization that spoils and rots society in the cities of the world. It also held that churches must respond to the needs of these new conditions and stand with the poor and oppressed.

> In response to this situation some churches have begun to seek for new expressions of their life, service and witness. New forms of missionary presence have emerged. An important group of such ministries and projects are engaged with different aspects of urban-industrialized society. They are denoted here "urban and industrial mission" (1968:4).
>
> . . . the most significant development has been that churches begin to realize that these ministries, which so far have been peripheral enterprises, must become the key part of a total strategy for mission in the modern society (*ibid*:5).
>
> A threefold objective was stated:
> 1. to stimulate the churches' interest in and commitment to urban and industrial mission.
> 2. to indicate criteria for priorities in the future development of urban and industrial ministries by the churches.
> 3. to prepare the way for a common ecumenical strategy based on joint action in a given area, metropolitan zone or among a particular group of people (*ibid*.).
>
> If the churches and the ecumenical movement want to continue as a constructive instrument of God's mission, they must break out of these limitations and overcome their cultural and sociological captivities. Positively, they must learn to speak relevantly and more effectively to the issues and events of a new urban-industrial society by relating to the forces and structures of modern society.

The churches must involve themselves more deeply with the new groups—the new poor, the workers, the new marginal groups and become a servant Church among them. They must also influence the planners, the decision-makers, the technocrats, that they may become instruments of a more just society.

The biblical call is to participate in God's mission in history so that the love, power and justice of Jesus Christ work for humanization among man. The goal, the objective, is mature manhood, when the fulness of Christ is attained. God has told us what our aim is to be: a new humanity already born in Jesus which forms part of the promise, "Behold I make all things new!" The Church's mission is to hold before men and institutions Christian hope. In order to make it understood and realized, there must be offered in word and action specific goals and specific programmes to accomplish these goals. Hope is not real unless it finds expression in new communities and changed lives. From this goal follow some clear priorities.

. . . God speaks to the church and the world through the voices of the poor and the weak. . . . The Church needs to engage with workers, union leaders, managers, government executives, scientists and teachers: for humanization of . . . Christian mission has not only to deal with people but with the organizational structures which determine in part the goals and values of society, as well as the fate and future of people (*ibid*:7–8).

The document, as a blueprint for action, called the whole Church to engage in this new kind of mission intended to make relevant what the churches were to say and do in the new secular world. It anticipated approval for its views by Uppsala.

In the period after Uppsala the churches will be confronted even more dramatically with the challenge to play a relevant role in city and industry. This will demand a radical shift in priorities and allocation of resources in terms of personnel and funds at all levels (*ibid*:13).

APPENDIX

The Advisory Group on Urban and Industrial Mission met in Kyoto, Japan, in August, 1970, to reflect on progress and direction. Excerpts from the report of this meeting follow.

We have felt that the Gospel message has demanded that we be actively present among those sectors of our societies which have been isolated from or corrupted by the advantages of technology and wealth, a necessary response to God's perfect expression of man's humanity in Jesus Christ. It is this Christ who is active in history even today, who we experience in our fellow man and to whom we are called to give living expression through our daily actions. *This is our proclamation* of the resurrected Christ, a word which is meaningless unless it finds expression in actions which contribute to the creation of a just, human, society . . . .

We resist imposed development schemes designed to make some quantitative improvements, but which leave the present system of international economic exploitation untouched. This means we are open to and frequently called to promote revolutionary change (i.e. basic changes of the power structures of society) in which we participate along with the people with whom we live and work . . . .

Many of the recommendations made in the 1968 document have been applied at local levels by UIM teams who, in the process, have had new experiences and gained new understanding. As we move forward we must bring our thrusts, policy priorities and structure into line with these new insights, and in so doing we strongly reaffirm our commitment to grassroots involvement which makes authentic response to real needs possible (WCC 1970:1).

It is now necessary to question ministries which are exclusively devoted to social service. We should emphasize ministries which enable groups and communities to organize themselves for action, avoiding paternalistic approaches, so that they might become aware of their oppression and voice their own challenges to the existing structures. Thus our mission is best defined as participating, enabling the movement of the people and assisting the poor to become their own best advocates.

Such an approach requires openness to creative conflict and avoids easy compromise, the acceptance of palliatives which do not remove the causes of oppression throughout the world.

Though we recognize growth and progress in our understanding and realization of mission, we are aware that history is a dynamic process with which we must move. Therefore, as we plan for the future action, we seek to respond more fully to the needs of the peoples who are lifting their eyes to a vision of a new society (*ibid*:2) (1970:2).

We reject the present dehumanizing structures of the world which divide the poor and oppressed along national, racial, or geographical lines. . . . Ours is a "mission in six continents" and we have been providing channels through which the clear international dimensions of issues could be seen and experienced in each regional context. UIM projects have in fact acted concretely in the light of that knowledge and interacted with people on other continents in a joint effort to bring about worldwide human justice . . . .

UIM has been an important influence on the life of our churches. This has been so because in many senses churchmen involved in UIM have been sensitive to the moment of history, a fact acknowledged by many of our secular contemporaries, and willing to commit themselves to the most crucial areas of modern society. We are eager to improve our communications with congregations, denominations, NCC's and other sectors of the church, many of whom look to us for challenges and guidance with regard to their own restructuring for more effective mission.

We are conscious of the fact that our responsibility to the churches is to remain at the critical limits of the present and moving into the future. We realize, as well, that we must frequently take positions which are subject to criticism. But we are encouraged to continue this by the response of many denominational and ecumenical bodies to our initiative (*ibid*:3).

A later report by this Advisory Group resulted from its meeting in Vancouver, June, 1976. The report begins with a theological reflection:

> God acts and speaks to the world through suffering and struggling people. To hear what God is saying we must learn to listen carefully to the people (WCC 1976b).
>
> Here is the crucial link between the biblical story and our story. Reflection on it strengthens and unites those who struggle one with another, and with other hopeful strugglers in different parts of the world (*ibid*:2).
>
> The struggle for economic justice is the central thrust of UIM in all regions.
>
> We identify two major issues:
>
> The operation of *multinational corporations* . . . and *unemployment*. The changes that must be achieved are, therefore, clearly aimed at both political and economic structures. But the struggle will not be successful unless the interdependence and interrelatedness of developed and developing countries is fully taken into account and unless the struggle is carried out simultaneously in all regions.
>
> Capital is increasingly organizing itself on an international level, there is an international solidarity of management, whereas the people have not yet achieved international co-operation and solidarity.
>
> Unemployment is a worldwide issue in developed and developing countries.
>
> It is necessary to organize people to fight for: 1) their right to work, especially to reinforce the bill of "right to work. . . ."
>
> It is our goal to achieve an economic order in which it is possible for people in all countries of the world to derive human dignity from work, to develop their creative and social faculties, and to have sufficient time outside work for private and public functions.

. . . We want to emphasize that the churches' concern for human rights should take the form of engagement and participation in the on-going action of groups of people working as part of, with, or on behalf of the poor, industrial workers, peasants and farmers in their struggles for justice and human fulfillment.

Our work to protect individual freedoms and to help persons whose right to speak and eat have been violated must be done in the context of the continuing strategies and actions for attacking injustice and for building just social, economic, and political structures.

Organizing People for Power:
Organizing has been a predominant method of UIM operations and will remain so. . . . Where there is widespread social and political revolutionary ferment, organizing is regarded by UIM as a process of being with the people and learning from them. Here UIM is very much part and parcel of a people's movement, making real the Christian's desire to be involved in the struggle of the people.

However, in a more stable situation, organizing is regarded by UIM as a process of enabling the people to have power, in order to make real the principle of participation (*ibid*:4–5).

This important development has strengthened UIM's ability to survive and to be more effective, and has driven us to more serious theological and ideological reflection.

In the coming years, an aspect of organizing which will be given more attention is that of partnership, or "who are our allies?" UIM has generally reached a stage in which a trust relationship with the people has been established. The people are asking, "Now what?" Hence the need to deal in depth with theology, ideology and partnership (*ibid*:5).

The Advisory Group reported to the CWME at its meeting in 1975. In a short, two-page report it spoke without ambiguity, confirming the stable understanding of UIM about itself and its work in the light of God's work.

Mission is understood not simply in terms of moving across geographical frontiers. It now involves the Church in penetrating all the diverse social milieux of mankind. It involves us in the process which we perceive more clearly in our own generation of the movement of mankind from old enslavements to new freedoms.

Mission is our participation in the action of God for the liberation of man.

Mission involves a process of movement back and forth between action and reflection or between context and text. . . . Action takes place in the sphere of politics but the motivation for action lies in the process of theological and sociological reflection (CWME 1976:2).

The Core Group of the CWME, and later the Advisory Group as a whole, made suggestions for the future carrying out of UIM programs. The report speaks of new thrusts for UIM:

Certain trends in UIM thinking and organization which have been in process for some years are now more clearly identifiable:

a. *Project and Movement.* There is a strong sense around the regions that we are all involved in a major movement of history. Increasingly, projects are being assessed by their partners in their own region or in other continents as to how far they are participating in the general movement. Generally, projects arise in response to purely local situations which may not form part of any widely spread phenomenon. The great danger with this kind of project is that it may become routinized and institutionalized after the situation which created it in the first place, has passed. The UIM movement across the world is accompanied by a sense of togetherness in the pursuit of shared aims and often even by similar strategies. Individual projects may emerge from insights central to this general movement—we might describe them as "movement oriented" projects.

b. *Rural/Urban Nexus.* There is a stronger sense that the lot of the urban poor and that of the rural poor are both part of one common situation. As the Bangkok document spoke in terms of the one mission of God, we recognize increasingly, *the one mission* which the Church *must undertake* in the common liberation struggle of rural and poor (*ibid*. Emphasis by the author).

We want to communicate to the Executive Committee of the CWME, our conviction that this Desk (UIM) requires the strongest possible support in organizational status, staff assistance and the resources necessary to fulfill the tasks assigned to it. We believe that it may not be sufficiently appreciated in this whole issue of staffing, that the Desk works closely with committees and full-time staff in three regions and with working committees in other world regions.

We call to the attention of the Executive Committee of CWME the recommendations for staffing in the 1972 report of the UIM Advisory Group and the action of the CWME itself at Bangkok in advocating adequate staffing and resources for the UIM work related to WCC (WCC Archives).

This strong advocacy by the UIM Advisory Group to CWME is doubly apparent in view of the financial crisis the entire WCC was then facing, calling for reduction of programs and staff wherever possible.

PERSONAL EVALUATION

UIM is frequently held up as a model for evangelism in an urban and industrial society. But if the reports from the Advisory Group are to be accepted at face value, the primary focus of this program is not on evangelism, but upon social action.

Back in 1969 when the director of CWME made an exhaustive report covering the world and the priorities for mission, UIM merited just one lonely sentence.

> Initiating experimental programmes of a temporary character (e.g. Urban and Industrial Mission), or sponsored agencies on clearly defined concerns for limited periods (WCC 1969).

During that same meeting, the question was asked: how could the UIM program be developed to further Joint Action for Mission and strengthen the local churches? However, approval was given for the direction in which the UIM Desk was moving as indicated in the documents.

I sense some continuing concern in CWME about an imbalance in the UIM program, and the degree of independence UIM displays in its very indirect accountability. I believe the Central Committee is aware of the dangers in this independent type of relationship with financial resources for which it is accountable only to an Advisory Group which cannot exercise the kind of unbiased judgment and appraisal of UIM policy and program needed to give it the balance it may be lacking.

That the Central Committee has its eye on the UIM program is apparent by its approval of two major committee recommendations concerning UIM. The Unit I Committee on Faith and Witness recommended and Central Committee agreed:

> The work of Urban and Industrial Mission of CWME should be fully reported to the Central Committee in 1977. The proposed study and action programme on transnational corporations should note the ongoing activity of CWME's Urban and Industrial Mission in this field (WCC 1976:27).

The important Review Committee of the WCC reported:

> Further information is needed before this Committee can provide an adequate appraisal of the work of Urban and Industrial Mission. It is requested therefore that a full report on this programme be provided to the Central Committee in 1977, including a consideration of CCPD's initiatives in this field (WCC 1976a:100).

It seems obvious that the Central Committee is concerned about the overlapping between UIM activities and those of the newly formed Commission on the Church's Participation in Development.

Searching in UIM official reports, I did not find much to indicate that a central, even marginal purpose of its program is to ensure an effective witness to the Gospel. UIM has one objective: to bring about a new social order by attacking the unjust structures of society and by enabling people to exercise power and display initiative to fashion a new society which is more just and humane.

I see in the UIM a model of commitment, vision, and practical working out of program and relationships that could well be duplicated by six great programs focused on evangelism among unreached peoples in six great continents. The churches concerned that their WCC and its member churches play an active part in efforts to communicate the Gospel are waiting for just such programs. The UIM model challenges the WCC and its member churches to make available similar finances to churches in Third World countries to enable cross-cultural evangelists to be sent out among peoples not yet reached. The same kinds of monies need to be made available for evangelism as are available for programs of social action.

Appendix H
Service Programs and Projects

Service and Mission have from the beginning been the two terms to describe the life and work of the WCC. Life & Work and Faith & Order were the movements that had come together to become the World Council of Churches in Amsterdam in 1948. The missionary movement, the third strong part of the ecumenical movement, was integrated into the WCC in 1961. All that the member churches are now doing together is presumably represented in the world body. Faith & Order remains small, the missionary movement has become small, but the service aspect (now combined with the emphasis on justice) has grown tremendously. This is illustrated by budget and income comparisons.

The Justice & Service Unit of the WCC receives approximately 60 percent of the total budget. Total income expected by this unit in 1977 exceeded $17 million. The same year the CWME expected to receive approximately $900,000. Of that amount, CWME gives approximately half to other WCC programs such as Dialogue, Program to Combat Racism, and Faith & Order/Joint Action for Mission. The amount of money that CWME has available to support the churches in their missionary and evangelistic task is manifestly small.

Most of the work of Justice & Service is financed by what is known in the WCC as the project system. (Discussion continues within the WCC on ways to get away from this approach to churches sharing together.) CWME and CICARWS are also represented in the project system. The work of UIM is totally supported without difficulty, but Faith & Order has a hard time to get enough funds for its important work. Very few projects with a strong evangelistic component are included among the projects.

Projects represent work for which local churches, or a group of churches and (less frequently) non-church groups appeal to the WCC for financial assistance. The projects do not originate in Geneva; they originate from within the life of the churches. Geneva processes the applications and divides them into three categories. For those in Category I, Geneva guarantees 90 percent (sometimes 100 percent) support. For Category II projects, Geneva will seek designated support and will provide as donors are found. Category III projects, not necessarily less important, will be supported only after the other two categories are met. Support for such projects may come from other sources. As projects in Category I are met by designated gifts, some of the guaranteed funds are released for projects in II and III.

These projects represent a very wide range of activities of WCC member churches around the world. In effect they represent the priorities of churches for work they want to do, but cannot do without assistance from affluent donor churches and agencies.

The other side of the project system is that it reflects what donor churches and agencies are prepared to support. Projects are presented in the perspective of what the prospective donor is most likely to support. It has been learned that projects that can be tied to "hunger" and "development" are more likely to find support than others.

Projects with a strong evangelistic element are reputedly rare on the project list. Several reasons are usually given: most Third World churches do not make a sharp distinction between mission and service; evangelism is deemed to be "holistic"; large donor groups (e.g. Bread for the World in Germany, Christian Aid in Britain, CROP in America), because of the public-appeal nature of their support, find support of specifically evangelistic projects impossible. But the Nairobi "Call" has created a new situation.

The WCC project list is one immediate, practical way that Geneva could respond to the intent of the Nairobi "Call." Member churches—particularly Third World churches—should be encouraged to make their plans to evangelize peoples where existing churches do not exist. They should be encouraged to do this in the confidence that Geneva would give priority to such projects and seek to relate them to affluent, donor churches from the West. This could indicate conclusively that the WCC really does have a heart for evangelism. Probably no other action could make a greater immediate impact on the ability of Third World churches to do their part to carry forward the missionary movement—with missionaries and evangelists from their churches being sent out to cross remaining frontiers. The Central Committee of the WCC has the authority to make it happen.

Appendix I
Survey
WCC Staff Views
WCC Evangelism
Program/Projects
in the Context of
Nairobi

This survey is made in the context of a worldwide Christian community renewing its commitment to evangelism. Among the many "signs" that this is so are the worldwide meetings in Lausanne, Rome, Bangkok and Nairobi.

Many among the member churches of the WCC concerned for worldwide evangelism were heartened by the emphasis given to evangelism evidenced in the Nairobi assembly. Without lessening its commitment to the social implications of the Gospel, Nairobi was seen as a positive response to a concern within its membership that the WCC place a greater emphasis upon evangelism in its life and work.

In 1961 in New Delhi when the International Missionary Council was integrated into the World Council of Churches, it was confidently predicted that henceforth "the missionary and evangelistic emphasis will be at the very centre of the integrated World Council."

With the adoption of the new constitution by the WCC in Nairobi, the process of integration involving the restructuring of the WCC in such a way that the Commission on World Mission and Evangelism is involved in the entire life and work of the WCC, including the sharing in the financing of various programs/projects, is said to have been completed.

Heartened by the call to evangelism made in Nairobi, member churches concerned for evangelism are watching critically and expectantly for reflections of intent to become programs of action in which the WCC encourages and assists its member churches to implement this "call."

Objectives. This survey is being made among WCC staff working in Geneva. A survey similar to this one will be conducted among WCC member churches. These are part of a larger study being done in the doctor of missiology program of the School of World Mission at Fuller Theological Seminary, Pasadena, California, USA.

The larger study of which this is a part concerns the subject How the WCC and Its Member Churches Work Together in Evangelism. The study is limited to the WCC and its member churches of the West and those non-Western member churches whose historic roots are in the missionary movement.

The larger study is being made to learn more about the ways in which these WCC member churches relate to one another and their interaction in the WCC. We hope it will provide useful information about the things these churches are currently doing together in their understanding of God's mission for them. We want to learn particularly the relative importance of evangelism in the things they are doing together. We want to know how much of their evangelism concerns "cross cultural" evangelism and the "unreached peoples." We want to learn in what ways the churches' participation in the struggle for liberation and a just society affect the work of evangelism in local congregations.

Although it is recognized that the WCC cannot itself be an evangelizing agency, we want to know more about how its programs help the work of evangelism in local churches. We hope to learn more about the kind of programs local churches need from the WCC to assist them in their work of evangelism. We hope the study may shed some light on the kinds of additional structures and relationships that may be necessary if all the churches on six continents are to be engaged in "mission in six continents."

This particular survey questionnaire is designed to gather and collate information from WCC staff in Geneva about WCC programs/projects to help ascertain the degree to which they reflect a concern for and an involvement with member churches in evangelism. Its two foci are: 1) To ascertain the degree to which WCC programs/projects prior to Nairobi reflected a concern for and an involvement in evangelism. 2) To ascertain what the understandings of the WCC staff are as to the intent of Nairobi's call to evangelism and how this intent is affecting present programs and to what extent this intent may be reflected in forthcoming programs of the WCC.

It is hoped that the survey will provide the churches with that kind of information that will assure them that they can have confidence that their concerns for evangelism are being met by the WCC and are reflected in their programs/projects.

Definition of Terms. In this survey, by "evangelism" we mean "holistic evangelism" an essential aspect of which is "naming the Name" in such a way that the good news from God about Jesus Christ, according to the Scriptures, is effectively communicated so that those who hear may believe in him and become his disciples.

In this survey, by "unreached peoples" we mean those who have no way to hear the Gospel effectively and in most cases have no chance to hear it at all . . . peoples who for various cultural, linguistic, geographical or political reasons are beyond the reach of existing evangelistic programs of churches anywhere in the entire world. This is not to imply that in the West there are no "mission fields with their pagan peoples" which should not be of deepest concern to the whole Church. Rather it is to draw the sharpest distinction between those who *cannot* hear and those who *do not* hear.

In this survey, by "cross-cultural evangelism" we mean evangelism that involves the Church crossing cultural barriers to communicate the Gospel in new communities. Frequently, but by no means always, geographical distance is involved. (For a full discussion of E^0, E^1, E^2, and E^3 types of evangelism in relation to the concept of "cross-cultural evangelism" see Ralph Winter's address, "Cross-cultural Evangelism, Highest Priority," in *Let the Earth Hear His Voice,* official text of addresses given at the Lausanne Conference on Evangelism.)

SURVEY QUESTIONNAIRE—WCC STAFF GENEVA

Personal Data   Date _____

1. At what level are you working for the WCC?
   Executive   ____
   Administrative   ____
   Secretarial   ____

2. How long have you worked for the WCC?
   Geneva:
   Elsewhere:

3. What country do you consider your home country?

4. What languages do you speak?

5. What is your church or religious affiliation?

6. Do you work in programs/projects of the CWME or in which CWME shares in financing?
   CWME _____   Other _____

HOW WCC STAFF, PROGRAMS/PROJECTS REFLECT A CONCERN FOR AND AN INVOLVEMENT IN EVANGELISM

On a scale from *one* to *five* indicate your response when applicable. Key to scale values:
1 = substantially so
2 = moderately so
3 = marginally so
4 = not at all
5 = question irrelevant to your work, or you have no basis upon which to answer.

1. The program/project in which you are working relates to WCC member churches primarily at what level?
   —with local congregations   ____
   — " Regional Conferences   ____
   — " National Councils   ____
   — " World Confessional bodies   ____
   — " government agencies   ____
   — " non-church, secular   ____

2. Most of your interaction with church workers is through what means? Indicate 1, 2, 3 as to order of frequency with *one* indicating highest frequency.
   —written correspondence   ____
   —contacts church leaders their visits Geneva ____

APPENDIX

—visits to member churches ____
—ecumenical meetings various places ____
—not listed ____

3. In your interaction with church leaders to what extent has the subject of evangelism in local congregations of WCC member churches been a topic of major concern?
    —with pastors and workers in local churches ____
    — " Regional Church Conference leaders ____
    — " denominational leaders—Western ____
    — " member church leaders—non-Western ____
    — " world confessional body leaders ____
    — " WCC staff members ____

4. In your interaction with church leaders to what extent has the subject of "cross-cultural evangelism" among "unreached peoples" been a topic of major concern?
    —with pastors and workers local churches ____
    — " Regional Church Conference leaders ____
    — " denominational leaders—Western ____
    — " member church leaders—non-Western ____
    — " world confessional body leaders ____
    — " WCC staff members ____

(For questions 5, 6, 7, 8 use a scale from *one* to *six*.)
Key: 1 = 100%; 2 = 75%; 3 = 50%; 4 = 25%; 5 = less than 25%; 6 = none

5. In the period from Uppsala to Nairobi in the program/project in which you are now working, what proportion of the program/project had as its function:
    —to encourage and assist the work of evangelism in local congregations? ____
    —to encourage and assist local congregations to participate in "cross-cultural evangelism" among "unreached peoples"? ____
    —to assist and encourage Regional Conferences* of churches in helping their member churches in the work of evangelism in local congregations? ____
    —to assist and encourage Regional Conferences of

*and/or Church Councils

275

churches in helping their member churches to participate in "cross-cultural evangelism" among "unreached peoples"? _____

6. To what extent would you agree that in the period since Nairobi WCC staff is making a serious response to the intent for Evangelism expressed at the Fifth Assembly of the WCC, indications of which are evident in the continuing discussions and conferences in which WCC staff are engaged as well as in the plans being projected when in several important meetings the concern for Evangelism will be of major importance, and that this response is being and will continue to be reflected in WCC programs and projects? _____

(Note: Questions 6 ff. use Key suggested on page 271)

7. In the light of Nairobi's call to evangelism, to what extent do you anticipate changes being made in your program/project reflecting the intent of Nairobi with respect to evangelism:
   —so that your program/project places more emphasis upon encouraging and assisting the work of evangelism in local congregations? _____
   —so that your program/project places more emphasis upon encouraging and facilitating the participation of WCC member churches in "cross-cultural evangelism" among the "unreached peoples"? _____

8. To what extent in principle would you support the view that more funds from richer churches should be made available to poorer churches among the WCC member churches for their use in their work of evangelism? _____

9. To what extent would you agree with a suggestion that WCC staff explore in depth ways in which relevant programs/projects can be modified to give encouragement and assistance to member churches in such a way that people from non-Western churches may do the work of evangelism among "unreached peoples"? _____

10. To what extent would you agree that WCC staff

should play a major role in helping its member churches on six continents find ways of working together in cross-cultural evangelism in "mission in six continents" in which, in all likelihood, the preponderance of personnel would be from the congregations of non-Western churches? ____

11. Recalling the lament of Bishop Arias that "Evangelism has become the Cinderella of the WCC" and in the context of John R. Stott's challenge to the WCC to "provide evidence that it has a heartfelt commitment to evangelism," to what extent would you say the program/project in which you are working reflects such a commitment? ____

12. While acknowledging that "paid evangelism" is not without its pitfalls, in view of the fact that in reality most missionaries have been able to work in cross-cultural evangelism because they are paid, to what extent would you agree that WCC member churches should develop programs and structures through which finances are available to make it possible for "missionaries" from non-Western churches to work in cross-cultural evangelism among "unreached peoples"? ____

13. To what extent do you feel that existing programs and structures of WCC member churches may be inadequate? ____

14. To what extent does the program/project in which you are working represent a response to requests for this kind of program from WCC member churches? ____

15. To what extent is your program/project more of a prophetic, catalytic nature to conscientize the churches to dimensions of discipleship which you feel the churches need but for which they have not yet expressed a need? ____

16. In the period from Nairobi until now in the program/project in which you are working, to what extent has there been any reallocation of funds within your program/project or in other programs/projects making available additional funds for those aspects of your program/project designed to encourage and

assist the WCC member churches in their evangelistic task? _____

17. During the period from Uppsala to Nairobi a number of new programs/projects were created by the WCC and existing programs/projects were modified to implement the emphasis given at Uppsala to the churches' responsibilities with reference to the social implications of the Gospel.
To what extent do you anticipate in the period from Nairobi until the next full Assembly of the WCC that its programs/projects will reflect a comparable response to the emphasis given to evangelism at Nairobi? _____

18. A commonly voiced concern with reference to "holistic evangelism" is that in practice that aspect of it which involves "naming the Name" frequently became of marginal significance.
In the program/project in which you are working to what extent would you say that this concern is justified? _____

19. To what extent would you say that the program/project in which you are working has an integrity of its own and in a marginal way only can be said to relate to evangelism? _____

20. In the program/project in which you are working, insofar as the program/project involves what may be in the nature of an ecumenical sharing of personnel, to what extent are the people moving about from churches in one part of the world to churches in other parts of the world engaged in activities:
   —specifically concerned with cross-cultural evangelism among "unreached peoples"? _____
   —in which they themselves are "missionaries" or cross-cultural workers engaged in cross-cultural evangelism among "unreached peoples" as it were in field work? _____
   —relating to the teaching, pastoral work of church or relating to its own functioning as an institution? _____
   —relating to institutions such as schools, hospitals,

etc. which churches have inherited from the various missions? _____

—relating to work that has traditionally been the work of interchurch aid in response to hunger, earthquakes, fire and flood? _____

—relating to churches working together with others in their local communities in projects that implement the social dimension of the Gospel? _____

—relating to governmental agencies of various kinds? _____

—relating to secular, non-church groups and organizations in whose projects the churches do not participate directly, but which the WCC assists in one way or another because these groups have goals and objectives which the church supports in its concern for a just society? _____

—relating to activities useful and necessary in the life and work of the WCC and its member churches? _____

21. To what extent in the programs/projects in which you are working does a major element of the program/project relate to:

—the life and work of local churches . . . teaching, pastoral, administrative, etc.? _____

—the life and work of WCC member churches at the regional or national level? _____

—the participation of a local congregation in the struggle for human rights and a just society? _____

—the interchurch aid type of work relating to tragedies like, famine, flood, earthquake, tornado, etc.? _____

—the work of evangelism leading to church growth by expansion of existing churches? _____

—the work of evangelism leading to church growth resulting from the planting of new churches made up of new believers? _____

—the evangelistic outreach into new communities in which cultural, possibly linguistic and geographical, barriers are crossed to communicate the Gospel among "unreached peoples"? _____

22. At Nairobi, J. R. Stott responding to Bishop Arias's

address on Evangelism said there were in his view *five* things the WCC needed to recover: 1) A recognition of the lostness of man. 2) Confidence in the truth, relevance, and power of the gospel of God. 3) Conviction about the uniqueness of Jesus Christ. 4) A sense of urgency about evangelism. 5) A personal experience of Jesus Christ.

Making due allowances for the fact that each of us might not view his assertions as of equal importance and that we might express ourselves in a slightly different manner, to what degree do you find yourself responding favorably to what Stott is trying to say? ____

23. Although the World Council of Churches cannot be expected to be an evangelizing agency, to what extent would you concur with the view of many who believe that the WCC's "finest hour" in evangelism has dawned affecting all its life and work, bringing with it the "sunrise" of a new day of joyful, expectant evangelism in many of her member churches? ____

24. In the period from Uppsala until now, of the persons whose names are listed below, which three would you say have probably exercised the greatest impact on the reflection/action in the program/project in which you are working? Please check *three*. Write in vote permitted!

Karl Barth ____
Bonhoeffer ____
Guevara ____
Calvin ____
Freire ____
Gatu ____
Hoekendijke ____
Rahner ____
Marx ____
Nyerere ____
Stott ____
Mao Tse-Tung ____
Moltmann ____
Takenaka ____
Gutierrez ____

Cone   ——

Not listed   ——

WCC Staff members:

My very deep sense of gratitude to each of you for your cooperation and assistance shown in your response to this survey. With every kind wish to each of you, I am sincerely,

Harvey T. Hoekstra 3/4/77

Appendix J
A Study of the WCC and its Member Churches— The Unfinished Missionary Task of Cross-Cultural Evangelism Among Unreached Peoples

This survey is part of a larger study on how the WCC and its member churches work together in evangelism. It is made in the context of a worldwide Christian community renewing its commitment to evangelism. The study focuses on the WCC and its member churches in the West and those non-Western member churches whose historic roots are in the missionary movement. This survey believes that such evangelism that disciples the nations is essential and helpful to efforts to achieve a more just and peaceful society.

The missionary-sending movement in which missionaries go out largely from Western churches can be said to have ended. Most remaining missionaries from the West working with WCC member churches are no longer on the "cutting edge" in evangelism among unreached peoples.

Churches are a fact on six continents. Many are growing rapidly. At the same time, in many places churches are small and Christians represent tiny minorities of total populations. Because of the cultures or subcultures represented by the membership of some churches evangelism by them among unreached peoples becomes difficult and unlikely. The fact is that perhaps *as many as 85 percent of the unreached peoples cannot effectively hear the Gospel through existing evangelistic efforts of churches anywhere in the entire world.*

Without creative new efforts in which churches from the

West and their mission societies and the churches of Africa,
Asia and Latin America and their mission societies work together in the unfinished missionary task of cross-cultural
evangelism, there is no real possibility of vast multitudes of
those who remain unreached by the Gospel coming to know
Christ and becoming his disciples. Nairobi's call to evangelism
challenges WCC member churches to find new ways to carry
forward the missionary task of taking the Gospel to the ends of
the earth to the end of time until all persons everywhere shall
have had an opportunity to hear the Gospel, believe in Christ
and become his disciples.

Definitions. For purposes of this survey, by "evangelism" we
mean to communicate the Gospel in such a way that the good
news from God about Jesus Christ, according to the Scriptures, is made plain so that those who hear may believe in him,
become his disciples and members of his church.

By "unreached peoples" we mean those who because of
culture, language, geography, status in society, or for various
other reasons, have no way to hear the Gospel effectively.
They are unreached because no churches exist having members representing the cultures and subcultures of these unreached peoples allowing the Gospel to be gossiped and
spread. They remain unreached because no churches or too
few churches have been planted among people of their kind.
They cannot hear the Gospel.

By "cross-cultural evangelism" we mean evangelism that
involves a missionary or evangelist crossing cultural barriers to
communicate the Gospel in new communities. Frequently, but
by no means always, geographical distance is involved and
linguistic problems must be surmounted.

*Your response to this survey can make a vital contribution to
efforts being made to find new ways and methods by which
churches in the West and the churches of Africa, Asia and
Latin America can work together in the unfinished missionary
task of cross-cultural evangelism among unreached peoples.*

SURVEY QUESTIONNAIRE

Personal Data   Date _____

Your name _____ Your position _____

Your country _____ Your mother tongue _____

Your second language _____ Your third language _____

Your Church's Profile and Related Questions

1. Church for which you are reporting? _____

2. Country in which your churches are located? _____

3. Province or districts in which your church is located? ___
   _____

4. Estimated total communicant membership (adult baptized members) of your churches? _____

5. Number of congregations served by ordained pastors? __

6. Number of evangelists working under the direction of your churches? _____

7. How many evangelists mentioned in question 6 are engaged in evangelism intended to plant new churches? __

8. How many evangelists mentioned in question 6 are planting churches among peoples whose language is different from the mother tongue of the evangelist? _____

9. In towns and cities where your evangelists are planting new churches do these begin as "house churches" (i.e. small groups meeting for Bible study, fellowship and prayer)? (Underline correct answer.)

   Always   Frequently   Sometimes   Seldom   Never

10. During the next ten year period what unreached peoples can your churches *without outside assistance* evangelize and plant new churches among? _____

11. During the next ten year period what unreached peoples could you evangelize and plant churches among *if you received assistance* from outside sources? _____
    _____
    _____

12. Please name the denominations (churches) and countries from which you would welcome missionaries and evangelists to work with your church's missionaries and evangelists in evangelism intended to plant new churches among unreached peoples?

Denomination Example: Presbyterian	Country Korea	For which unreached people? Shako
1		
2		
3		
4		
5		

13. Do you feel that outside financial assistance could be safely used to enable your churches to send out your own missionaries and evangelists to otherwise unreached peoples in your district without hindering local congregations supporting pastors and staff in their local churches?

14. In principle do you believe affluent churches should make funds available for churches anywhere on six continents to enable such churches with this financial assistance to send out their missionaries and evangelists to do cross-cultural evangelism and plant new churches among otherwise unreached peoples?

15. Does the WCC's Program, Ecumenical Sharing of Personnel, help your churches to send missionaries and evangelists to engage in cross-cultural evangelism and planting new churches among unreached peoples?

16. Does the WCC's Program, Urban Industrial Mission, in places where your churches are involved, help your congregations to grow or new congregations to be formed made up of new believers?

17. Would you welcome new efforts by the WCC, its member churches and mission societies to fashion new structures and find new ways to enable the churches from the West and the churches from Asia, Africa and Latin America to work together in cross-cultural evangelism in such a way that the resources and personnel from all the churches

could be part of a common effort among the unreached who remain without the effective knowledge of Christ?

18. Do your churches, both locally and regionally, have structures devoted to evangelizing unreached peoples that may be comparable to mission societies in churches in the West?

19. Does your church have a missionary society which can work with existing missionary societies in sister churches enabling you to work together in cross-cultural evangelism intended to bring multitudes from among the otherwise unreached peoples to faith in Jesus Christ and into the membership of his Church?

20. Please name the programs or projects in which *from the WCC* you receive funds or personnel to enable your churches to send out your own people to evangelize otherwise unreached peoples . . . peoples who without such assistance you cannot evangelize?

1 _____ 2 _____
3 _____ 4 _____
5 _____

21. Please name the programs or projects in which *from sister churches* (not the WCC itself) with which you maintain "church-to-church" relations or *from mission agencies* you receive funds or personnel for cross-cultural evangelism among unreached peoples?

1 _____ 2 _____
3 _____ 4 _____
5 _____

22. Please send me your concrete proposals on how the WCC or its member churches can best assist your churches to do the work of evangelism among unreached peoples? (Personnel, finances, technology, structure, etc.) Be as specific as possible.

SURVEYING THE TASK

Country of _____

Homogeneous Unit**	Its Size	District	Language	Number of Churches	Membership	Pastors	Evangelists
Example: Shako	20,000	Masha	Shakoinya	2	250	0	2
1							
2							
3							
4							
5							

Name each homogeneous unit in your area which has significant numbers of unreached persons where existing churches are either small or few, or whose members are from tribes or castes or segments of society that make it difficult if not unlikely that they can successfully evangelize these people and multiply congregations of believers among them.

Homogeneous Unit	Its Size	District	Language	Number of Churches	Membership	Probable Attitude Toward the Gospel*
1						
2						
3						
4						
5						
6						

*Indicate whether likely to be: receptive, hostile, or indifferent.

**By Homogeneous Unit we mean a segment of society whose members speak the same language, have common interests, same ethnic group . . . people who naturally group together etc. Examples might include: sailors, coal miners, taxi drivers, a particular tribe, religious group, student group.

BIBLIOGRAPHY

ABRECHT, Paul
  1961 *The Church in Rapid Social Change.* Garden City, Doubleday and Co.

ADLER, Elisabeth
  1974 *A Small Beginning, An Assessment of the First Five Years of the Program to Combat Racism.* Geneva, WCC.

ALAN, Richard
  1928 *Jerusalem: A Critical Review of the "World Mission of Christianity."* London, World Dominion Press.

ALTHAUSEN, J.
  1973 "The Ecumenical Task in Education. A Test for the European Churches." In: *Study Encounter,* Vol. 9, no. 3, 1973.

ALVES, R.
  1969 *A Theology of Hope.* Cleveland, Corpus Books.

ANDERSON, Gerald H., ed.
  1961 *The Theology of the Christian Mission.* New York, McGraw-Hill.

ANDERSON, Whilhelmn
  1955 *Towards a Theology of Mission: A Study of the Encounter between the Missionary Enterprise and the Church and Its Theology.* London, SCM Press Ltd.

AREVALOS, G. G.
  1972 *Theology in Action,* Urban and Industrial Mission Manila Conference.

ARIAS, Mortimer
  1976 *That the World May Believe,* International Review of Mission, Jan. 13–16.

BARKAT, M. and JONES, Philip E.
  1974 An article on the "Chinese Experiment," *Study Encounter,* 1974.

BARTH, Karl
  1938 *The Church and the Churches: To the Second World Conference on Faith and Order.* Grand Rapids, Wm. B. Eerdmans Publishing Co.

BATE, H. N., ed.
  1927 *Faith and Order: Proceedings of the World Conference, Lausanne, Aug. 3–21, 1927.* London.

BEAVER, R. Pierce
  1968 *All Loves Excelling.* Grand Rapids, Wm. B. Eerdmans Publishing Co.
  1970 *North American Protestant Ministries Overseas Directory,* 9th ed.
  1973 ed. *The Gospel and Frontier Peoples.* South Pasadena, CA., Wm. Carey Library.

BELL, G. K. A., ed.

1926   *The Stockholm Conference 1925,* London.
BERKHOF, Hendrik
1968   "Report on the Development of the Study 'The Finality of Jesus Christ in the Age of Universal History,'" *The Ecumenical Chronicle* XX:464–465.
BEYERHAUS, P. and LEFEVER, H.
1964   *The Responsible Church and the Foreign Mission,* Grand Rapids, Wm. B. Eerdmans Publishing Co.
BEYERHAUS, P. and HALLENCREUTZ, C. F.
1969   *Of the Church Crossing Frontiers,* Lund, Gleerup.
BEYERHAUS, Peter
1971   *Missions: Which Way?* Grand Rapids, Zondervan Publishing House.
1972   *Shaken Foundations: Theological Foundation for Mission.* Grand Rapids, Zondervan Publishing House.
1974   *Bangkok '73.* Grand Rapids, Zondervan Publishing House.
BIBLE
1957   Revised Standard Version. T. Nelson for National Council of Churches.
BLAKE, Eugene Carson
1969   *The Ecumenical Review* 21, no. 4, October.
BOCK, Paul
1974   *In Search of a Responsible World Society, the Social Teachings of the WCC.* Philadelphia, The Westminster Press.
1975   *Doing Theology in a Revolutionary Situation.* Philadelphia, Fortress Press.
BRISTONE, Keith R. and WAGONER, Walter D., ed.
1963   *Unity in Mid-career.* New York, The Macmillan Co.
CASTRO, Emilio
1964   "Evangelism in Latin America," *International Review of Mission,* Vol. 53, 452–456.
1973   *Amidst Revolution.* Belfast, Christian Journals Ltd.
1973   "Bangkok, the New Opportunity," *International Review of Mission,* 1973:140.
1974   CWME Director's Report, Geneva, WCC Archives.
1975a   CWME Director's Report, Figueira de Foz, Geneva, WCC.
1975b   Document 3 CWME files, Geneva Archives.
1976   CWME Director's Report, Geneva, WCC.
CONE, James H.
1970   *A Black Theology of Liberation.* Philadelphia, Lippincott.
COSTAS, Orlando E.
1974   *The Church and Its Mission, Shattering Critique from the Third World.* Wheaton, Tyndale House Pub.
COX, Harvey
1965   *The Secular City: Secularization and Urbanization in Theological Perspective.* New York, The Macmillan Co.
1967   *The Church Amid Revolution.* A selection of the Essays prepared for the WCC, Geneva Conference on Church and Society. New York, Assoc. Press.
DOUGLAS, J. D., ed.
1974   *Let the Earth Hear His Voice.* Minneapolis, World Wide Pub.
DURHAM, J.

1973 "Editorial Correspondence," *International Review of Mission*, Vol. LXII, October 1973, 487–490.

FEY, Harold E., ed.
1967 *A History of the Ecumenical Movement, 1948–1968.* Philadelphia, The Westminster Press.

FREIRE, Paulo
1970 *Pedagogy of the Oppressed.* New York, Herder and Herder.
1972 *Conscientisation and Liberation: A Conversation with Paulo Freire.* Document 1. Geneva, Institute of Cultural Action.
1973 *Education for Critical Consciousness.* New York, The Seabury Press.

FUNG, Raymond
1975 "Industrial Mission and Evangelism," *International Review of Mission,* April, 1975.

GILL, David J., ed.
1968 "The Secularization Debate Foreshadowed," *International Review of Mission,* Vol. 57, 344–357.
1970 *From Here to Where? Technology, Faith and the Future of Man.* Geneva, WCC.

GLASSER, Arthur F.
1969 *What Has Been the Evangelical Stance, New Delhi to Uppsala?* Evangelical Missions Quarterly, No. 3, Spring 1969: 129ff.

GOODALL, Norman
1953 *Missions Under His Cross,* Willigen Papers, London, IMC Edinburgh House.
1968 *The Uppsala Report 1968,* official report of the Fourth Assembly of the WCC, Geneva, WCC.
1972 *Ecumenical Progress,* A decade of change in the Ecumenical movement 1961–71. London, Oxford University Press.

GRUBER, Pamela H.
1970 *Fetters of Injustice. Report of a Conference Held at Montreux,* Jan. 1970. Geneva, WCC.

GUTIERREZ, Gustavo
1973 *A Theology of Liberation.* New York, Orbis Books.

HALLENCREUTZ, Carl F.
1970 *New Approaches to Men of Other Faiths, 1938–1968.* A theological discussion. Geneva, WCC.

HENNES, Gerhard
1977a *Let's Have Another Look at ESP, CWME, Document #9, Feb., 1977.* Geneva, WCC.
1977b *What Has ESP Done?* Geneva, WCC.

HOEKENDIJK, J. C.
1950 "The Call to Evangelism," *International Review of Mission,* April, 1950: 162–175.
1952 "The Church in Missionary Thinking," *International Review of Mission,* Vol. 41, April 1952: 324–336.
1966 *The Church Inside Out.* L. A. Hoedemaker and R. Tijmes, editors. Translated by J. C. Rottenberg. Philadelphia, The Westminster Press.

HOEKSTRA, Harvey
1977a Survey Questionnaire, WCC Staff, Geneva.

1977b A study of the WCC and its member churches—the unfinished missionary task of cross-cultural evangelism among unreached peoples.

HOGG, Wm. R.
1952 *Ecumenical Foundations*. New York, Harper & Bros. Publishers.

HOLLENWEGER, Walter J.
1956 *Evangelism Today*. Belfast, Christian Journals.

HUBBARD, David Allan
1975 "An Evangelical Evaluation of the World Assembly," *Religious News Service*, 12/23/75.

INTERNATIONAL MISSIONARY COUNCIL
1928 *Report of the Jerusalem Meeting of the IMC, 1928*. 8 Volumes. London, Oxford University Press.
1938 *The Madras Series:* Presented Papers Based upon the Meeting of the IMC at Tambaram, Madras, India, 1938. New York, IMC.
1952 *Minutes of the Enlarged Meeting and the Committee of the IMC, Willingen, Germany 1952*. London, IMC.
1961a *Minutes of the Assembly of the IMC, Nov. 17–18, 1961 and the First Meeting of the CWME, WCC, Dec. 7–8, 1961 at New Delhi*, WCC.
1961b *New Delhi Work Book.*

JOHNSON, David Enderton
1975 *Uppsala to Nairobi, The Official WCC Account*. New York, Friendship Press.

JOHNSTON, A. P.
1974 *World Evangelism and the Word of God*. Minneapolis, Bethany Fellowship, Inc.

KANE, J. Herbert
1971 *A Global View of Christian Missions*. Grand Rapids, Baker Book House.

KENNEDY, James W.
1975 *Nairobi 1975*. Cincinnati, Forward Movement Publications.

KNUTSON, Kent S.
1972 *The Shape of the Question. The Mission of the Church in a Secular Age*. Minneapolis, Augsburg Publishing House.
1976 *Gospel, Church, Mission, 1924–1973*. Minneapolis, Augsburg Publishing House.

KODR, George Metopolitan
1971 "Christianity in a Pluralistic World," *Living Faith and the Ecumenical Movement*. Geneva, WCC.

KRAEMER, Hendrik
1963 *The Christian Message in a Non-Christian World*. 1st ed. 1938. Grand Rapids, Kregel Publishers.

LATOURETTE, K. S. and HOGG, W.
1948 *Tomorrow is Here* (Whitby Report). New York, Friendship Press.
1969 *Christianity in a Revolutionary Age: A History of Christianity in the 19th and 20th Centuries:* Vols. I–V. 1st ed., 1961.

LEHMANN, Paul L.
1951 "Renewal in the Church," *Theology Today*, Jan., 1951:472–485. Princeton, N. J.

LOCHMAN, Jan
1977 *Encountering Marx*. Belfast, Christian Journals Limited.

LOEFFLER
1962 *Layman Abroad in the Mission of the Church*. London, Edinburgh

House Press.
1967   "Conversion in an Ecumenical Context," *The Ecumenical Review,* XIX July, 1967:252-260.
1968   *Secular Man and Christian Mission,* Commission on World Mission and Evangelism Study Pamphlet. Geneva, WCC.

MACKIE, Steven G.
1970   *Can Churches be Compared?* Geneva, WCC.

MARC
1974   *That Every Man May Hear. A Ministry of World Vision.* Monrovia, Marc.

MARGULL, Hans Jochen
1962   *Hope in Action,* tr. by Eugene Peters, Philadelphia, Muhlenberg Press.
1968   "Presence and Proclamation," European Consultation on Mission Studies, European Consultation No. 7, April, 1968:1-11.

MCGAVRAN, Donald A.
1965   "Wrong Strategy: The Real Crisis in Missions," *International Review of Mission,* October, 1965:451-461.
1968   "Church Growth Strategy Continued," *International Review of Mission,* July, 1968:335-343.
1972a ed. *Crucial Issues in Missions Tomorrow.* Chicago, Moody Press.
1972b ed. *Eye of the Storm: The Great Debate in Mission.* Texas, Word Book Publishers.
1977   ed. *The Conciliar-Evangelical Debate: The Crucial Documents 1964-1976.* Pasadena, Wm. Carey Library.

MIGUEZ, Jose Bonino
1974   "A Latin American Attempts to Locate the Question of Unity," *What Kind of Unity,* Geneva, WCC.

MOLTMANN, Jurgen
1967   *Theology of Hope.* London, SCM.

MORGAN, G. Campbell
1970   *The Missionary Manifesto.* Grand Rapids, Baker Book House.

NEEDHAM, Joseph
1973   In *Anticipation,* No. 14.

NEILL, Stephen Chas.
1958   *The Unfinished Task.* London, Edinburgh House Press.
1959   *Creative Tension.* London, Edinburgh House Press.
1966   *Colonialism and Christian Missions.* New York, McGraw Hill.
1970   *Call to Mission.* Philadelphia, Fortress Press.
1975   "The Nature of Salvation," *The Churchman,* Vol. 89, No. 3:225-234.

NEWBIGIN, Lesslie
1960   "Mission and Missions." *Christianity Today,* August 1, p. 23.
1966   *Honest Religion for Secular Man.* London, SCM.

NILES, D. T.
1962   *Upon the Earth: The Mission of God and the Missionary Enterprise of the Churches.* New York, McGraw Hill.

NISSEN, Karsten
1974   "Mission and Unity," *International Review of Mission,* Vol. 63, 539-550.

NYERERE, Julius K.
1967   "Education for Self-Reliance," *Ecumenical Review,* Vol. 19, No. 4, October 1967:382-403.

OLDHAM, J. H.
1937 *World Conference on Church, Community and State, Oxford 1937.*
The official report. Chicago, New York, Willett, Clark & Co.
ORCHARD, Ronald K.
1958 *The Ghana Assembly, IMC.* London, Edinburgh House.
1959 *Out of Every Nation,* A discussion of the internationalizing of missions. London, SCM Press.
1964 ed. *Witness in Six Continents, Mexico City, CWME 1963.* London, Edinburgh House Press.
PARMER, Samuel L.
1974 "The Limits of Growth Debate in Asian Perspective," *The Ecumenical Review,* Vol XXVI, No. 1, Jan. '74.
PATON, David M., ed.
1976 *Breaking Barriers Nairobi.* London, SPCK; Grand Rapids, Wm. B. Eerdmans.
POTTER, Philip
1969 "Towards Renewal in Mission," *The Church Crossing Frontiers,* Uppsala, Erup Lund.
1972 *Christ's Mission and Ours in Today's World.* A mimeographed paper. Geneva, WCC Archives.
RANSOM, C. W., ed.
1948 *Renewal and Advance, IMC.* London, Edinburgh House Press.
1954 "The Christian World Mission in the Perspective of History," *International Review of Mission,* Vol 43, 381–389.
ROBINSON, John Arthur Thomas
1963 *Honest to God.* Philadelphia, The Westminster Press.
ROSTAGNO, Sergio
1977 *Essays on the New Testament, a 'Materialist' Approach.* World Student Federation, Goodwin Press Ltd. (TU), 135 Fonthill Rd, London.
ROUSE, Ruth and NEILL, Charles
1967 *A History of the Ecumenical Movement 1517–1948.* Philadelphia, The Westminster Press.
ROWE, Richard C.
1969 *Bible Study in the WCC.* Geneva, WCC.
SAMARTHA, Stanley J.
1971 *Dialogue Between Men of Living Faiths.* Papers Presented at a Consultation held at Ajaltoun, Lebanon, March, 1970. Geneva, WCC.
SHAULL, Richard
1965 "The Christian World Mission in a Technological Era," *The Ecumenical Review,* Vol XVII, July:14–21.
1967 *Revolutionary Change in Theological Perspective.* A paper written for Geneva Conference 1966. Edited in *The Church Amid Revolution.* Cox, editor (see bibliography under Cox).
SIDER, Ronald J.
1974 ed. *The Chicago Declaration.* Carol Stream, Illinois, Creation House
SLACK, Kenneth
1961 *Dispatch from New Delhi.* London, SCM Press Ltd.
1976 *Nairobi Narrative.* London, SCM Press Ltd.
SPEER, Robert E.
1933 *Rethinking Missions-Examined.* New York: Fleming H. Revell Co.
STOTT, John R.
1975 *Christian Mission in the Modern World.* Downers Grove, Ill., Inter-

varsity Press.
1976 "Response to Bishop Mortimer Arias," *International Review of Mission,* Vol 65:30–33.

STRINGFELLOW, Wm.
1973 *An Ethic for Christians and Other Aliens in A Strange Land.* Texas, Word Books, Waco.

STRONG, Robbins
1977 *CWME Financial Askings,* Geneva, WCC.

SUNDKLER, Bengt
1965 *The World of Mission.* London, Lutterworth Press.

THAN, U Kyaw
1958 "The Christian Mission in Asia Today," *International Review of Mission,* Vol 47, 153–162.
1967 *Report to the Continuing Committee, East Asian Christian Conference, November, 1966.* Bangkok, Thailand, EACC.
1969 "Mission Hour in Asia," Address delivered to the 62nd Annual Meeting of the American Baptist Convention, Seattle, Washington. Geneva, WCC Archives.

THERESA, Chong-Carino
1975 Notes on Student Protest and Education in S/E Asia Today. Singapore, Student Christian Movement in the Philippines. In *Jesus Christ Frees and Unites,* WCC Dossiers, 1975.

THOMAS, M. M.
1964 "Christianity and World History." *The Ecumenical Review,* Vol XVI, No. 5, October.
1966 *World Conference on Church and Society,* Geneva 1966. (Official report with description of the Conference by M. M. Thomas) Geneva, WCC.

THOMAS, M. M and ABRECHT, Paul
1966 *The Structure and Work of the Conference. World Conference on Church and Society,* Geneva, 1966.

TIPPET, Alan R.
1969 *Verdict Theology in Missionary Theory.* Lincoln, Lincoln Christian College Press.

TOMKINS, Oliver S.
1950 *The Church in the Purpose of God: An Introduction to the work of the Commission of Faith and Order.* London, SCM Press Ltd.

UDO, S. R. Ladny
1972 *Report to the Assembly of the World Student Christian Federation in Addis Abba, Dec. 28, 1972–Jan. 9, 1973,* Minutes. Geneva, WCC Archives.

VAN BUREN, P. M.
1963 *The Secular Meaning of the Gospel: Based on an Analysis of its Language.* New York, The Macmillan Co.

VAN DUSEN, Henry P.
1940 *For the Healing of the Nations.* New York, Scribners.
1957 *World Christianity (Yesterday, Today, Tomorrow),* New York, Abingdon Cokesbury Press.
1961 *One Great Ground of Hope,* Philadelphia, Westminster.

VAN LEEUWEN, Arend
1964 *Christianity and World History.* Translated by H. H. Hoskins. New York, Charles Scribner's Sons.

VAN RANDWIJCK, Graff
    1958   Mimeographed papers Ghana Assembly file, Geneva, WCC.
    1961   "Inter Church Aid (A Challenge to Missions)," *International Review of Mission,* Vol 50, 385–394.
VANDEN HEUVEL, A., ed.
    1969   *Unity of Mankind.* Speeches from the Fourth Assembly of the World Council of Churches, Uppsala 1968. Geneva, WCC.
    1973   *The Conversation of Truths, Communication in the Ecumenical Movement. EASC.* WCC Archives Geneva.
VANDER BENT, Ans J.
    1973   *The Utopia of World Community. An Interpretation of the World Council of Churches for Outsiders.* London, SCM.
VERKUYL, J.
    1972   *The Message of Liberation in Our Age.* Grand Rapids, Wm. B. Eerdmans.
VICEDOM, George F.
    1965   *The Mission of God,* Saint Louis, Concordia Publishing.
VINCENT, J.
    1974   "The Para-Church: An Affirmation of New Testament Theologies," in *Study Encounter,* Vol. X, No. 1, SE 55.
VISCHER, Lukas, ed.
    1971   *Faith and Order Louvain, 1971: Study Report and Documents.* Geneva, WCC.
VISSER 't HOOFT, Wm. A., ed.
    1949   *The First Assembly of the World Council of Churches 1948.* London, SCM Press.
    1948   ed. *Man's Order and God's Design: I–IV.* The First Assembly of the WCC held at Amsterdam, 1948. New York, Harper & Brothers Publishers.
    1956   *The Renewal of the Church,* Philadelphia, The Westminster Press.
    1962   *The New Delhi Report;* The Third Assembly of the World Council of Churches 1961. New York, Association Press.
    1963   *No Other Name: The Choice between Syncretism and Christian Universalism.* Philadelphia, Westminster Press.
    1974   *Has the Ecumenical Movement a Future?* Belfast, Christian Journals Limited.
    1977   Taped Interview in Geneva, March 1977.
WAGNER, Peter
    1971   *Frontiers in Missionary Strategy.* Chicago, Moody Press.
    1972   *Church/Mission Tensions Today.* Chicago, Moody Press.
WAKATAMA, Pius
    1976   *Independence for the Third World Church,* Downers Grove, Ill. Intervarsity Press.
WARREN, Max
    1976   *I Believe in the Great Commission.* London, Hodder and Stoughton.
WEBER, Hans Rudi
    1963   "God's Arithmetic," *Frontier,* Vol. 6, Winter, '63:298–301.
WEBSTER, Canon Douglas
    1973   Address on "Use of the Bible" delivered on occasion of United Bible Societies' Anniversary. WCC Archives, Geneva.
WIESER, Thomas, ed.
    1966   *Planning for Mission,* Working Papers of the New Quest for Missionary Communities. Geneva, WCC.

1972 *Salvation Today and Contemporary Experience*, Geneva, WCC.
WILLIAMS, Colin W.
  1963 *Where in the World?* Office of Pub. NCC in USA.
  1964 *What in the World?* Office of Pub. NCC in USA.
WINNINGE, Ingrid and Carol
  1976 *The International Church Worker*, Tierps Tryckeri, AB 1976.
WINTER, Ralph
  1970 *The Twenty-Five Unbelievable Years 1945-1969.* South Pasadena, William Carey Library.
  1972 "The Planting of Younger Missions." Chapter in *Church/Mission Tensions Today* (see Wagner, ed.).
     ed.
  1973 *The Evangelical Response to Bangkok*, South Pasadena, William Carey Library.
  1974 "The Highest Priority: Cross-Cultural Evangelism" In J. D. Douglas (ed.) *Let the Earth Hear His Voice*, 213-241.
WORLD COUNCIL OF CHURCHES
  1948 *The Ten Formative Years*, Geneva, WCC.
  1954 *The First Six Years 1948-1954.* Prepared for the Second Assembly of the WCC. A Report of the Central Committee of the WCC on the Activities of the Departments and Secretariats of the Council. Geneva, WCC.
  1957 *Transcribed Notes* covering Ghana debate on integration. Geneva, WCC Archives.
  1961a *Minutes of the Assembly of the IMC, Nov. 17-18, 1961, and of the First Meeting of the CWME, WCC Dec. 7-8, 1961 at New Delhi*, WCC.
  1961b *Evanston to New Delhi 1954-1961.* Geneva, WCC.
  1966a *Central Committee Minutes.* Geneva, WCC.
  1966b *CWME Director's Report*, 1966. Geneva, WCC.
  1967a *The Church for Others:* Department on Studies in Evangelism. (A Quest for Structures for Missionary Congregations. Final Report on the Western European and the North American Working groups.) Geneva, WCC.
  1967b *All Things New, Fourth Assembly Uppsala*, Geneva, WCC.
  1968a *New Delhi to Uppsala:* Official Report on Activities of the WCC from 1961-1968. Geneva, WCC.
  1968b *Drafts for Sections*, Uppsala, Sweden, 1968. Geneva, WCC.
  1968c *Workbook for the Assembly Committees*, Geneva, WCC.
  1968d *Uppsala Speaks:* The Reports from Uppsala, 1968. Geneva, WCC.
  1968e *Becoming Operational in a World of Cities*, Geneva, WCC.
  1968f *Conference on World Cooperation for Development, Beirut, 1968.*
  1969 *Director's Report to CWME, 1969.* Geneva, WCC Archives.
  1970 *Report of Advisory Group on UIM Thrusts, Policy, and Structures, Kyoto, Japan, Aug. 1970.* Geneva, WCC Archives.
  1971a *Faith and Order, Louvain, 1971: Study Reports and Documents.* Faith and Order Paper No. 59, Geneva, WCC Archives.
  1971b *Planning for Bangkok*, 1971-72. Geneva, WCC Archives.
  1972a *WCC Consultation in Cardiff, Wales.* Published Dec. 13, 1972 in Anticipation, "Global Environments, Economic Growth and Social Justice."
  1972b *Salvation Today and Contemporary Experience.* CWME. Geneva, WCC.

BIBLIOGRAPHY

1972c *Comments Stimulated by the Collection of Texts on Salvation Today and Contemporary Experience.* CWME. Geneva, WCC Archives.

1972d *The Report of the CWME: From Mexico City to Bangkok, 1963–1972.* Geneva, WCC.

1973a *The Bangkok Assembly,* Geneva, WCC.

1973b *Core Group, CWME, 1973.* Geneva, WCC Archives.

1973c *Faith and Order Commission,* "Unity of Mankind," July, 1973. Geneva, WCC Archives.

1973d *Letter to Constituents,* Secretariat for Evangelism, 1973. Geneva, WCC Archives.

1973e World Council of Churches Language Service, *Report of the Working Party of the Berlin Ecumenical Institute,* 1973. Geneva, WCC.

1973f *Violence, Non-Violence,* statement from WCC Central Committee, (also see: "Violence, non-violence and the Struggle for Social Justice," *The Ecumenical Review,* Vol XXV, No. 4, Oct. 1973).

1973g Working Papers for a Consultation on "Education and Theology in the Context of the Struggler for Liberation," 1973. See Preparatory materials Fifth Assembly, Dossiers, Geneva, WCC. 1975.

1974 *Service Programme and List of Projects 1975,* Geneva, WCC.

1975a *CWME Director's Report, 1975.* Geneva, WCC Archives.

1975b *Preparatory Materials for Fifth Assembly, Dossier,* "For the Liberation of the Indian," The Declaration of Barbados, International Review of Mission, Vol LX, No. 238, Apr. '71.

1975c *Giving Account of the Hope That is Within Us,* printed in Switzerland by La Concorde, Lausanne.

1975d WCC Dossier, Sec. I, 1975, *Introduction.* Geneva, WCC.

1975e WCC Dossier, Section V, 1975. *Introduction.* Geneva, WCC.

1975f *Orthodox Contributions to Nairobi,* Geneva, WCC.

1975g *Report of Advisory Group UIM to CWME, '75.* Geneva, WCC Archives.

1975h *Report of a Consultation on Human Rights and the Churches of Latin America, Puerto Rico, Feb. '73.* From WCC Dossier with Preparatory Materials for the Fifth Assembly, Geneva, WCC.

1975i *Some Reflections on Canada's Relationship with the Third World,* WCC Dossiers Fifth Assembly, 1975, Geneva, WCC.

1975j *Work Book* for Fifth Assembly of WCC. Geneva, WCC.

1975k *The Nature of the Church and the Role of Theology.* Imprimerie Corbaz s.a. Montreux.

1975l *Jesus Christ Frees and Unites,* Dossier Section I, Geneva, WCC.

1975m *Jesus Christ Frees and Unites,* Dossier Section II, Geneva, WCC.

1975n *Jesus Christ Frees and Unites,* Dossier Section III, Geneva, WCC.

1975o *Jesus Christ Frees and Unites,* Dossier Section IV, Geneva, WCC.

1975p *Jesus Christ Frees and Unites,* Dossier Section V, Geneva, WCC.

1975q *Jesus Christ Frees and Unites,* Dossier Section VI, Geneva, WCC.

1975r *Target,* the Official Fifth Assembly Newspaper printed daily for delegates and participants.

1975s *International Review of Missions,* Vol. 64.

1976a *Minutes of Central Committee,* Aug. 1976. Geneva, WCC.

1976b *Report of Ad Hoc Advisory Group on UIM, CWME,* June, '76. Geneva, WCC Archives.

1976c *Service Programme and List of Projects 1977.* Geneva, WCC.

1977 *Alone You Get Nowhere,* An assessment of CWME and CICARWS involvement with personnel in the Sudan. Geneva, WCC.

Harvey Thomas Hoekstra was born on November 20, 1920. He was the fourth of six brothers. His boyhood was spent on the farm where he grew up in the atmosphere of a Christian home. He was out of school for four and one-half years between grade school and high school. During this time he had three major operations and spent some forty-five days in the hospital. Through this experience he came to know Christ as personal Savior and was called to the ministry.

He began high school in 1938 and graduated with honor completing his work in two and a half years. He graduated Cum Laude with an A.B. degree from Hope College, and received his B.D. degree from Western Theological Seminary of the Reformed Church. He was student pastor of the Hope Reformed Church in Grand Haven, Michigan for three years while taking his theological training.

Post graduate work included the Summer Institute of Linguistic course with Wycliffe at the University of Oklahoma, a year of post graduate study at Scarrit and Peabody Colleges in Nashville, Tennessee. He also studied during two furloughs, with a term at Princeton Seminary and a semester at the Kennedy School of Missions in Hartford, Connecticut.

As part of his research for his doctor of missiology, he attended the Fifth Assembly of the World Council of Churches in 1975. In 1977 he spent two months at the Ecumenical Centre in Geneva interviewing WCC leaders and studying unpublished materials in the WCC archives. He has recently completed his studies at the School of

World Mission of Fuller Theological Seminary. When he received the Doctor of Missiology degree in June 1978, he was awarded the Donald Anderson McGavran Award in recognition of the excellence of his dissertation, which formed the basis of this book.

While in college, he was married to Lavina Irene Hoffman. With their children they have served as missionaries in the Sudan and Ethiopia for 28 years. In the Sudan he reduced the Anuak tribal language to writing, worked in the area of literacy and evangelism and translated the New Testament into the Anuak language. He also translated into the Murle language Mark, John, Acts and Romans which was printed by the United Bible Societies using both the Roman and Arabic script.

In Ethiopia he, with his family, pioneered work among the Mesengo forest people in the Southwestern part of the country. Here he developed the use of cassettes in evangelism aimed at reaching a number of previously unreached tribes with the Gospel, each in its own language. He and Mrs. Hoekstra returned to Africa in December 1977 with Portable Recording Ministries' new World Cassette Outreach programme. The aim of this programme is to assist Third World churches to use the cassette for evangelization of yet unreached peoples.

At the last meeting of the Reformed Church General Assembly, Mr. Hoekstra was elected moderator. He and his wife and youngest teenage son are now living in San Diego where he finalized his dissertation manuscript and edited it for publication.

The Hoekstras have six children, four of whom are married.